SCOTTISH ADVERTISING WORKS 4

Proving the effectiveness of marketing communications

OTHER TITLES IN THIS SERIES

Advertising Works And How
ed. Laurence Green

Advertising Works 13
ed. Alison Hoad

Advertising Works 12
ed. Marco Rimini

Advertising Works 11
ed. Tim Broadbent

Scottish Advertising Works 3
ed. James Best

Scottish Advertising Works 2
ed. Diane Lurie

Scottish Advertising Works 1
ed. Diane Lurie

AREA Advertising Works 5
ed. Katrina Michel

AREA Advertising Works 4
ed. Mike Rayner

AREA Advertising Works 3
ed. Roger Ward

SCOTTISH ADVERTISING WORKS 4

Proving the effectiveness of marketing communications

Cases from the Scottish IPA Effectiveness Awards 2005

Edited and introduced by

James Best

Chairman and Convenor of Judges

WARC
World Advertising Research Center

Scottish IPA

First published 2005 by the World Advertising Research Center
Farm Road, Henley-on-Thames, Oxfordshire RG9 1EJ, United Kingdom
Telephone: 01491 411000
Fax: 01491 418600
E-mail: enquiries@warc.com

Copyright © 2005 IPA, Institute of Practitioners in Advertising

All rights reserved. No part of this publication may be reproduced or transmitted in any form or by any means, electronic or mechanical, including photocopying, recording or any information storage or retrieval system, without prior permission in writing from the publishers.

The contents of this book are believed to be correct at time of printing. Nevertheless the publisher, editors and the Scottish IPA can accept no responsibility for errors or omissions, changes in detail given or any expense or loss thereby caused.

A CIP catalogue record for this book is available from the British Library

ISBN 1 84116 178 0

Typeset by Godiva Publishing Services Ltd, Coventry
Printed and bound in Great Britain
by Biddles Ltd, King's Lynn

Contents

Scottish IPA Effectiveness Awards, 2005 *James Best*	vii
The Judges	xi
Acknowledgements	xii
Sponsors	xiii
Prizes	xiv

SECTION 1: GOLD WINNERS

1	*Children's Hearings – Panel membership*	3
2	*Blood Donation – New strategy, new blood*	17

SECTION 2: SILVER WINNERS

3	*Baxters – The personal touch pays dividends*	33
4	*Broadband for Scotland – Turning* Braveheart *into* Blade Runner	43
5	*National Trust for Scotland – Reversing 10 years of decline*	57
6	*Oral Cancer Campaign – How Henry helped save lives*	69
7	*Seriously Strong Cheddar – How advertising created a seriously big impact on seriously strong cheese*	79
8	*University of Dundee – Academic brand creation*	97

SECTION 3: BRONZE WINNERS

9	*Anderson Strathern Solicitors – 'From this day forward, we leave our green wellies at home'*	111
10	*Broadband Registration Drive – The HIE road to broadband*	121
11	*Grolsch – You can't rush these things*	143
12	*My First Bed – A media strategy you can trust*	157
13	*Nambarrie – Going from strength to strength*	165
14	*Overgate – The drive of your life*	179
15	*s1jobs.com – Leading from the front*	187
16	*Scotch Beef – Raised the way you want it*	201
17	*ScottishPower – Energising The Energy People*	209
18	*Standard Life – It's not easy to be liked*	221

How to Access the IPA dataBANK	235
World Advertising Research Center	236
Scottish Effectiveness Awards Cases in the IPA dataBANK	237
Index	239

Scottish IPA Effectiveness Awards 2005

Scottish advertising works. The evidence in this book and its predecessors shows us that it does. But these cases are only the tip of the iceberg: the vast bulk of campaigns are not submitted to the torture test of an IPA jury and it would be foolhardy to claim that all Scottish advertising works every time. Things can always get better, and that is where this book comes in. There are some impressive stories in this 2005 collection and, like all such IPA cases since the Effectiveness Awards began in 1980, they are intended to provide learning about advertising – about how it works, how much it works, and how we can measure how much it works. These impressive stories provide the learning that, individually and collectively, can help bring the standard of *all* Scottish advertising up to their own high level.

But there's a curious thing about us advertising – and marketing – people. On the one hand, we are always looking for the magic formula, the 'how to guarantee great results' or '10 rules for successful copywriters'. On the other, we are very bad at learning from our and others' experiences. Brought up, perhaps, to challenge conventions, break rules and be original at all costs, we want each day to be a new dawn, each brief a new beginning. Certainly, originality is vital in our business, but that does not mean ignoring the lessons of experience: history is not 'bunk', nor does it 'begin with me'. There is freedom for creativity within a framework of learning from our predecessors.

Of course, every winning case in the Awards is unique, as is every brief we get from our clients, but we can learn some general lessons from the hundreds – actually over a thousand now – of different submissions in the IPA archive. Les Binet of the IPA's Value of Advertising Committee, who has overseen development of the IPA dataBANK and is a multiple award winner himself, has analysed the 1065 submitted cases, comparing those that won prizes with those that, despite being instances of successful advertising, did not make the final cut. He has drawn a number of conclusions from his analytical comparison, several of which are echoed in these 2005 Scottish Effectiveness Awards.

Our winning papers tend to possess a blend of the success factors identified by Les Binet's analysis, which shows, for instance, that campaigns with few objectives have been more likely to win than those with many. More focused campaigns – that is, those with one to three objectives – are more effective than those with many goals: so be single-minded in what you set out to achieve. Not a new lesson, you may say, which makes it all the more surprising that it is too often ignored and clarity of purpose too often compromised.

Another conclusion is that campaigns aiming to change behaviour are more effective than those aimed at changing attitudes. So have a behavioural objective, a call to action – buying, visiting, contacting – over and above attitudinal ones such as awareness, approval or positive imagery. Marketing communications are about provoking a change in people's behaviour, or sometimes preventing one that would otherwise take place to the brand's disadvantage, and although attitudinal changes may be indicative, they are not a proxy for the actions that actually drive revenue gains or losses.

Again, seeking new customers is more likely to bring success than trying to increase loyalty, so make penetration gains your aim, find new buyers rather than expect to change the habits of existing ones (something that Professor Andrew Ehrenberg has been telling us for years). By all means seek to transform brand friends into brand lovers, but the way to do so is nearly always by recruiting new friends to your brand.

Further, to secure growth, spend ahead of share of market: share of voice matters more than absolute spend and an aggressive approach is more likely to bear fruit. Easily said and not always easy to do, but responding to competitive weakness or aggression can be critical; budgets should be set with attention to the brand's competitive context.

Binet also shows that emotion is as effective a lever as reason. Previous IPA analysis has shown that few campaigns whose approach was 'mostly rational' were among the winners; the majority sought to occupy emotional territory and this remains true in Les's work. Again, not a surprise result when we consider recent academic work on human motivation and behaviour, which shows how our decisions are made by a combination of emotion and reason: the brain's reasoning capacity cannot operate separately from its emotional components.

The analysis indicates that ads work better if people like them, so go for likeability ahead of standout as a predictor of effectiveness. The US Advertising Research Foundation reached the same conclusion several years ago, so it is reassuring that hard IPA cases reinforce this finding.

Not surprisingly, many executional styles can work, but of those categorised, testimonials and 'slice of life' were the least effective, while humorous and sexy ads were most likely to win. Since IPA judges do not give marks for how much they enjoyed the advertising they are evaluating, the fact that this conclusion emerged from Les Binet's work is all the stronger proof.

Curiously, considering the success of so many research techniques, pre-testing neither predicts nor guarantees effectiveness. The lesson: don't waste research money there when maybe you can use it more rewardingly at earlier exploratory and later evaluative stages. Certainly, the papers in this book show the value of research early in the strategy development process to understand 'people in life', rather than later to test people on advertising.

Finally, a lesson about creativity. What sort of campaigns are these prize-winningly effective ones? Well, a high proportion – far higher than a random sample would throw up – of the top effectiveness winners are also creative award winners. It's roughly 50% over the years. By the normal law of averages, of the 30 IPA Effectiveness winners in 1998, maybe two would also have been creative award winners. In fact, 16 out of 30 were, and seven out of the 15 top winners in 2000, 13 out of the 23 Gold and Silvers in 2002 and nine out of the 19 in 2004.

It certainly seems that creativity – originality of thought, unexpected ideas, the fresh expression of a proposition, surprising executional treatments – plays a big part in effectiveness. Of course, Bill Bernbach was there long ago, he wrote:

'Properly practised, creativity must result in greater sales more economically achieved. Properly practised creativity can make one ad do the work of ten. Properly practised creativity can lift your claims out of the swamp of sameness and make them accepted, believed, persuasive, and urgent. Is creativity some obscure, esoteric art form? Not on your life. It's the most practical thing a businessman can employ.'

Which is, of course, its only justification in a commercial context: that a creative approach connects better with consumers and communicates more convincingly.

So there is a framework of learning, even in our business, that we should all be aware of. Within that framework, we have the freedom to exercise our creativity. There is no magic formula, but there is still magic.

A few comments about our Gold and Silver winners. Interestingly, but maybe a reflection of the client 'diet' of Scottish agencies, both Gold awards went to public-sector cases. Both, too, are about recruitment – in one case for members of Children's Hearings Panels and in the other for donors to the Blood Transfusion Service. Both demonstrated real focus on understanding people, revealing insight, clear strategy and smart work to overcome serious barriers. Both demonstrated definite results that met definite objectives and made public money work hard for the public good.

Our Silver winners were more diverse, spanning a cheese, a soup, a university, new technology, oral cancer and Scotland's heritage. This diversity of subjects was mirrored in the diversity of stories told, from turning 'internet rage' to positive effect in stimulating the take-up of broadband, to the role of a very suave mouse in building Seriously Strong Cheddar across the UK.

In selecting these cases for the highest accolades, the judges assessed them on seven criteria. Among the seven, the most critical were the scale of the campaign's effect in the context of the difficulty of its task – the magnitude and efficiency of its effect – and the exploration and proof of that effect. Only if the judges were convinced of the unbreakable chain of causality between the agencies' work and the real-world effects, could other factors like the strength of the solution, strategically and in its expression, or innovation in measurement and channel exploitation, really come into play.

A word on the judging. Our jury admired and enjoyed the shortlisted entries in all their variety and had no hesitation in naming some worthy winners. Particularly interesting this year were the many examples of multi-disciplinary and multi-channel campaigns, where agencies and clients had combined different media and different communication skills to good effect. Nowadays the winners in IPA Effectiveness Awards use four different 'channels' on average and this number has been growing steadily over the years. So mastery of the more complex ways in which consumers may now experience brands is a critical motif of contemporary marketing and it was good to see evidence for it in these Scottish cases. The subtitle of this book is, after all, 'proving the effectiveness of marketing communications' and, although consumers naturally refer to all such activities as 'advertising', the Scottish marketing community should be proud of the way its agencies have grown their capabilities to good effect, well beyond their traditional skills.

But in looking at the judges' notes, one constant refrain is evident: 'Where is the evidence for return on marketing investment (ROMI)?' The value of advertising depends on its effect outweighing its cost, either directly through enhanced revenues at a margin delivering profitability or more indirectly through an economic impact over time that justifies the expenditure. Demonstrating this value, as our best papers did, is critical to the objectives of the Awards, as it is to the IPA's wider strategy of bolstering the commercial and financial communities' appreciation of the contribution of marketing communications to business and the economy. Public service advertising, of course, is expected to deliver a return in terms of savings or tangible benefits to the taxpayer and electorate, equivalent to the ROMI for a commercial venture. Future case writers are urged to focus more on the value of their campaigns by presenting evidence of successful ROMI.

Having made that rather critical point, I shall reiterate a more unreservedly positive one from my introduction to the 2003 edition of *Scottish Advertising Works*: the winning authors convinced the judges that their agencies and their clients knew what they wanted to do, how they expected to do it, and how they knew they had done it. The results of their work benefited Scottish society, business and marketing. Our congratulations go to them all.

The Judges

James Best
Chairman and Convenor of Judges
Group Chairman, DDB London

Alistair Cunningham
Director of Brand Valuation & Strategy Department, Interbrand

Jim Law
Managing Director, Market Research UK

Alan MacKenzie
Head of Intermediary Brands & Communications, Abbey

Sandra Mitchell
Director of Marketing for Tennents, Interbew UK

Barbara Moyses
Director, Barbara Moyses & Partners

Sven Olsen
Chairman of IPA Value of Advertising Committee
EVP, FCB Europe

Martin Raymond
Head of Public Affairs, NHS Health Scotland

Menekse Suphi
Managing Director, Scott Porter Research

Acknowledgements

Many people worked hard to make the awards a success, in particular the core team at the Scottish IPA, Sara Robertson and Sonja Mclean, and at the IPA, Jill Bentley and Anna Foster.

The IPA's thanks are also due to our judges and to the Scottish IPA Committee, especially Chairman Phil Adams, Vice Chairman Helen Hourston, and David Amers.

Sponsors

The success of the Scottish IPA Effectiveness Awards 2005 owes a great debt to our sponsors. The Scottish IPA would like to thank the following companies whose support made the presentation possible, in particular our main sponsors, *The Scotsman Publications* and SMG Television.

MAIN SPONSORS

THE SCOTSMAN
SCOTLAND'S NATIONAL NEWSPAPER

smg television

CO SPONSORS

Posterscope UK

Summerhall

GRP

THE DRUM

Prizes

GRAND PRIX
Barkers for Children's Hearings (Scottish Executive)

CHAIRMAN'S AWARD
Citigate SMARTS for Anderson Strathern Solicitors

BEST DIRECT/BRAND RESPONSE
The Bridge for Blood Donation (Scottish National Blood Transfusion Service)

BEST INSIGHT AND INNOVATION
The Leith Agency for Standard Life

BEST INTEGRATION
*Spiritmedia Scotland for Broadband Registration Drive
(Highlands and Islands Enterprise)*

BEST MEDIA THINKING
The Union for Baxters (Baxters Food Group)

BEST NEW AUTHOR
Giles Moffat, The Union (Broadband for Scotland and Scotch Beef)

BEST NEW CLIENT
1576 for Seriously Strong Cheddar (McLelland)

BEST BRAND REJUVENATION
1576 for National Trust for Scotland

GOLD AWARDS

Barkers for Children's Hearings (Scottish Executive)

The Bridge for Blood Donation (Scottish National Blood Transfusion Service)

SCOTTISH IPA EFFECTIVENESS AWARDS 2005

SILVER AWARDS

The Union for Baxters (Baxters Food Group)

The Union for Broadband for Scotland (Scottish Enterprise)

1576 for National Trust for Scotland

*The Bridge for Oral Cancer Campaign
(West of Scotland Cancer Awareness Project)*

1576 for Seriously Strong Cheddar (McLelland)

Frame C for University of Dundee

BRONZE AWARDS

Citigate SMARTS for Anderson Strathern Solicitors

*Spiritmedia Scotland and Arrow Creative for Broadband Registration Drive
(Highlands and Islands Enterprise)*

The Leith Agency for Grolsch (Coors Brewers UK)

Feather Brooksbank for My First Bed™ (Silentnight)

The Leith Agency for Nambarrie

family for Overgate (Lendlease)

The Union for s1jobs.com (Newsquest)

The Union for Scotch Beef (Quality Meat Scotland)

The Bridge for ScottishPower

The Leith Agency for Standard Life

Section 1

Gold Winners

Section 1

GOLD
GRAND PRIX WINNER

1

Children's Hearings
Panel membership

Principal author: Michael Kemsley, Barkers
Collaborating author: Emma Taylor, Consultant
Media agency: Feather Brooksbank

EDITOR'S SUMMARY

If understanding your audience is the principal step to advertising effectiveness, then this case proved the point. Reassessing the audience, and consequently changing the tone of the advertising to appeal to a broader demographic group, made all the difference in attracting enough of the right volunteers to put themselves forward for membership of Children's Hearings Panels. Barkers made the Scottish Executive's money work harder with a new campaign that achieved better results, and made a simple and effective argument for the value of its work that certainly convinced the judges.

BACKGROUND

This paper explains how Scotland's Children's Hearings system has used advertising to inspire and motivate local people in local communities. The Children's Hearings system works not only with offenders but with children who have been neglected or abused.

For several years the number of people applying to join Panels had been in desperate decline. The future of the system hung in the balance and morale among those in the field was low. An urgent call to action was required that would strike a chord with people from all walks of life.

This paper will demonstrate how a change in advertising led to a dramatic turnaround in fortune for the Children's Hearings system. We will prove that advertising became the driving force for recruitment. We will show how an advertising strategy with a positive rather than negative focus effected a massive shift in the entire culture and philosophy of the Hearings system.

THE PROBLEM

Supporting, and where necessary reprimanding, children who become involved in crime or public misbehaviour is by its nature a very sensitive issue.

What makes the Children's Hearings system so unique is that each case is heard before a Children's Panel. The Reporter, an official employed by the Scottish Children's Reporter Administration, oversees the hearing but it is the Panel members that discuss the case and make recommendations for the future of the child.

Every Children's Panel includes three members of the local community. The aim is that these are three people who represent the local area and who each bring experience and fresh thinking on how the needs of the child can best be met. Their decision is informed through discussion with the child and those with parental responsibilities, with social workers and through reports from other appropriate parties. The Children's Panel is about finding the best outcome for each child that comes before it.

Panel members have to be committed to their role. Although full training and support is given, the demands placed upon each member should not be underestimated. The role entails exposure to highly traumatic cases, weekend work, time away from work for training courses and a general demand on free time. It is also unpaid. There are some 30 Children's Panel groups operating throughout Scotland, each one dependent on the cooperation of local volunteers for its ability to function and its very existence.

MARKETING OBJECTIVES

The initial objective was to reverse the decline in respondents, which threatened to bring about the demise of the Children's Hearings system.

A secondary objective was to bring together a broad cross-section of the community on the Panel. In general, would-be Panel members consisted of a high

CHILDREN'S HEARINGS

percentage of women, older people and people from higher socio-economic groups. This left a large part of the community under-represented, going against the whole ethos of the system.

Applications for the Panel could be made by telephone through a response-handling centre or the campaign website.

THE TASK

Attracting new blood to the Panel is crucial, and this has taken place annually with a recruitment campaign for Panel members every September throughout Scotland. A small media campaign including national and local press and radio had, for a while, been performing adequately. However, from 1998 onwards, the response level declined until it reached the point where the number of applicants became so low that the minimum Panel membership was in direct jeopardy. Among authorities it had been agreed that, in general, at least 4000 applicants per annum were required to generate sufficient numbers to maintain Panel membership.

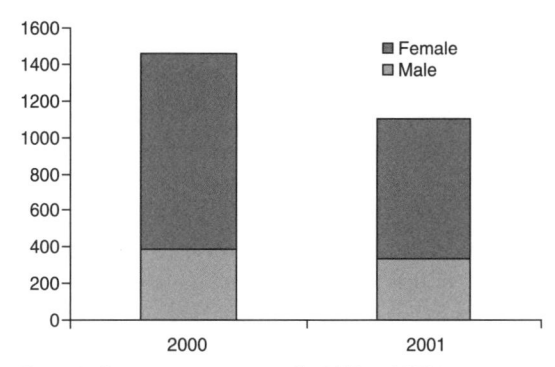

Figure 1: *Campaign response rate for 2000 and 2001*

As shown in Figure 1, the total responses to the handling centre for the 2000 campaign were 1460, falling further to 1105 in 2001. Of these, in 2000 only 8% came from C2DE groups, while in 2001 this dropped even further, to 6%.

Clearly the decline was dangerously close to profoundly damaging Scotland's unique system. The challenge was set.

THE STRATEGIC SOLUTION

With applicants at such a low level and a massive increase in budget out of the question, a new creative brief was developed for the 2002 campaign.

It was recognised that the role of research in developing this brief should be an important one. A qualitative programme was conducted among seven groups in the primary target: 25–45 BC1C2D. Given the desire to boost applications from those under-represented on the Panel, the ratio of groups was weighted towards men and lower socio-economic groupings.

To enhance understanding of the motivations to join the Panel, groups of Panel members who joined in 2001 were also consulted. A substantial stakeholder consultation was under way that encouraged blue-sky thinking. What could we do better? Where did we need to be giving our messages? Was advertising failing? Perhaps it wasn't a job for advertising after all? These questions and more were thrown open to discussion, leaving no stone unturned. Local Children's Panel Advisory Committees (CPACs) were a key focus and their extensive knowledge of the subject matter was probed deeply.

Research and advertising planners worked tirelessly to tease out the issues, in particular the negative associations people had with the Panel. It seemed that to study the negatives would be crucial in finding a long-term solution to the recruitment problem.

In developing the new brief, a massive number of stimuli were tested at research and in stakeholder consultation. A vast range of ideas featured, including those the agency felt to be uninspiring, so we could truly get behind the reasons why they were rejected. The creative from earlier years was also redrafted and resubmitted as a concept for testing. The following points summarise the outcome.

- We found a lack of awareness that the Children's Hearings system was unique to Scotland. Once this was explained, there was a real feeling of national pride that Scotland was at the cutting edge in this field.
- People were far more likely to apply to join their local Panel than they would be to apply for a national Panel. It was less intimidating and more relevant.
- The perceived amount of time that would have to be allocated to Panel duties was a major barrier to applying. There was extremely low awareness of what this would amount to in reality – people didn't really know if it would be 10 minutes a week or six hours.
- Most people perceived Panel members to be educated, middle-class and slightly elitist, which discouraged those in lower socio-economic groups from applying. They felt that anything they would have to say would have less value than those from higher socio-economic groups and that it generally wasn't a role for people like them.
- The concept of 'policing' young criminals was thought to be frightening and problematic, and there was a lack of awareness about the caring and positive side of the Panel work.

We discovered that the main motivations to join the Panel were clear and very strong, very personal drivers. People wanted to help children – especially those local to their area. They wanted to make a difference, to give something back to society. There was a thirst for knowledge about the system, its successes and what it could do. More generally there were a substantial number who wanted to use membership as an opportunity for personal development and lifelong learning, particularly to develop an existing interest such as childcare or social work.

It became clear that previous creative work had done nothing to address these issues. The use of black-and-white images, as shown in Figure 2, had actually put across a message of depression and helplessness rather than that of a caring and inspirational role. The use of vocabulary such as 'trouble' and 'challenge' reaffirmed the more confrontational aspects and said nothing of the help that members give to young people. The advertising had, correctly, sought to advise of the serious and important nature of the role but had inadvertently created a new barrier to applicants.

It was also apparent that we needed to produce less of what would be considered a traditional recruitment campaign and more of a product-based advertising campaign. New thinking and research showed that a recruitment-led format was in fact counterproductive.

A new strategy was required that would engender wider appeal for the Panels. We had to make the broadest audience possible interested in the system and its

Figure 2: *'Alone'*

work, emphasising the positives of the Panel rather than the negatives. We had to associate a new set of brand values with Children's Hearings.

We had to deliver this locally and we had to speak to people about their community. Above all, we had to show that it was a worthwhile journey to go on, and we had to take into account that each individual has a different idea of what constitutes worthwhile. The new brief was an extremely difficult one: to turn current perceptions upside down. We had to appeal to new people and we had to engage them in a deeply emotive, positive way.

THE IDEA

A more open, caring and accessible approach needed to be taken towards the creative. We needed to encourage people to do their bit for their local community, for young people from their own part of town. As such it had to become less intimidating and more inspirational.

The new Children's Hearings had to stand for 'my local area and the kids that live here', it had to be 'for people like me' and it had to show the philanthropic value. What was needed was optimism, and all advertising and marketing collateral would need to be reframed as such.

Consultation work was again under way. It was imperative that those involved in the management of the Panels, in particular CPACs, bought into, and more importantly understood, the new focus.

It went deeper than advertising. CPACs were guided through the process of preparing more positive and welcoming packs. The new optimistic essence of the work cascaded down to all levels. Expertise was shared on engaging elected officials and local media, and on developing public information points such as libraries and supermarkets. The new optimism about Children's Hearings would permeate at all levels and create a new wave of applicants, vying for recognition as one of society's enablers.

As a result of all this work, the ads shown in Figures 3–6 were developed for the 2002 campaign.

THE COMMUNICATION ACTIVITY

2002

For 2002 the advertising activity was split into two parts, to allow for both an awareness and a recruitment campaign. The awareness campaign used national and regional titles for one week commencing 26 August, while the recruitment campaign took advantage of local and national press and 16 Scottish radio stations.

The agency negotiated a supplement in the *Sun* to support the advertising. Every effort was made to ensure that the *Sun* grasped the philosophy of the campaign, and case studies were produced that highlighted individuals and how the role had enriched their lives.

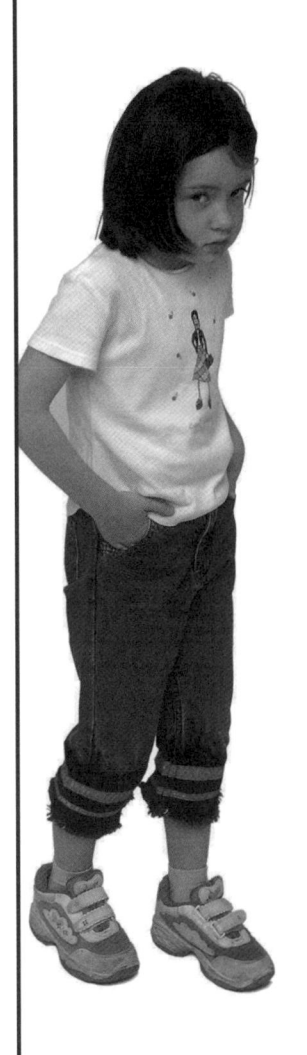

Figure 3: 'Lauren'

Figure 4: *'Growing pains'*

Figure 5: 'Priceless'

SCOTTISH ADVERTISING WORKS 4

Figure 6: 'What kind of ...'

Campaign guides were distributed across all local authority areas and included an overview of the campaign, artwork that could be tailored for local use and tips on making the campaign successful at a local level.

The awareness campaign achieved coverage among all adults of 67.4% at 2.1 OTS. The recruitment strand of the campaign achieved 78% at 5.8 OTS among all adults for press and 68% cover at 8.5 OTH for radio. The total media budget was

CHILDREN'S HEARINGS

£178,196.87 (excluding VAT, ASBOF and agency fees) and the paid-for media activity lasted for a total of five weeks.

2003

In 2003 the campaign received a cut in overall budget while still requiring high response rates to ensure the Panel's success. An extra creative execution was added to those used in 2002. This execution was produced with the specific aim of halting the decline in male applicants and appeared within the sports pages of press titles.

National and local press were used, plus local radio for the general campaign. From a total media budget of £148,730 the campaign achieved 68% at 8.5 OTH among all adults on radio and 67% at 2.1 OTS. Paid-for media activity lasted for a total of three weeks.

THE RESULTS

According to the data presented in Figure 7:

- in 2000 a total of 1460, 27% male (390) and 73% female (1070), respondents were logged;
- in 2001 a total of 1105, 30% male (334) and 70% female (771), respondents were logged;
- in 2002 a total of 4133, 23% male (938) and 77% female (3195), respondents were logged;
- in 2003 a total of 3816, 30% male (1118) and 70% female (2698), respondents were logged.

An overall increase in respondents of 374% was achieved from 2001 to 2002.
According to the data presented in Figure 8:

- in 2000 the breakdown of respondents by age can be shown as 18–30 23% (343), 31–40 35% (519), 41–50 26% (378) and 51+ 16% (220);
- in 2001 the breakdown of respondents by age can be shown as 18–30 27% (293), 31–40 37% (403), 41–50 25% (272) and 51+ 12% (137);

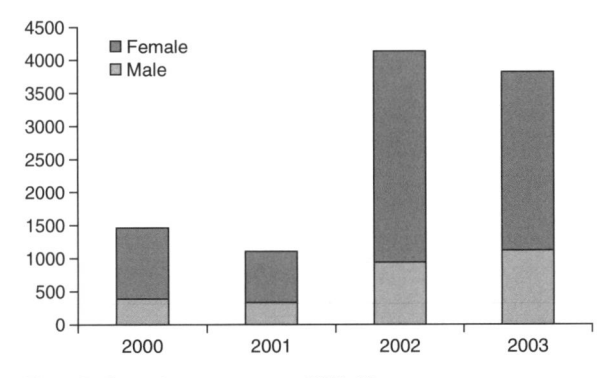

Figure 7: *Campaign response rates 2000–03*

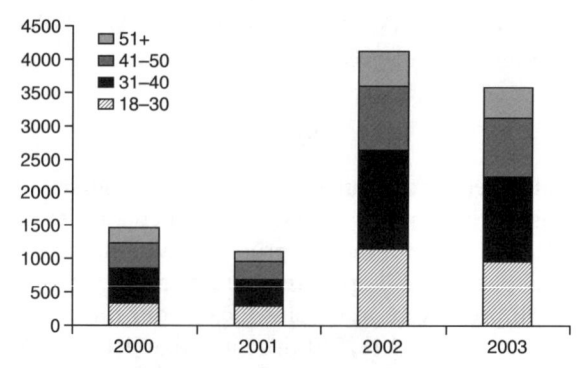

Figure 8: *Responses by age*

- in 2002 the breakdown of respondents by age can be shown as 18–30 28% (1146), 31–40 36% (1492), 41–50 23% (954) and 51+ 13% (541);
- in 2003 the breakdown of respondents by age can be shown as 18–30 25% (954), 31–40 34% (1297), 41–50 23% (878) and 51+ 12% (458) and unknown 6% (229).

According to the data presented in Figure 9:

- in 2000 the breakdown of respondents by socio-economic group can be shown as AB 32% (465), C1 34% (506), C2 4% (52), DE 4% (58) and F 26% (379);
- in 2001 the breakdown of respondents by socio-economic group can be shown as AB 53% (587), C1 15% (161), C2 4% (47), DE 2% (27) and F 26% (283);
- in 2002 the breakdown of respondents by socio-economic group can be shown as AB 30% (1246), C1 32% (1315), C2 5% (208), DE 6% (257) and F 27% (1107).

Please note that there is no comparable socio-economic information available for 2003 due to a change in classification used for that year's figures.

These figures demonstrate the actual level and type of respondents contacting the response centre. Although local authorities were encouraged to build upon the success of the advertising campaign through localised promotion using campaign creative work, there has been no other promotional work to which we could attribute such a massive increase in response levels.

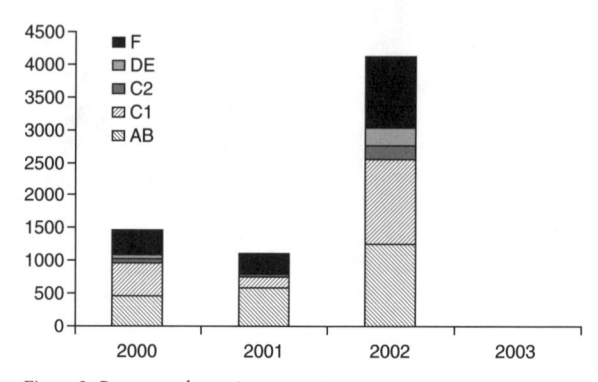

Figure 9: *Responses by socio-economic group*

CHILDREN'S HEARINGS

No significant change to length or composition of media was observed throughout the four-year period, which suggests that it is the creative execution that has brought about such an upturn, rather than a change in media strategy.

In 2002, national press advertising reaped dividends with as many as 508 people citing the *Daily Record*, and 363 people the *Sunday Mail* as their reason for calling. The special *Sun* supplement performed extremely well, with the number of respondents driven by the *Sun* totalling 239. Local press yielded over 171 respondents from the *Glasgow Evening Times* and 158 from the *Edinburgh Evening News*. Radio also performed extremely successfully, with 346 respondents who had heard advertising on Radio Clyde, 330 on Real Radio and 209 on Radio Forth.

To put this in context, only 44 people contacted the response centre as a result of word of mouth.

PAYBACK/RETURN ON INVESTMENT

For this we can simply presume that the total amount of budget spent on media advertising can be divided by the number of respondents to the handling centre. This gives us a straightforward cost per respondent. The breakdown for this year on year is shown in Table 1.

TABLE 1: COST PER RESPONDENT CALCULATIONS

Year	Total respondents	Total budget	Cost per respondent
2000	1460	£89,629	£61.39
2001	1105	£99,375	£89.93
2002	4133	£178,197	£43.12
2003	3816	£148,730	£38.98

SUMMARY

Getting people to sacrifice their free time and expose themselves to potentially upsetting situations without pay is no mean feat. We have proven that small budget doesn't equate to small campaign, and the magnitude of the work required us to reach out throughout Scotland. Response growth from 2001 to 2002 was 374%.

It's a simple campaign, the results are straightforward and it's extremely effective. We can clearly show how advertising achieved goals and revolutionised recruitment to the Children's Hearings system.

GOLD
BEST DIRECT/BRAND RESPONSE

2

Blood Donation
New strategy, new blood

Principal author: David Watson, The Bridge
Media agency: MediaCom

EDITOR'S SUMMARY

The challenge of reversing donor decline was a big one for the Scottish National Blood Transfusion Service and an important one to resolve. That The Bridge's campaign contributed substantially to the turnaround in donations achieved, and did so with a remarkable improvement in cost-effectiveness, was the case made convincingly in this paper. Learning from international experience to gain consumer insight prompted an excellent response-generating campaign that combined TV with radio to achieve enhanced mutual effect. Its results could not fail to impress: a threefold increase in calls and all the donors needed at a cost per response that had halved.

BACKGROUND

On 16 March 2004, the Health Secretary John Reid announced that all those people who had had blood transfusions since 1980 would be excluded from future blood donation. This policy was introduced as a measure to reduce the possible risk of vCJD (new variant Creutzfeldt-Jakob disease) transmission by blood transfusion. People who have been the recipients of blood transfusions tend to be more likely to become blood donors themselves. These previously transfused donors (PTDs) made up a significant proportion of existing blood donors. To exclude them from the donor base in Scotland would have a major impact on the blood supply.

In addition, the extent of the problem did not extend only to PTDs. Previous experience had shown that adverse publicity (such as that in connection with the HIV virus in the 1980s) would have a considerable secondary impact on blood donor recruitment. It was estimated that the issue of vCJD transmission in blood would lead to a loss of up to 10% of the Scottish donor base.

The immediate effects of this crisis were serious enough. However, it occurred at a time when the donor base had been declining for broader social and demographic reasons. In 1991, donors aged 17–24 accounted for 26% of the donor base, but by 2001 accounted for only 20%. At the same time, an ageing population required more operations and hospital care. In addition, trends such as exotic travel, body-piercing and tattooing had also affected donor numbers (deferral periods can be up to 12 months following any of these activities). Deferral rates among new donors had more than doubled since 1993 and currently nearly one-third of all new donors are turned away at their first session.

Therefore the vCJD crisis took place at a time when there had been an overall decline in the level of blood donations in Scotland over many years. The crisis in blood stocks was alleviated only in 2003/04 with an emergency appeal. This drastic and unusual step was taken because donor attendances were expected to be only 300,000 (see Figure 1). Yet, this was something undertaken as a last resort and could not be repeated every year.

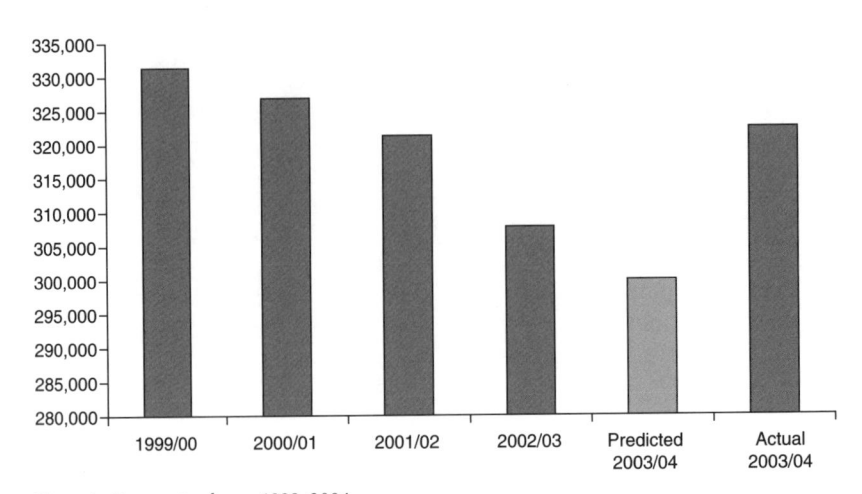

Figure 1: *Donor attendance, 1999–2004*

BLOOD DONATION

The combination of the deferral of PTDs and long-term erosion of the donor base meant that there were no longer enough blood donors to reliably support Scottish healthcare. The Scottish National Blood Transfusion Service (SNBTS) had to recruit donors, and quickly developed an integrated marketing strategy to stimulate the recovery of the Scottish blood donor base.

THE NEW STRATEGY

SNBTS estimated that it needed to attract 58,000 new and returning/lapsed donors in order to repair the donor base and to offset the effects of the vCJD crisis. (Returning/lapsed donors are those who haven't given for more than two years.)

However, as Figure 2 makes clear, this was a massive task. Over the last 15 years, the annual number of new and returning donors has fluctuated only slightly and was part of a longer-term decline. Between 1989/90 and 1999/2000, new donor levels averaged 42,994. By 2003/4, this figure was only 38,381.

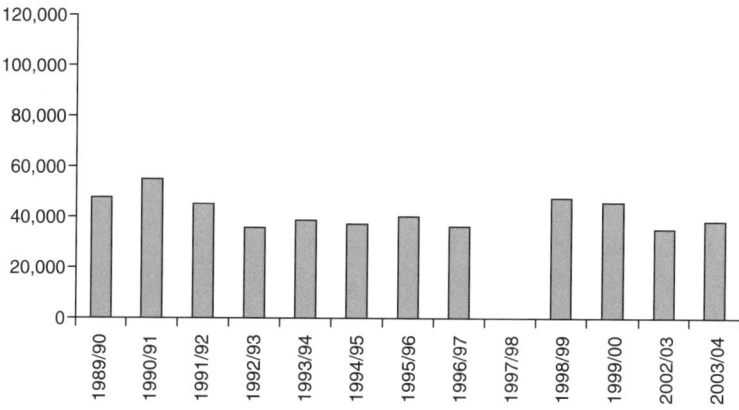

Figure 2: *New and returning donor attendances, 1989–2004*

Put into this historical context, the target of 58,000 new and returning donor attendances was incredibly challenging. It meant delivering over 50% more new and returning donors than had been achieved in 2003/04. It was clear that in order to affect such a step-change in donor numbers, a step-change in strategy was required.

The first task of The Bridge's marketing strategy was to separate out a clear role for the advertising (to ask people to register to become a blood donor) and a clear role for the below-the-line activity (to manage the database) (see Figure 3).

At the heart of the strategy was the idea of personal relevance. Extensive desk research of blood collection campaigns around the world revealed a common theme: the importance of making a personal connection with the (potential) donor.

Only 6% of the Scottish population are blood donors. Blood donation just isn't at the top of people's minds. Most people in Scotland agree that giving blood is a good thing. They also understand the need for blood donors, yet for 94% of the population the concept of blood donation is clearly not something they are actively

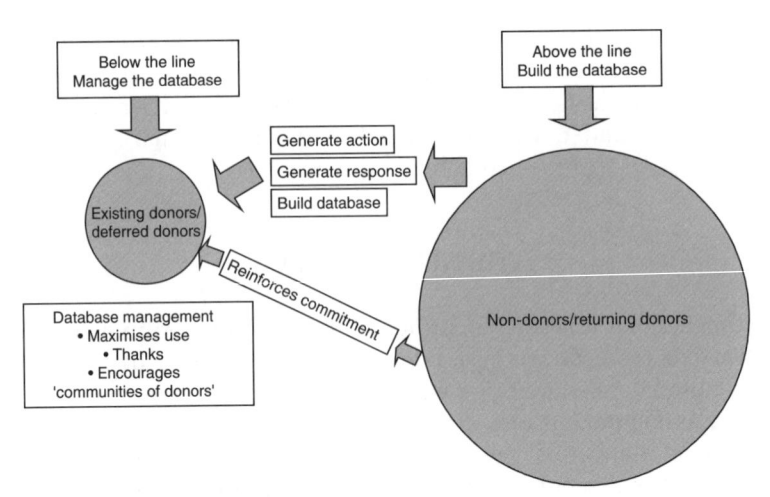

Figure 3: *A model of how The Bridge's strategy would work*

engaged in. It was crucial that the advertising engaged with people and made them think that their contribution would be important. The strategy needed to make the issue of blood donation personally relevant.

Research from worldwide donor recruitment campaigns revealed a stunning insight: when questioned, the biggest single reason non-donors gave for not giving blood was that they felt they had never been asked. Although people were aware of a general request or 'asking' for blood donors, they didn't feel it was actually directed at them. They felt the advertising was asking someone else. Clearly, success in reaching the new donor targets would depend on making it obvious to the viewer that it was they who were being asked to donate blood. It needed to feel like a personal request. This would give blood donation a personal relevance that it previously didn't have.

EXECUTING THE STRATEGY: THE CREATIVE WORK

For the new strategy to deliver results, there were four fundamental issues that the creative work needed to address. First, it needed to leave the viewer in no doubt that it was they who were being asked to register to become blood donors. Second, it needed to do this in an emotive and engaging manner. Third, in order to deliver the stiff response targets, it was crucial that the direct response element of the commercial didn't feel tagged on. It needed to be integral to the commercial. Finally, it was vital that the message was delivered without causing anxiety. Any hint of crisis would only lead to donor fatigue.

Although it was important for the new commercial to generate as many blood donations as possible, donor attendances (and consequently blood stocks) needed to be manageable. Blood has a limited shelf life of only a few days and collecting too much blood would mean that the SNBTS would be faced with higher than acceptable levels of wastage. Therefore the strategy needed to work like a tap – able to turn the donor supply on and off, and airing the commercial only when there was a need for blood.

BLOOD DONATION

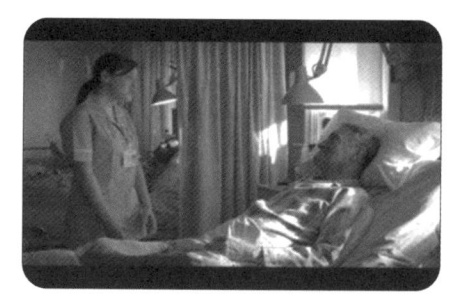

Nurse: I'm sure they'll call

Dad: She's bound to call soon son

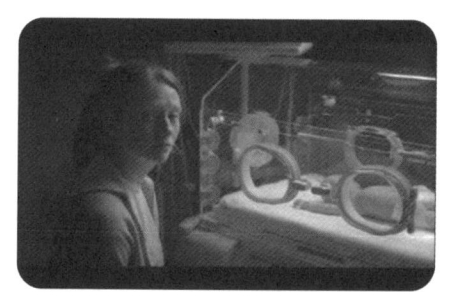

Doctor: Don't worry, he'll call in a while

VO: It's not someone else they're looking for. It's you. Scotland needs you to give blood. Whether you've never given before or just haven't given for a while, call 0845 90 90 999.

Figure 4: *'Call'*

Following qualitative research, 'Call' was identified as the television script that resonated most with new and lapsed donors. The campaign was launched on 2 August 2004 and ran until 31 August at a weight of 500 TVRs across Scotland (see Figure 4). Blood supplies were healthy until later in the year, when two radio commercials, 'Your Call' and 'Accident' ran in November and December. The TV commercial 'Call' was broadcast again in January 2005.

THE RESULTS

Prior to developing the new creative work, the SNBTS had been using a rebranded version of a National Blood Service (NBS) commercial, featuring Gary Lineker and other celebrities. The effectiveness of the new strategy would be measured against the effectiveness of the Lineker commercial and also against targets set by SNBTS.

The new strategy was an immediate success. A pre and post test using the TNS Omnibus reported that the commercial was demonstrating considerable cut-through. Between the pre and post test, unprompted awareness of advertising for blood donors rose from 62% to 73%. Furthermore, the new commercial hit a prompted awareness level of 57% after just one month of advertising. This is compared to prompted awareness of the Lineker commercial of 54%, after three years of airtime.

RESPONSE DATA

Television activity: August 2004

The NBS commercial last ran in July 2004, the month before 'Call' was launched. Therefore a direct comparison of effectiveness can be made between the two. Figure 5 illustrates the comparative spend and Figure 6 the level of response for each commercial.

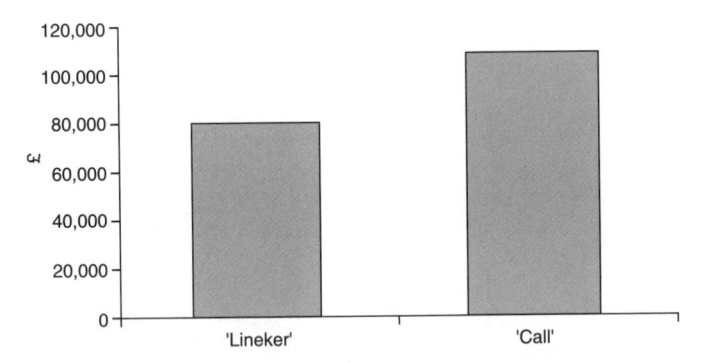

Figure 5: *Comparative spend between 'Lineker' (July) and 'Call' (August)*

Figures 5 and 6 offer clear evidence of the increased effectiveness of 'Call' in generating response: a 35% increase in media spend between the two commercials resulted in nearly a 300% increase in responses. Yet the success of the new commercial wasn't just measured in increased response – it was also far more efficient, as a comparison of cost-per-response data makes clear (see Figure 7).

Furthermore, in-depth analysis of the response data makes it clear that the new commercial was more than four times as effective in recruiting the key target of new donors (see Figure 8). Significantly, 'Call' also proved twice as effective in motivating returning donors to register.

The new commercial played the major role in motivating people to call the donor line: 74% of new donors cited it as their reason for calling. The success the

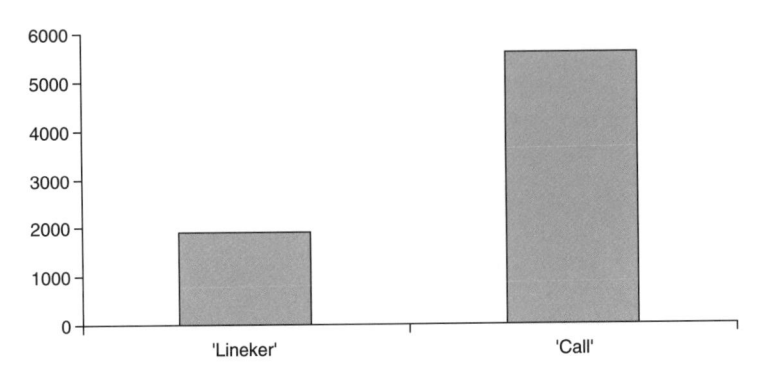

Figure 6: *Calls generated by 'Lineker' (July) and 'Call' (August)*

BLOOD DONATION

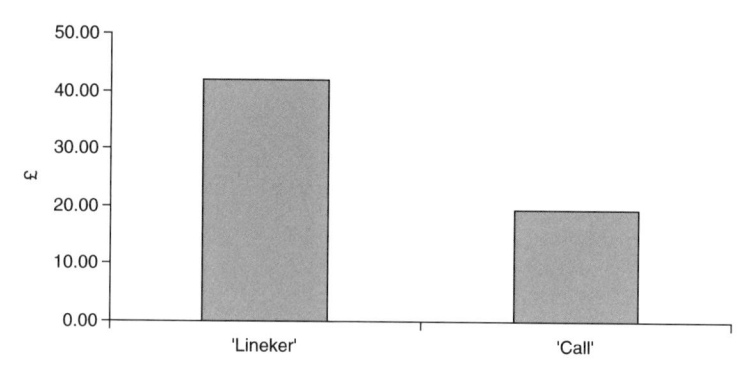

Figure 7: *Cost-per-response comparison between 'Lineker' (July) and 'Call' (August)*

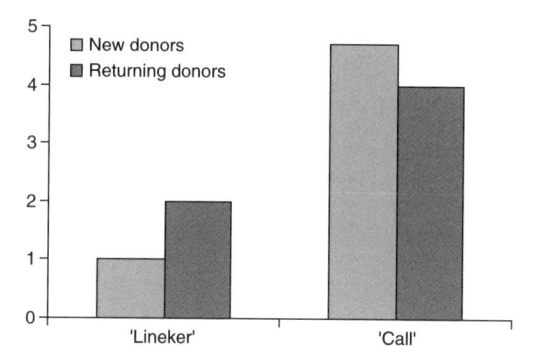

Figure 8: *Comparison of responses per TVR between 'Lineker' (July) and 'Call' (August)*

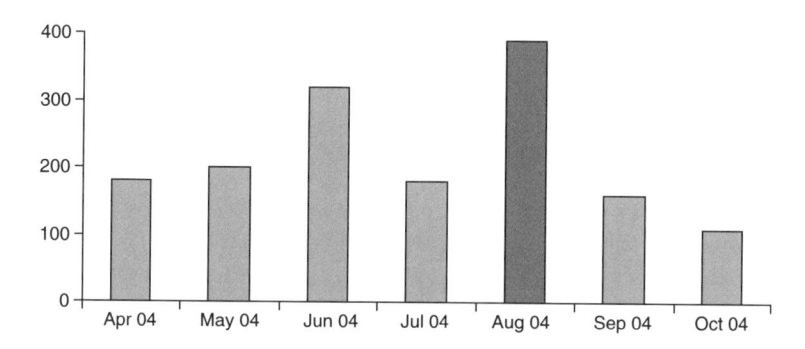

Figure 9: *Website registrations per month, 2004*

new commercial had in attracting calls to 0845 90 90 999 was mirrored in the success it had in generating registrations on the website (see Figure 9).

Radio advertising: November and December

The success of the new strategy was reinforced by the responses generated by the new radio commercials. Their launch in November saw the highest call numbers since August (see Figure 10).

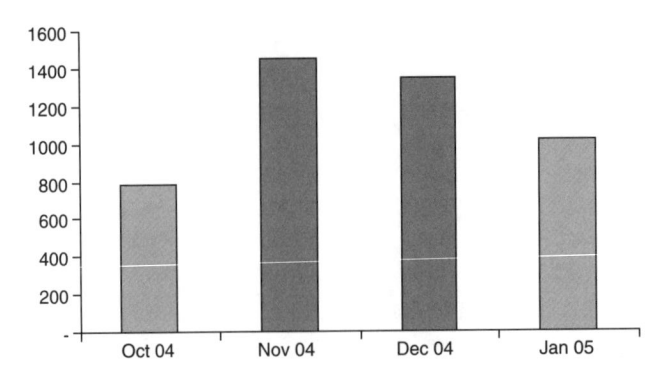

Figure 10: *Calls to 0845 90 90 999 (by month), October 2004–January 2005*

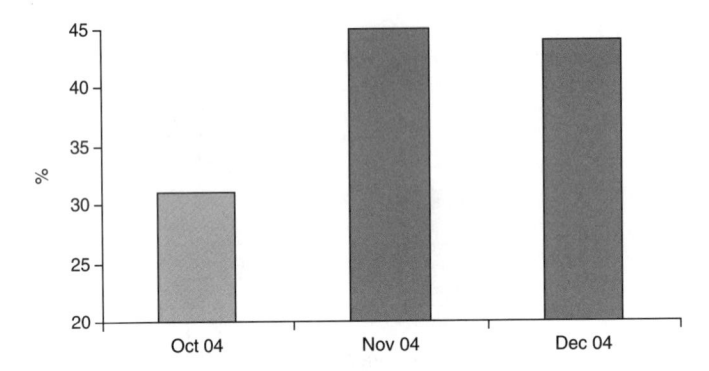

Figure 11: *Percentage of new donors calling 0845 90 90 999*

The new radio commercials also proved effective in recruiting those all-important new donors (see Figure 11).

Just like the new television commercial, the cost per response of the new radio commercials was proving the efficiency of the new strategy against the old one (see Figure 12).

The effectiveness of the new strategy in generating calls was further underlined by the response data for January 2005, which showed that 'Call' was continuing to deliver over three times the number of calls per TVR than the Lineker commercial.

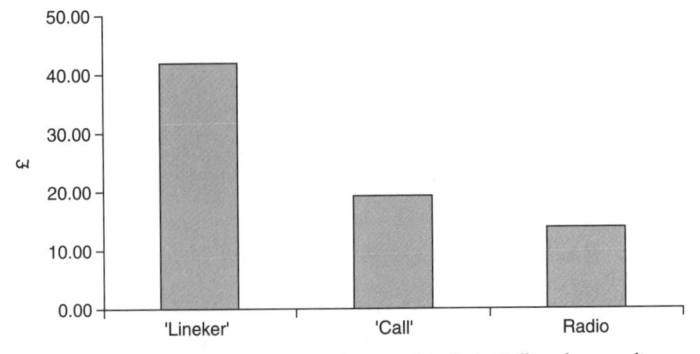

Figure 12: *Cost-per-response comparison between 'Lineker', 'Call' and new radio commercials*

BLOOD DONATION

Donor attendances and blood collection

But what was really important was increasing blood donations. The new strategy was equally effective in motivating people to become blood donors. It had an immediate impact on donor attendances – bearing out the 'tap on, tap off' strategy – and it helped the SNBTS surpass its exacting targets for August (see Figure 13).

This upturn in donor numbers in August is in comparison to the figures for July 2004 when the NBS commercial was running. It delivered only 96% of the month's overall target (see Figure 14).

The SNBTS had hoped that the new strategy would have a significant effect on donor numbers and had expected an upturn. However, the success of 'Call' was beyond its expectations, delivering 23% over the projected target for the week following the launch of the commercial and 15% over the projected target across the whole month (see Figure 15).

Furthermore, a profile of donor attendance shows that the new strategy was also working in terms of attracting increased numbers of returning donors as well as the all-important new donors (see Figure 16).

And it wasn't just new and returning donors that were motivated to action by the new commercial. It also appears to have helped build donor loyalty by persuading regular donors to give more often (see Figure 17).

This resulted in a considerable increase in the number of donations (see Figure 18).

The success of the television advertising in increasing donor attendances was matched by the radio advertising in November (see Figure 19).

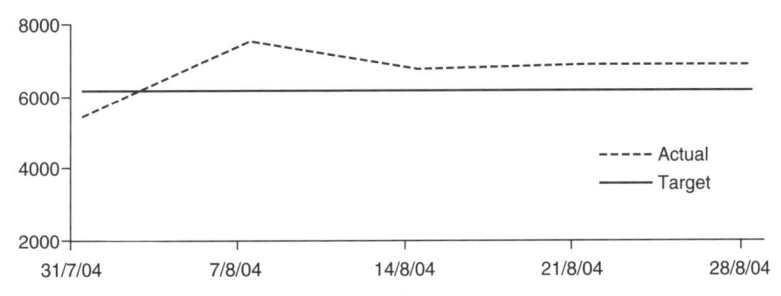

Figure 13: *Donor attendances vs target, August 2004*

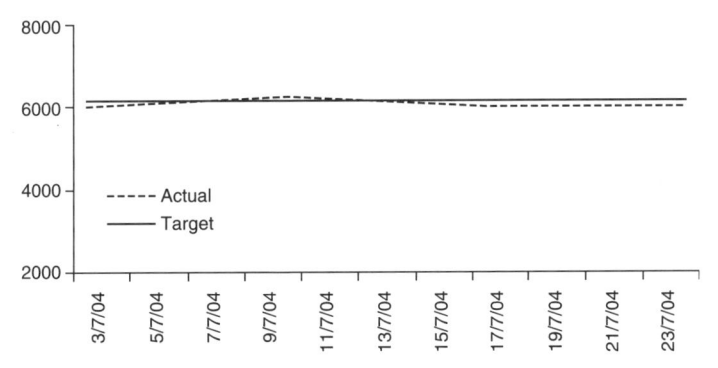

Figure 14: *Donor attendances vs target, July 2004*

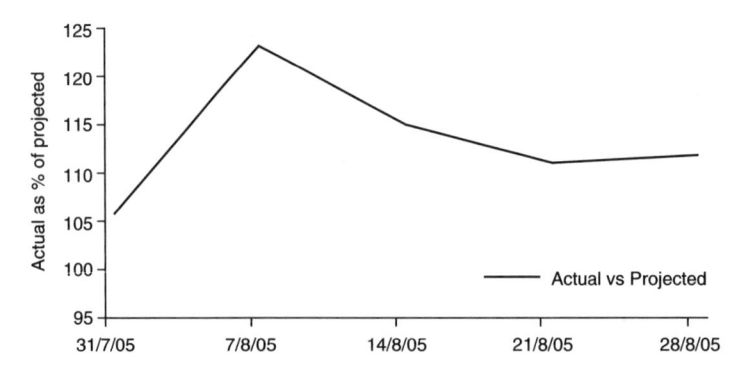

Figure 15: *Donor attendances, actual vs projected, August 2004*

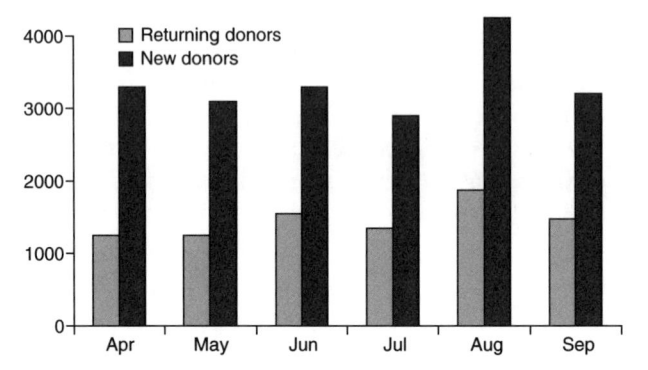

Figure 16: *New and returning donor attendances, April–September 2004*

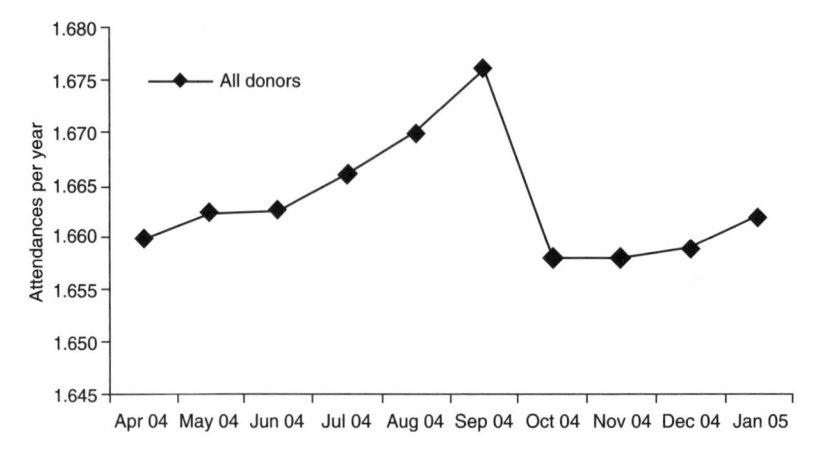

Figure 17: *Annual attendance frequency (all donors)*

BLOOD DONATION

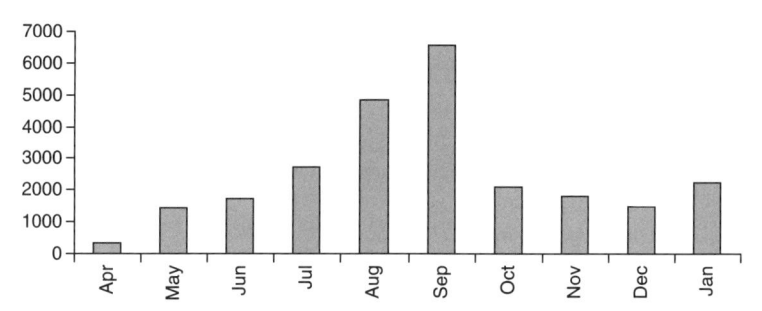

Figure 18: *Additional donations from regular donors*

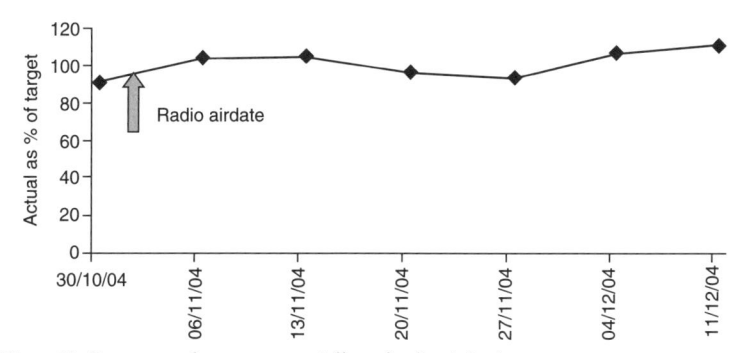

Figure 19: *Donor attendances vs target (effect of radio airdate)*

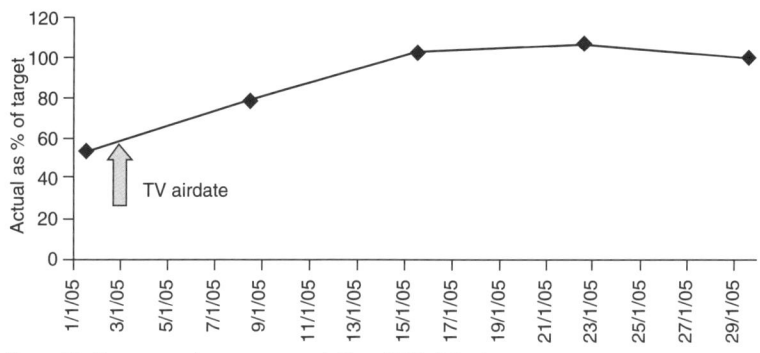

Figure 20: *Donor attendances vs target (effect of TV airdate)*

A further burst of television in January also boosted donor numbers from the traditional New Year low (see Figure 20).

By 31 January 2005, the SNBTS was well on its way to reaching its targets. Year-to-date figures show that donor attendances were on target for the year and up 2% from 2003/04, and that the number of new donors was up 9% on the previous year. The number of new and returning/lapsed donors currently stands at 46,527, an average of 5170 per month. Taken over a 12-month period, this equates to 62,040 new and lapsed donors for the year – some 7% over the target of 58,000 that was required in order to repair the donor base and offset the effects of the vCJD crisis.

Other factors

Holiday periods and major sporting events are detrimental to blood donation. Anything, in fact, that disrupts people's routine will affect blood-donation levels. The new campaign was launched on 2 August 2004, 11 days before the start of the largest sporting event in the world: the Olympic Games. The Games ran until the end of the month. Not only that, but August is a significant holiday period with one bank holiday at the end of the month. Despite these obstacles, the new strategy delivered responses, donors and attendances well over target.

There is also evidence to show that in May (when there was no advertising, but there was a bank holiday as in August) blood donations failed to meet the target for most weeks (see Figure 21).

Likewise, in October, when there was no advertising, calls and donor numbers were down and below target (see Figures 22 and 23).

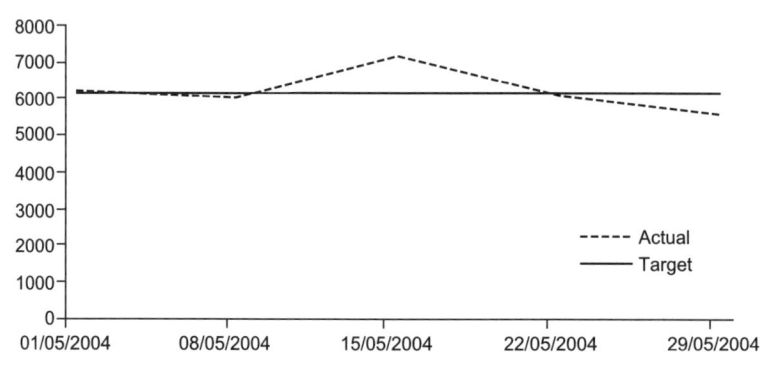

Figure 21: *Donor attendances vs target, May 2004*

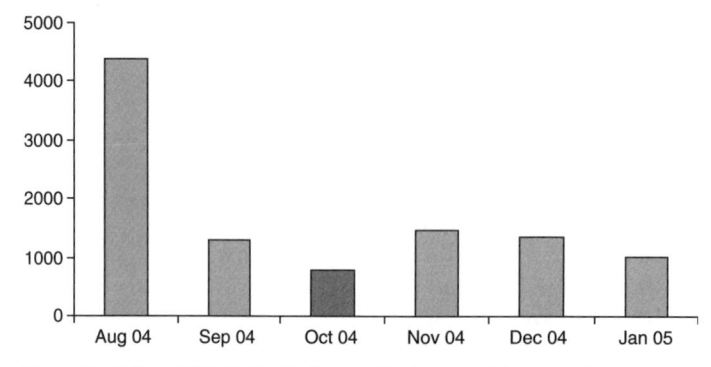

Figure 22: *Calls to 0845 90 90 999 (by month), August 2004–January 2005*

BLOOD DONATION

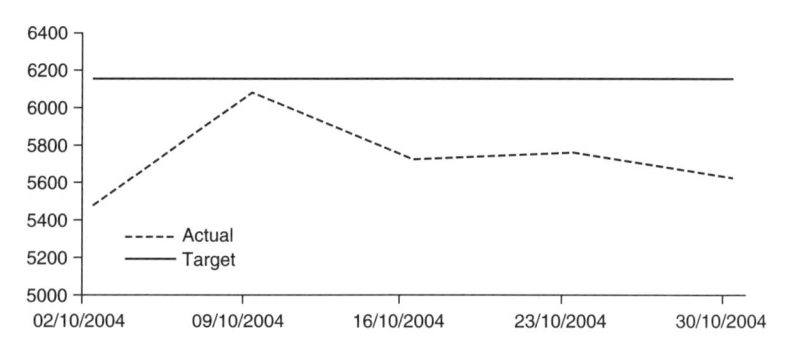

Figure 23: *Donor attendances, October 2004*

RETURN ON INVESTMENT

The maintenance of blood stocks is vital to Scottish healthcare. They are used in all aspects of the health service – from operations such as hip replacements to treatment for leukaemia to accident and emergency units. All depend on having blood stocks available. This paper demonstrates what a clear and unambiguous role advertising has played in ensuring healthy blood stocks in Scotland. The new advertising strategy has proved extremely effective and, without it, there is no doubt that the SNBTS would have had to issue an emergency appeal for donors (as it did in October 2003). In this context, the return on investment cannot be quantified in monetary terms, but in far more significant terms: without it, the health service in Scotland may well have ground to a halt.

Section 2

Silver Winners

SILVER
BEST MEDIA THINKING

3

Baxters
The personal touch pays dividends

Principal author: Mark Reid, The Union
Collaborating authors: Beverley Hart and Rebecca Harrison, The Union
Media agency: MediaCom

EDITOR'S SUMMARY

An excellent IPA case from The Union, its key point of interest being the bold decision to switch funds from TV and print into the 'more personal' medium of radio in support of a particular creative approach. A good story of resulting sales growth, substantiated by some clear-cut econometric analysis of the brand's performance in Sainsbury's stores, convinced the judges of Baxters' claim to a Silver award, despite their frustration at the lack of real ROI data.

INTRODUCTION

Baxters Food Group has been making fine quality foods since 1868. Throughout this period the company has remained entirely in the hands of the Baxter family. Over the years the company has developed an enviable reputation for producing top-quality preserves, chutneys, beetroot and, particularly, soup.

What this paper demonstrates is how in its advertising campaign from October 2003 to March 2004, Baxters leveraged real consumer insight to develop a hugely impactful advertising campaign using radio – a relatively new medium for the brand. The campaign successfully built on existing Baxters advertising equity in a persuasive and memorable way that had a strong positive impact on the health of the brand.

THE MARKET CONTEXT: DAVID TAKES ON GOLIATH

In autumn 2003, the company was facing increasing competition from competitors Heinz and Campbell's. With its aggressive marketing and huge budgets Heinz had amassed a dominant market share of 57.5% (MAT) of the wet ambient soup category (WAS). Campbell's, the US food giant, enjoyed a UK market share of 17.0%, leaving Baxters behind in third position with 11.5% share.[1]

Undeterred by the size and weight of the competition, Baxters set itself the task of narrowing the share gap between itself and Campbell's, while continuing to improve consumer disposition to the brand.

HARNESSING THE BRAND'S EQUITY

In the 12 months leading up to the 2003 soup season (traditionally October–March) Baxters invested in research that would enable the marketing team to fundamentally leverage the brand's core equity in a relevant and modern way.

Extensive usage and attitude studies helped identify consumer motivations and core brand properties. The team conducted research into both category and brand perceptions across the UK. As a result it gained a deeper understanding of the uniqueness of the brand and its relevance to today's consumers.

What it found was that the real driver of the brand's appeal was the company's relatively small size but, more importantly, the commitment and personal involvement of the Baxter family. This brand truth set it apart from the giants it was up against.

But this wasn't really new news. In recent years the brand communication strategy had struggled with how to leverage the Baxter family's involvement. The memorable 'Ena Baxter' campaign, while achieving standout, was not relevant to today's consumer.

Being a family business, which still believed and valued its heritage, did have potential strengths for brand communication. The family was shorthand for personal care, expertise and integrity – things that more and more consumers are being turned on to in an increasingly mass-market, impersonal and faceless world. It was still the great-tasting food that was the consumer benefit, but the personal touch of the family was the core essence, the primary reason to believe.

---

1. Source: ACNielsen.

Figure 1: *The Baxters brand pyramid*

THE CREATIVE AND THE MEDIA BRIEF

Baxters' marketing objectives were to drive reappraisal of this 137-year-old brand, generating fresh relevance and triggering trial.

The creative brief was simple: 'Real Food from Real People'. The aim was to strike up a dialogue and generate warmth and passion.

Up to this point the communication channel thinking had been media neutral. In previous years the brand had tried to maintain a presence on TV – this was driven by retailer pressure, but limited advertising funds had always meant that a potent weight, given sufficient share of voice, was difficult to achieve at a national level.

Figure 2: *The Baxters logo*

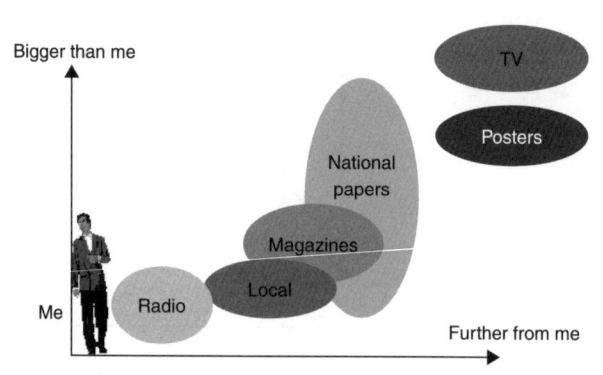

Figure 3: *Media selection criteria*

To reinforce the personal touch, the communication channel also needed to use a close and personal medium. The channels needed to be 'conversational', 'personal' and more intimate to the consumer. Also, to stimulate reappraisal, Baxters needed a high frequency of message, but on a tight budget.

The media selection was born out of considering each medium's 'natural operating area' (see Figure 3).

Radio provided the perfect solution. It had a strong strategic fit. It is an intimate medium and it gave the opportunity to build cheap frequency. It also provided flexibility when it came to regional weighting, allowing the 'volume' to be turned 'up' when required (in regions of opportunity such as southern Wales, the West and South-West, Yorkshire and the Midlands) or 'down' in, for example, Scotland – the Baxters heartland.

However, the lack of visual content meant that a radio advertising campaign needed to have particularly strong impact to be effective. This is even more the case with food brands.

THE CREATIVE DEVELOPMENT PROCESS

Beginning with one core proposition, seven development routes were identified and presented as concepts only. From these, four routes were taken to the next stage of script development. Two survived this next stage and were put forward for creative research.

THE CREATIVE IDEA: IT'S THE WAY YOU TELL IT

The final creative idea took the family's commitment and passion, and expressed it as 'the extra lengths the Baxter family goes to, to make its soup so good'.

With radio it isn't just what you say, it's how you say it. It's a tonal medium and the listener is sensitive to how brands speak to them:

> 'Advertised brands are like guests at a singles party – they try to impress with their appearance – hair, make-up, clothes, etc. But with radio, they are talking to the blind guest at the party.'
>
> *RAB website*

BAXTERS

The use of humour had to be pitched very carefully. It had to be appropriate for the Baxters brand and appeal to its traditionally older audience, yet it still needed to achieve standout. Six 40-second scripts were finally produced.

THE RESULTS

The campaign impacted positively on a number of key brand health measurements for Baxters. In pure sales terms, if we look at figures for the year ending February 2004 versus the year ending February 2003, we see that sales of Baxters tinned soups were over £2,120,000 higher. This represents a 7.8% increase in terms of year-on-year sales.[2]

However, this growth in volume sales was not simply down to underlying growth within the soup category. This is demonstrated by the fact that Baxters' market share in the year ending February 2004 was 13.5%. This was up from 12.0% in the year ending February 2003.[3]

The objective of eating into Campbell's market share in order to become the number-two brand in the soup market was also becoming a reality. In the 12 months ending February 2002, Campbell's share of the soup market was 17.0%; by February 2004 it had fallen to 13.5%.[4]

Historically the Baxters brand has had a base of consumers who have a relatively old age profile. As a consequence there has always been a requirement to recruit new consumers to the brand.

BRINGING NEW CONSUMERS TO THE BRAND

Reassuringly the brand's strong performance throughout 2003/04 was very much driven by the recruitment of new consumers to the brand. Specifically household penetration of Baxters in the year to February 2004 was 21.8%. This compares to a figure of 19.1% in February 2003.[5] This shift represents an additional 660,000 households being recruited to the Baxters brand during the course of the campaign.

During the same period both Heinz and Campbell's saw declines in their levels of household penetration: Heinz by 1% and Campbell's by 5%.[6]

These sales increases and share gains enjoyed by Baxters over the period were not simply a function of improved distribution for the brand. In March 2003 distribution as monitored by ACNielsen was 21.1% and in March 2004 it was virtually unmoved at 21.2%.

Clearly these are the 'hard' measures, the measures for the Baxters brand that have most impact on the bottom line. They demonstrate the commercial success of the campaign.

---

2. Source: ACNielsen.
3. Source: ACNielsen.
4. Source: ACNielsen.
5. Source: TNS.
6. Source: TNS.

ECONOMETRIC MODELLING: ISOLATING THE ADVERTISING EFFECT

In a quest to get a more in-depth understanding of the impact of the advertising, and to isolate the advertising effect, Baxters commissioned a market research agency (Tangible Branding) to carry out an econometric analysis of the effect of the Baxters advertising.

The analysis concentrated on the performance of Baxters' three main soup ranges – Vegetarian, Traditional and Healthy Choice – in Sainsbury's stores. Figures 4–6 plot the modelled/predicted share of the Baxters range in Sainsbury's stores

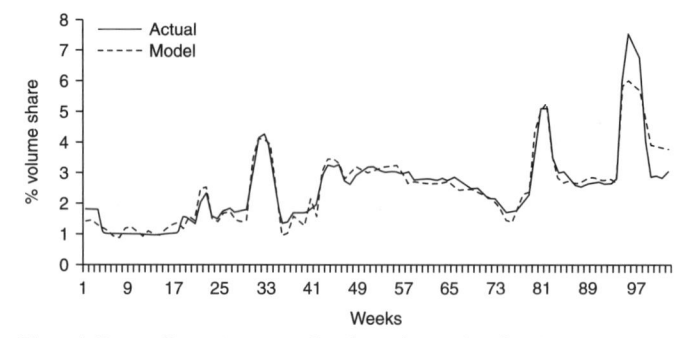

Figure 4: *Baxters Vegetarian soups: % volume share in Sainsbury's*
Source: Tangible Branding

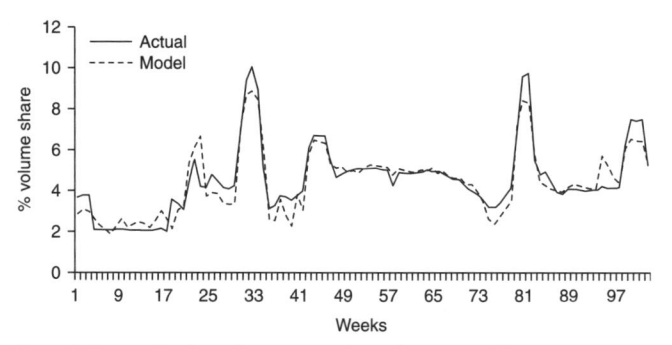

Figure 5: *Baxters Traditional soups: % volume share in Sainsbury's*
Source: Tangible Branding

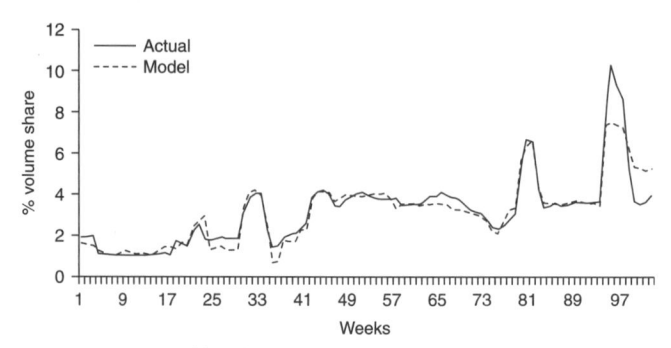

Figure 6: *Baxters Healthy Choice soups: % volume share in Sainsbury's*
Source: Tangible Branding

over the period (the broken line) and the actual sales of each of the ranges (the solid line). What Figures 4–6 show is that the market share is consistently above what the econometric model would have predicted.

When the model is deconstructed it shows that the volume attributable to advertising for each of the three ranges is as shown in Table 1.

TABLE 1: BAXTERS % VOLUME INCREASE IN SAINSBURY'S ATTRIBUTABLE TO ADVERTISING

Range	% volume increase
Healthy Choice	19%
Traditional	14%
Vegetarian	16%

Source: Tangible Branding

Again this is strong evidence of the powerful effect of the advertising campaign.

Equally the campaign impacted positively in some of the softer 'brand metrics'. While perhaps not as instantly commercially rewarding, these measures are very important to the health of the Baxters brand moving forward.

In order to monitor these softer measures Baxters conducts regular brand health surveys. The data, which follow, highlight the impact the advertising campaign has had on some of these key measurements.

AWARENESS

Perhaps the most compelling evidence of the cut-through of the advertising campaign is the improvement in advertising awareness.

Prior to the campaign, advertising awareness for Baxters was 47%. After the campaign, advertising awareness had increased to 71%. This represents a 51% increase.[7]

This increase in advertising awareness helped increase brand awareness of Baxters from 42% in October 2002 to 46% in March 2004.[8]

BRAND PREFERENCE

Probably the most impressive effect of the campaign has been its influence on brand choice, specifically when people were asked what would be their first, second, third and fourth choice of brand in the tinned soup market.

In October 2002 Baxters' combined score for being first/second choice was 49%. By March 2004 this had improved to 62%, an increase of 27%. Importantly

---

7. Source: Tangible Branding.
8. Source: Tangible Branding.

this shift elevated Baxters above Campbell's to become the number-two brand in the market so far as brand choice is concerned.[9]

BRAND IMAGE

Baxters has also seen improvements in consumers' attitudes to the brand. These improvements cover a range of image areas – spanning expertise, uniqueness and relevance. Again these types of image dimension are felt to be fundamental to the continued future success of the brand.

TABLE 2: BAXTERS CONSUMERS' ATTITUDINAL SHIFTS
(OCTOBER 2002–MARCH 2004)

	October 2002	March 2004
Offers something different	50	61
Innovative	38	49
A brand for me	57	60
Experts in making soup	52	70
Healthy brand	62	65

Source: Tangible Branding

When the data are dissected further, it again highlights the positive effect the advertising had on the brand image of Baxters. Specifically if those that are aware of the Baxters advertising are split out from those that are unaware of the advertising there are some significant differences in impressions of the Baxters brand.

TABLE 3: CONSUMERS' ATTITUDES TO THE BAXTERS BRAND
(MARCH 2004)

	March 2004 Unaware	Aware
Soup made by people who care about what they do	66	75
Offers something different	60	68
A brand with a sense of humour	30	46
Has interesting varieties	69	77
Goes to extra lengths	56	76
Great tasting	67	76
Soup made with the personal touch	65	77
A brand for me	56	78
Friendly	53	67
Innovative	47	58

Source: Tangible Branding

---

9. Source: Tangible Branding.

CONCLUSION

With smart use of media selection and a creative strategy that communicated the brand's equity in a relevant way, Baxters Food Group, based in the Highlands of Scotland, took on the big boys and did some serious damage.

Sales were up. Baxters' market share increased 12.5%. It welcomed 660,000 new consumers to the brand and household penetration went up – vital when its loyal target base is aged 50+.

The advertising also impacted very positively on some key brand health image statements. Attributes based around 'expertise' and 'innovation' enjoyed impressive shifts. That these shifts were very much a function of the advertising is demonstrated by the huge increase in advertising awareness.

Brand attributes such as 'a brand for me', 'goes to extra lengths' were dramatically higher among those aware of the advertising. This all translated into impressive improvements in brand choice.

That these shifts were achieved is demonstrated by an econometric modelling exercise conducted with Sainsbury's.

SILVER
BEST NEW AUTHOR

4

Broadband for Scotland
Turning Braveheart *into* Blade Runner

Principal author: Giles Moffatt, The Union
Collaborating authors: Wayne Oxley, Scottish Enterprise,
and Stewart Laing, Parallel 56
Media agencies: Feather Brooksbank/MediaCom

EDITOR'S SUMMARY

The confusion and clutter so often suffered in new technology markets were the villains of this piece, and a paper of admirable clarity from The Union shows how the Broadband for Scotland campaign cut through both. The judges liked the argument for a demand-generating strategy, the 'internet rage' creative idea and the well-integrated use of channels in the case, but what mattered most were the clear and convincing results, with Scotland outperforming the rest of the UK in its embrace of broadband.

PROLOGUE: BEWARE OF THE LUDDITE ...

'Luddism began on the night of 4 November 1811, in the little village of Bulwell, some four miles north of Nottingham, when a small band of men gathered in the darkness, counted off in military style, hoisted their hammers and axes and pistols, and marched to the home of a "master weaver" named Hollingsworth. They posted a guard, suddenly forced their way inside through shutters and doors, and proceeded to destroy a half-dozen weaving machines of a kind they found threatening to their trade. They scattered into the night, later reassembled at a designated spot, and at the sound of a pistol disbanded into the night, heading for home.

'That, at any rate, was the first attack on textile machines by men who called themselves followers of General Ludd, who would convulse the countryside of the English Midlands for the next 14 months – and would go down in history, and into the English language, as the first opponents of the Industrial Revolution and the quintessential naysayers to odious and intrusive technology.'

Kirkpatrick Sale (1999) *A brief history of the Luddites*, The Ecologist 29(5), August/September

INTRODUCTION

There has always been a certain amount of resistance to new technology. Ned Ludd remains the most notorious exponent. We are now in an age where innovation and new technology dominate our lives more than ever before. The irony is that despite a rich tradition of invention and innovation, Scotland's future was recently threatened by its national reluctance to embrace a new technology.

Broadband is recognised by all advanced and developing economies as being a key technology for economic growth and future prosperity. Governments around the world are investing billions in developing bandwidth and availability.

Before this campaign was devised, Scotland lagged well behind.

You may ask why a government body like Scottish Enterprise should spend taxpayers' money on promoting a product that is already widely advertised by the likes of British Telecom, AOL, Freeserve and Wanadoo. What is the motivation? What is the gain?

The purpose of this paper is to demonstrate how an integrated and impartial campaign was the differentiating factor in stimulating availability and take-up of broadband in Scotland. We will also demonstrate why this was of major economic importance in the first place. Lastly, we want to show why a successful outcome hinged on getting the communications message right, and using a multichannel approach in a strongly integrated way.

BACKGROUND

The internet took off properly in the mid-1990s. By 2000, as broadband began to flourish, governments around the world recognised the importance of this new technology. In the UK, the Broadband Steering Group (BSG) was set up to promote availability and take-up, and to give advice on the Government strategy to meet its target for the UK to have the most extensive and competitive broadband market in the G7 by 2005.

Similarly, the Scottish Executive and Scottish Enterprise took on the task of developing and promoting broadband in Scotland, where coverage and usage were both well below the UK average. This was done under the banner of Broadband for Scotland (BFS).

Many of us think of broadband as a means of entertainment, or simply 'posh internet access'. It is worth pointing out the serious economic benefits at this stage, to put the whole initiative in context.

TABLE 1: WHY IS BROADBAND IMPORTANT FOR THE ECONOMY?

Macro-economic

Increased GDP: the BSG reports that, by 2015, successful adoption of broadband in the UK will boost productivity by 0.5–2.5% and increase GDP by £22 billion. Accenture has calculated that, from 2003–10, broadband adoption has the potential to contribute $300–400 billion to European GDP.

Employment benefits: in the USA it is estimated that broadband technologies will directly create an additional 2.7 million jobs by 2012 (Criterion Economics, 2003).

Regeneration of rural areas: especially important for Scotland where the population is less than 14 per square kilometre.

TABLE 2: BENEFITS TO BUSINESS

- Time and cost savings
- Enabling teleworking
- Improved productivity
- Facilitate collaborative projects regardless of geography
- Reduction in overhead costs through increased teleworking
- Opportunity to hire people who are well qualified but do not want to relocate
- Reduction in absenteeism (up to 63%)
- E-learning: increased training opportunities
- Procurement: efficiency gains through streamlining supply chains
- Improved inventory control
- More effective communication
- E-CRM: lower cost of ongoing marketing
- Increased workforce collaboration
- Access to intelligence: news, research, competitive data

TABLE 3: BENEFITS TO CONSUMERS

- Communication: lower bills, simultaneous services
- Entertainment: increased download speeds and access to music, video, gaming
- Free software updates to optimise your PC/defend against viruses
- Educational aspects – the world's largest information database
- Shopping: fast, easy, safe transactions for cheaper products and services
- E-tourism: 'visit' places before you go there
- Managing utility bills – facilitating domestic administration

Tables 1–3 list the hard economic benefits of broadband adoption, which should explain the need for the public sector's intervention.

Scotland needed intervention more than other nations and more than any other region in the UK. Before the campaign, in 2003, coverage (availability) stood at only 57%. The take-up figures were even worse: 96% of homes were without broadband and, even more significantly, 87% of Scottish businesses *did not have broadband in the workplace*.

We outlined the *benefits* of broadband earlier. It's also worth considering the consequences of *failure* to achieve sufficient adoption (see Table 4).

TABLE 4: NEGATIVE OUTCOMES:
NATIONS WITH LOW BROADBAND ADOPTION

Business
- Productivity will trail that of other broadband-enabled economies
- Lack of bandwidth will discourage inward investment and relocation
- Workforce will leave – 'brain drain' to more competitive nations

Consumer
- Individuals' quality of life will be worse than elsewhere
- Social fragmentation: greater divide between urban and rural economies

Source: KPMG 2005

In short, big problem ... and big challenge.

THE BUSINESS STRATEGY

There are three distinct stages to the Broadband for Scotland initiative.

1. Achieve a marked increase in coverage – the target was availability to 90% of Scotland by 2005.
2. Increase take-up among business (target 30%) and domestic users (target 18%) by 2005.
3. Address the availability issue in rural/remote areas (the remaining 10%).

Stages one and two are the subject of this paper. Stage three is being dealt with in the next 12 months.

A total marketing budget of £5 million was made available. As the initial priority was to boost coverage, the first task was to persuade the telecoms network (BT wholesale) to enable telephone exchanges across the country.

Other regions of the UK (particularly the north-east of England) opted to use their budget to incentivise the telecoms company to do this (i.e. pay a set fee per exchange enabled). Scottish Enterprise chose to take a demand-led route: in other words, convince enough consumers and businesses to register their interest in broadband, and thus meet targets set by BT.

This approach was deemed to be more cost-effective in creating the coverage, but also had the added benefit of stimulating take-up. This was subsequently validated by a KPMG report in 2005.

To generate all this demand, a group of agencies was briefed to develop a comprehensive through-the-line campaign.

THE MARKETING CONTEXT

Broadband is to the 'noughties' what the mobile phone market was to the 'nineties'. The technology is still in the adoption phase, there are a myriad of suppliers offering different packages, performance, pricing and products. Many of them advertise heavily, and there is no shortage of direct marketing from ISPs (internet service providers) promoting their own broadband products. In short, the market is emergent, but already highly cluttered.

And like the mobile phone market in the mid-1990s, this clutter has led to a huge degree of confusion. The result of this confusion: paralysis and inertia. Consumers are faced with too much choice; too many packages; too many tariffs; too many suppliers – and all for a product they barely understand in the first place. The ISPs in the UK spend over £70 million a year promoting their products.

Our job was to stimulate demand for broadband, and the task was literally to cut through the clutter and noise. Perversely, the more active the suppliers were in their efforts to seduce consumers with deals, features, tariffs, packages, the harder our job would be. Our activity would have to complement their efforts by making the whole decision-making process clearer. An impartial website would form an important part of this.

THE STRATEGIC SOLUTION

We knew we had to stimulate demand. We knew we had to eradicate a lot of the confusion to achieve this. What we didn't know was how the public would react to a government body 'advertising' what was effectively a commercial product. As a result, there were several stages of research.

The first step involved two key pieces of insight work: a quantitative opinion poll and some qualitative groups across Scotland.

The findings confirmed our hypotheses on the market. Although heavy users of the internet had frustrations with slow speeds and blocked phone lines, the majority of people claimed they 'felt they could live with it' (Scott Porter, October 2003). The quantitative opinion polls corroborated the levels of inertia in Scotland. When asked, 'What's stopping you getting broadband?' over 14% of people without broadband claimed the main reason was that they had 'never got round to it'. A significant proportion of Scots (35%) legitimately claimed 'lack of availability'.[1]

The agency's brief was becoming clearer. If advertising was going to succeed in enabling exchanges, it was going to have to *provoke* the public enough to shake off their apathy. It would also have to be populist and accessible, given the breadth of the audience and the levels of confusion out there.

A number of initial routes were tested in December 2003. The first played on the Scots' reputation for inventiveness and intelligence, and questioned why, despite this, they weren't smart enough to get broadband. Although humorously treated, the idea alienated many (with hindsight, not surprisingly!).

The second route focused on speed, and lampooned 'slow' characters. People warmed to it, but felt it didn't tell them anything new about broadband. Everybody knew it was faster.

A third idea was entitled 'Why are you waiting?' It was designed to highlight the absurdity of using the internet in sub-optimal form. This came out as the strongest

---

1. Source: MRUK.

of the three routes. It touched a raw nerve, without making people feel foolish or backward.

However, we got more from the groups than we expected. At one point, one of the respondents launched into a major rant about how useless his computer was when going online. Others joined in, and there followed a freeform discussion on 'bad experiences' on the internet. We were amazed at the levels of 'internet rage' we could see, even in groups of seemingly reasonable people. ('Internet rage' subsequently became the theme for a major PR initiative, and received substantial press coverage.)

We realised that if you pushed the right buttons, people would confess to having 'lost it' with their computer at some point in their recent lives. Despite claiming earlier in the groups that dial-up was 'good enough', when the confession finally came it unleashed a tirade of abuse at inferior technology and an inferior experience.

As none of the routes we had researched fully tapped in to this, we amended our creative proposition to:

'Don't get mad, get broadband.'

Three more creative routes were developed along the lines of this proposition, including the Ford Kiernan 'Angry Man' idea (see Figure 1), which used the 'Ballistic Bob' character from the BBC's hugely popular sketch show, *Chewin' the Fat*. Populist and accessible, we thought he would be a great vehicle for building awareness rapidly.

The 'Angry Man' route dominated in the next round of research. Many people identified with the scenarios: one where Kiernan is trying to get through to someone whose dial-up connection is blocking the line; another where he waits patiently for a file download only for it to crash. In both instances, he loses the plot completely and trashes everything around him in a frenzy of rage.

People said things like:

'Been there, done that. Had to get a new laptop.' (Male, Glasgow)

'It's so true – there are times when you just want to punch the screen.' (Female, Edinburgh)

(*MRUK qualitative research, December 2003*)

We were pleased that we had found a very strong solution. It clearly tapped into something that would help break up the inertia. It also bore no resemblance to anything the suppliers were doing. While they were battling it out with claims on pricing, megabytes, ADSL, we took the high ground and concentrated on a fundamental consumer insight.

THE COMMUNICATION ACTIVITY

The whole Broadband for Scotland programme was quite an elaborate one, involving many media and many channels. Each channel had a slightly different role.

The first phase was designed to boost availability of broadband in Scotland. The chosen strategy was to build enough interest and physical registrations (businesses or consumers in all areas registering their details) (see Table 5).

Figures 2–5 show examples of the creative used in different media.

BROADBAND FOR SCOTLAND

TABLE 5: PHASE 1 – TARGET: BOOST COVERAGE IN SCOTLAND FROM 57% TO 70% (NOVEMBER 2003–JULY 2004)

Media	Role
TV	Consumer awareness (and visibility to suppliers)
Press	Consumer and business education
Posters	Consumer awareness
Radio	Consumer awareness
Online	Traffic to website
Website	Impartial advice, postcode checker and registrations
Other channels	
Field marketing	Capture business and consumer registrations
Door-drops	Lobbying consumers to register for broadband locally
Business incentives	Encouraging take-up of broadband in SMEs

Figure 1: *'Angry Man'*

SILVER SCOTTISH ADVERTISING WORKS 4

Figure 2: *'Billy' press ad*

Figure 3: *'Thinking Cap'*

Figure 4: *Mailing*

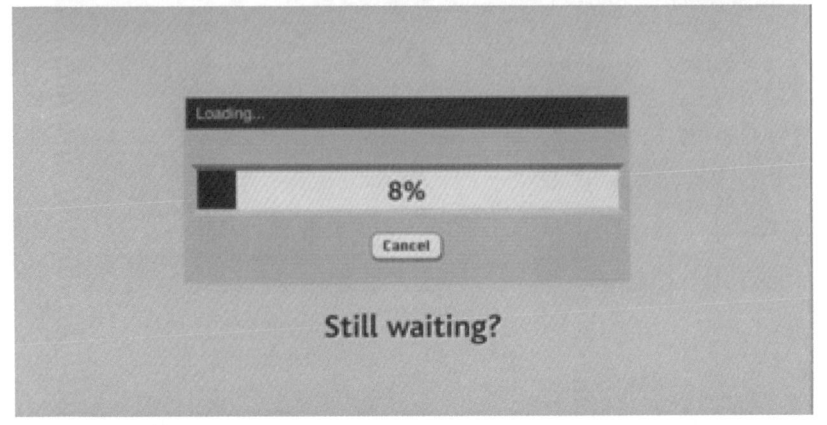

Figure 5: *Postcard*

50

THE RESULTS

The first objective (phase 1) was to increase coverage to 70% of Scotland (Table 5). The combined impact of 38,000 registrations and the scale of the activity convinced BT to enable far more exchanges than expected.

By the end of 2004, 92% of the country had the potential to access broadband through land-based services. This exceeded the 2005 target of 90% a year early.

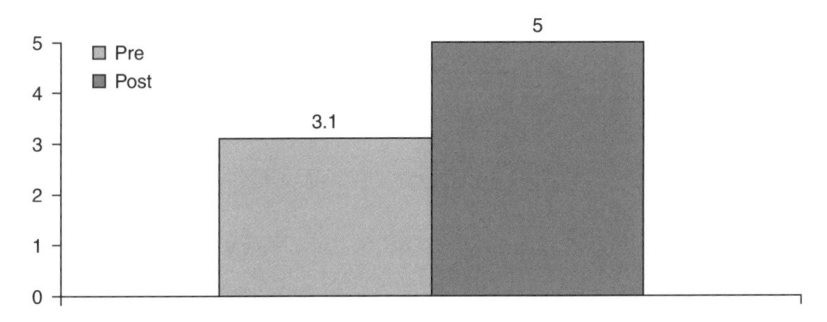

Figure 6: *Pre-/post-campaign population with access to broadband (millions)*

Figure 6 shows how many million Scots had potential access to broadband as a result of the campaign – about 95% of the population.

The efficiency of the demand-led strategy can be quantified. If you divide up the total marketing budget, the cost of enabling the exchanges works out at approximately £7000 per exchange. At the same time, that investment created widespread consumer and business awareness (as detailed below).

Other regions paid BT *significantly* higher sums to enable exchanges. This with absolutely no impact on consumer awareness or behaviour.

With the coverage job achieved so comprehensively in phase 1, the ongoing challenge was now to convince Scots businesses and home users to trade up to broadband. The take-up figures speak for themselves. Across the period measured, Scottish Enterprise data showed the increases illustrated in Figure 7. These figures show that business usage more than doubled (×2.54).

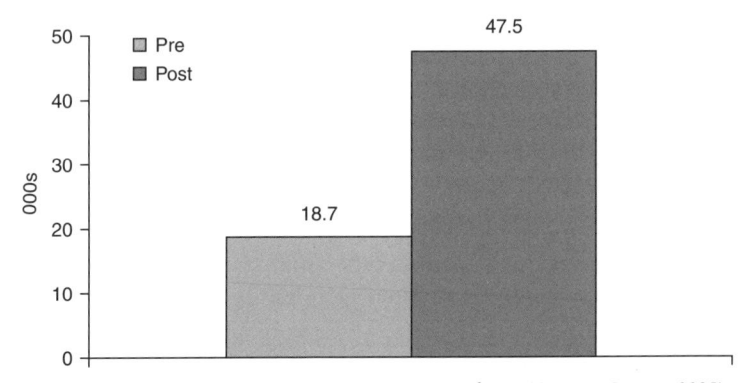

Figure 7: *Business users pre-/post-campaign (pre = December 2003, post = January 2005)*

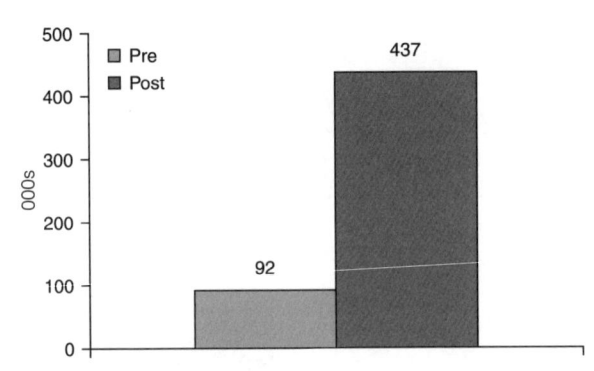

Figure 8: *Domestic users pre-/post-campaign*

A total of 33% of Scotland's businesses now use broadband daily. This is now higher than the UK figure of 25%.[2]

The increase in domestic users is even more dramatic, as is illustrated in Figure 8. The number of home users in Scotland increased almost fivefold (×4.75) across the period.

To put this particular growth figure in context, the figure for the UK as a whole for the period is only 191%.[3] The growth rate in Scotland was therefore *2.8 times that of the rest of the UK.*

HOW DO WE KNOW THE CAMPAIGN ACTIVITY WAS RESPONSIBLE FOR ALL THIS?

To demonstrate that the Broadband for Scotland campaign was the primary force behind these results, we will look at two other factors.

1. Supplier 'competitive' activity: we want to be sure that supplier advertising in Scotland had no greater effect than activity in the rest of the UK.
2. Proof that the individual parts of the campaign were effective in their own right, increasing the likelihood of a cumulative effect.

Pricing of broadband packages must also be taken into account. The cost has decreased slightly throughout the UK since the campaign started. Ofcom states that prices in July 2004 were between £20 and £40 per month, depending on the supplier and the package. By February 2005, prices were £15–£40, making entry-level packages marginally more accessible. Most importantly, broadband pricing is decided nationally. There is no evidence that pricing in Scotland was unduly lower than in any other area of the UK. Price variation can therefore be excluded from the results.

Supplier 'competitive' activity

Total UK spends are obviously considerably higher than Scotland-only activity. NMS figures for Scotland show a gradual increase in overall spending from 2001

---

2. Source: Ofcom.
3. Source: Ofcom, January 2005 Quarterly Update, pp. 5, 38.

BROADBAND FOR SCOTLAND

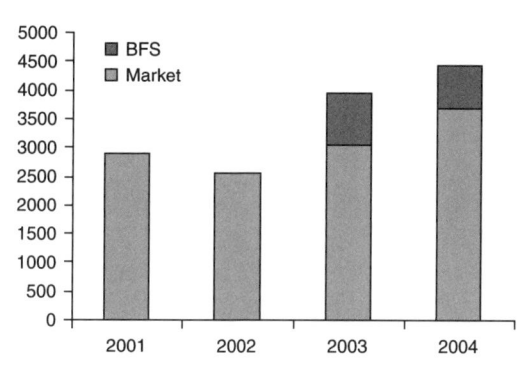

Figure 9: *Media expenditure Scotland (£000s) NMS*

through to 2004. However, the major significant increase in media expenditure in 2003 and 2004 came directly from the Broadband for Scotland campaign. Figure 9 demonstrates that the lion's share of incremental activity was actually ours. There was no sudden or massive increase in spending by suppliers that can be deemed to have influenced the marketplace any differently from previous years. Tiscali and Wanadoo did increase their spending by £500,000 (total for both brands) in response to the increased coverage that resulted directly from our activities.

Adoption of broadband in the UK

It is a key fact that the rate of broadband adoption in Scotland was 2.8 times greater than the rate for the UK as a whole (Figure 10).

This demonstrates that the stimulus provided by the campaign created a significant difference versus other 'control' regions. It's also worth noting that other regions of the UK *did* have supply-side programmes in place to stimulate broadband growth – none of them were *doing nothing*.

Campaign results

Advertising
The advertising clearly cut through and captured people's imaginations. Indeed, towards the end of the campaign, we got an unexpected indication of just how

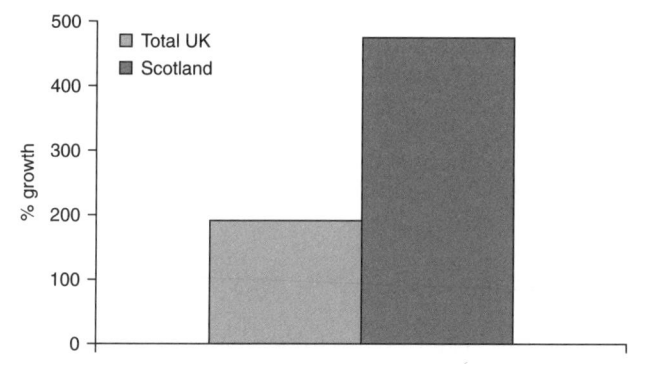

Figure 10: *Growth of broadband adoption, UK vs Scotland during campaign period*

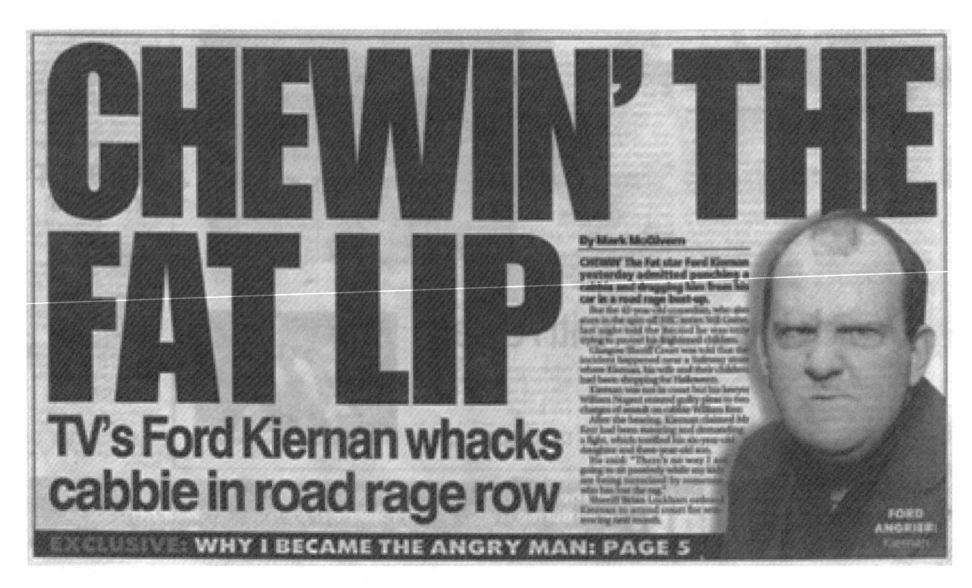

CHEWIN' THE FAT LIP
TV's Ford Kiernan whacks cabbie in road rage row

Figure 11: *Media coverage of the Ford Kiernan road rage incident*

popular the campaign had become. The media had a field day when Ford Kiernan (who played all the characters, including the Angry Man) was involved in a road rage incident in January 2005 (see Figure 11).

In December 2004, tracking from TL Dempster puts overall awareness of the campaign in excess of 70%. A recent quantitative survey conducted by BD Network's field marketing team showed an even higher result of 87%. Although the main media clearly served to drive awareness, other channels were critical in fulfilling key objectives. Each of them performed phenomenally well individually.

Field marketing
The field marketing conducted on a local basis in phase 1 allowed us to target specific areas where broadband was not available. Promotional teams visited the areas and captured registrations in a way that no conventional direct-response activity could have; 176 new areas were triggered as a result.

The second phase of field marketing was designed to create a broadband 'experience' – we knew from focus groups that 'until you've tried broadband, you probably won't buy'. The field marketing offered interactive demonstrations to 310,176 people, including 10,000 businesses. Data show that interactions lasted an average of six to seven minutes on bespoke broadband terminals. This kind of quality experience is usually unheard of in sales promotion. When surveyed on exit, 74% said they were 'more likely to get broadband' and 97% said they 'would get broadband within the next three months'.

PR
PR also contributed to the overall success. Early in the campaign it was used to support the 'anger' message. The PR agency seeded the media with stories of internet rage along with statistics. The resulting press coverage achieved just under 13 million opportunities to see.

Website

From the outset the website (www.broadbandforscotland.co.uk) was an essential tool. It was created to be an impartial resource providing comparisons of the different options, as well as a postcode checker and a facility for registering your interest in broadband if it happened not to be available in your area.

Since the campaign started, 170,000 people have visited the site meaningfully, with about 65% of them going on to use the postcode checker. On average they viewed six pages, and the 54% of them who weren't already set on broadband said they were 'more likely to get broadband' as a result of viewing the site.

Direct marketing

Direct marketing to industry sectors with low broadband penetration (retail, tourism and leisure) adapted the above-the-line ideas to reinforce the hard business benefits of broadband.

PAYBACK/RETURN ON INVESTMENT

The total spend on marketing was in the region of £2.5 million per annum over two years. The price of increasing coverage through a demand-led strategy was a fraction of that spent by other regions. So the strategy was cost-effective, but what about the return on investment?

We cannot measure ROI the traditional way – we were selling a category and not a product. The real measure of the campaign's value is its contribution to 'Scotland plc'.

By 2015, the value of broadband adoption will be 1.5–2.5% annual growth in GDP.[4]

Scotland's current GDP is £64 billion. Effectively the contribution of broadband and broadband-related businesses will be upwards of £960 million to £1.6 billion growth *per year*. These figures absolutely dwarf the initial investment. They also show how essential the programme was in the first place. We are talking about future payback in hundreds of millions, if not billions.

Using an integrated and holistic approach to communications, the Broadband for Scotland campaign made this technology available to the majority of Scotland's population and businesses. It also made them realise the value of trading up from dial-up, and shook them out of their apathy and inertia. Domestic use quadrupled during that time period, at over twice the rate of the rest of the UK. Business use doubled. Overall adoption of broadband outpaced the rest of the UK by almost three times the rate.

Could we have done it without this campaign? We could have 'bought' coverage, but this wouldn't have stimulated take-up or achieved any kind of shift in cultural attitudes towards technology. We could have focused on businesses alone, but that's what other regions did, with less success. We might even have chosen a different advertising idea, but then again, would it have resonated so strongly with the Scottish public? As one respondent said in the recent field marketing survey, 'the ads are so close to reality it's scary'.

Not as scary as a future without broadband.

---

4. Source: KPMG.

SILVER
BEST BRAND REJUVENATION

5

National Trust for Scotland
Reversing 10 years of decline

Principal author: Kenneth Fowler, 1576
Media agency: NTS/Mediashop

EDITOR'S SUMMARY

Turnaround stories, where decline is transformed into growth, are rare and powerful. Such was the National Trust case. A good strategic thought process, lively creative and imaginative use of ambient media and PR combined to attract a new family audience to the Trust's properties, without alienating its existing supporters. The Bannockburn event was particularly successful and 1576's well-presented evidence added up to make a convincing case. In the judges' opinion, more about other factors influencing visitor numbers and the commercial return of the activity might have taken this paper even further.

AN ORGANISATION WITH 'ISSUES'

The National Trust for Scotland was founded in 1931 with the aim of:

> 'Serving the nation as a cabinet into which it can put its valuable things where they will be perfectly safe for all time and where they are open to be seen and enjoyed by everyone.'
>
> *Sir John Stirling Maxwell, 1932*

Nobody doubts the value of the Trust in terms of its conservation work. It looks after more than 150 places of historical interest and natural beauty across an astonishing variety of properties, gardens and wilderness sites. The core ethos of the Trust is that it exists 'for the benefit of the nation'.

However, by early 2003, indications were that the people of Scotland did not agree with this sentiment. Visitor numbers to Trust properties were in systematic decline, down a massive 21% in the decade from 1992 to 2002, to less than 1.5 million (see Figure 1).

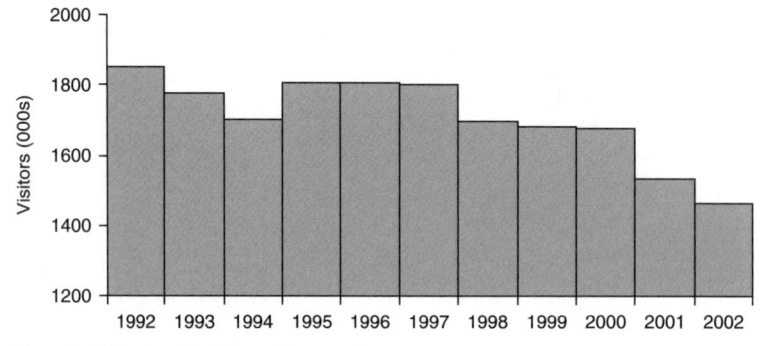

Figure 1: *A decade of declining visitor numbers*

As a charity dependent on visitor revenue, donations and legacies for income, the very future of the Trust in Scotland was in jeopardy.

Perception of the Trust was the main issue. Research had indicated that the general public in Scotland saw the NTS as 'elitist', 'exclusive' and 'not for me'. This sentiment was particularly prevalent among families with children.

Also, the Trust's advertising in previous years had been sporadic, minimal and lacked creative synergy. There was no consistent 'core thought' behind the Trust's marketing activity, resulting in disparate marketing communications with no common message or tone of voice.

In February 2003, when 1576 was appointed to work with the National Trust for Scotland, this was the situation.

OUR TASK

The brief was clear – 1576 was tasked with creating an advertising communications campaign that would:

NATIONAL TRUST FOR SCOTLAND

- arrest the decline in visitor numbers to Trust properties
- position the Trust as more 'inclusive' and relevant to a broader, contemporary Scottish audience
- specifically, help the Trust engage with a more family-orientated market as well as expanding its appeal among its core, older, audience.

Given the recent trading history of the Trust, this was going to be a major challenge.

SEARCHING FOR INSIGHT

Before any advertising creative was developed, 1576 worked closely with the Trust's new marketing team to develop a core proposition for the brand. To achieve this, rigorous research was essential.

First, we asked 'What do we already know?' We reviewed all available research that the Trust had previously commissioned, analysed the data the Trust gathers on its visitors and its members, and looked closely at broader economic and social trends that could impact on the Trust. This process highlighted gaps in the Trust's customer base and in its knowledge.

The Trust knew plenty about who was currently visiting its properties but virtually nothing about those who weren't. In particular, families with children were not engaging with the Trust and, alarmingly, the Trust was also missing out on a growing sector of the Scottish population: older 'empty nesters' with money to spend.

We needed to understand why. To do this, we conducted research (qualitatively and quantitatively) among those audiences that were not engaging with the Trust.

We also spoke to National Trust for Scotland staff (as a public-facing organisation, Trust staff form an important component of the brand) covering all levels of the organisation from the Chairman through to property guides and retail staff.

Finally, we spoke to Trust members, mindful of the fact that we had to be careful not to alienate existing members through the campaign we would subsequently develop.

Our research produced a wealth of information. However, from an advertising development perspective, there were four key insights.

1. There was a significant 'gap' between the 'reality' of the Trust and the common consumer perception. The Trust is bursting with enthusiastic staff who are keen to embrace a wider, more mainstream audience in Scotland. The public, on the other hand, don't see the Trust in this way. For them, the organisation was still 'elitist', a 'bit old-fashioned' and not particularly welcoming. The Trust was seen as 'not for the likes of us'.
2. There was a basic awareness of the work of the Trust, but the most common assumption was that it's all about 'castles, stately homes and that's it'. Awareness of the broader portfolio, such as wilderness areas like Glencoe, gardens like Inverewe, holiday lettings, cruises, and so on, was negligible.

3. Once consumers are made aware of the range of the Trust's offering and the range of work it does, they become motivated, energised and engaged.
4. Practically none of the general public were aware that the National Trust for Scotland is a charity. The common misconception was that the Trust is some sort of self-funded 'club' for the affluent upper-classes.

It was clear that there was a major communications job to be done.

USING THIS INSIGHT

We used this knowledge to develop a motivating core communication proposition for the Trust (a first for the organisation), which we could then use as the starting-point for creative development.

We needed to overcome the commonly held perceptions of the Trust, communicate a sense of shared ownership and position the Trust as a welcoming, worthwhile and, most of all, open organisation. We developed a simple and single-minded proposition: 'For You'. This proposition formed the core of the brand positioning template (the brand wheel) that we developed for the Trust (see Figure 2).

Tactically, we recommended focusing marketing efforts on the Trust's events programme – using the 'For You' brand message to give people a reason to believe in the Trust and the events programme to give them a reason to visit.

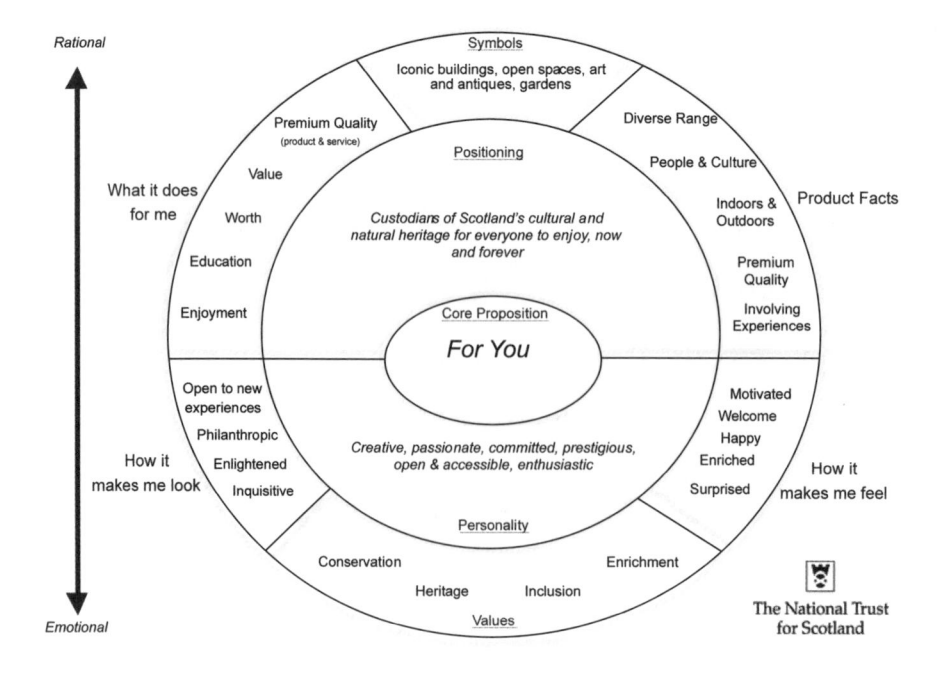

Figure 2: *Brand wheel developed for the Trust*

THE CAMPAIGN

We then went on to develop a campaign that would challenge not only existing consumer perceptions of the organisation as stuffy and elitist, but also the way the Trust had traditionally presented itself to the public.

The campaign deliberately adopted a surprisingly different tone of voice.

Out went recessive National Trust colours and shots of imposing country houses. In came humour, warmth and a contemporary 'clean' style of art direction. This was a departure for the Trust, but one aimed at helping the Scottish population reassess their perceptions of the brand.

All elements of the campaign were underpinned with the strap-line 'For You'.

The first test of the new campaign was the launch of the Trust's season in Easter 2003, when many of the properties in the portfolio reopen to the public after winter closure. We developed a press advertisement that embraced the new art direction style, tone of voice and brand proposition. We immediately challenged (albeit gently) the traditional perceptions of the Trust by featuring a suit of armour sporting a pair of bunny ears. This was accompanied by the line 'Are you ready for some fun this Easter? We are.' (See Figure 3.)

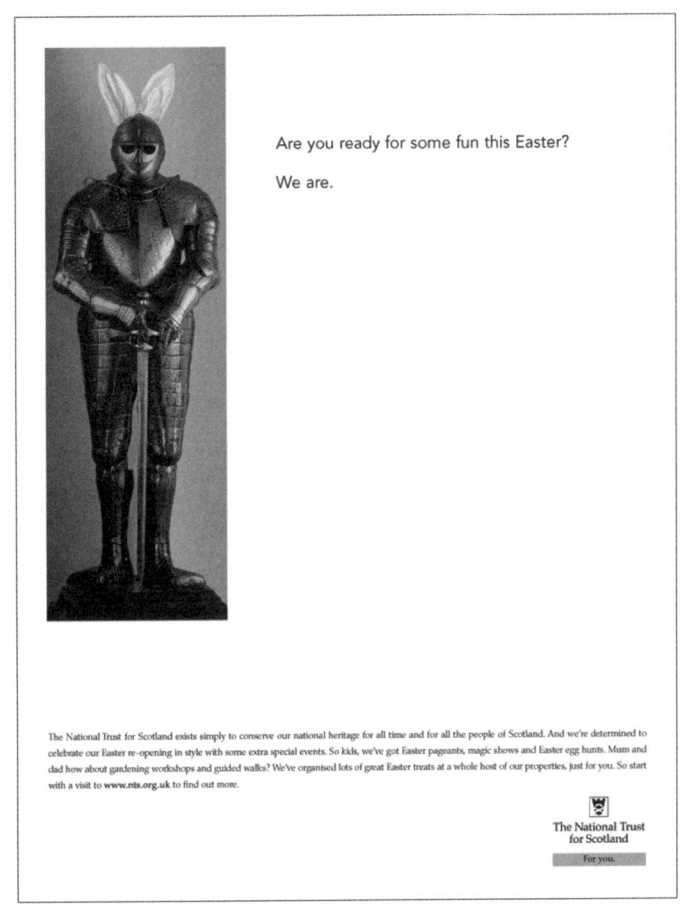

Figure 3: *Easter campaign launch press ad*

The Easter launch caused quite a stir within the Trust itself. Many long-serving staff members within the organisation needed convincing that this was the right direction for the brand; despite basing our creative campaign firmly on robust consumer insight, at 1576 we still had our fingers crossed.

Following quickly on the heels of the Easter launch campaign, 1576 developed press and radio executions to promote the Trust's annual 'open doors' day, when access to all properties is free of charge. We developed a sub-brand for the day ('The National Invitation'), and again utilised the new art direction style, welcoming tone of voice and underlying brand proposition. The campaign was starting to gain momentum (see Figure 4).

Figure 4: *'National Invitation' press ad*

NATIONAL TRUST FOR SCOTLAND

This execution ran in local and national Scottish press and was accompanied by radio advertising – a first for the Trust.

The campaign ran throughout summer 2003 and 2004, focusing on key events in the Trust's calendar such as the annual battle re-enactment at Bannockburn, jousting at Castle Fraser (see Figure 5) and the Palace of Magic event at Falkland Palace. This was supported by property-specific campaigns focusing on the most important properties in the Trust's portfolio, such as Culzean Castle and Country Park.

Figure 5: *Example of key event press advertising (jousting at Castle Fraser)*

The sponsorship with Mackies Ice Cream was another first for the Trust. Working with 1576 to make sure that the message was relevant, once again the emphasis on fun came through, backing up the tonal change we were adopting.

The campaign involved traditional media such as press and leaflets, but also introduced new media for the Trust such as radio and 'ambient' advertising. All of this was aimed at reaching a mainstream Scottish audience, with the emphasis on families with children.

BANNOCKBURN: THE STRATEGY IN MICROCOSM

One of the key events in the National Trust for Scotland's calendar is the annual re-enactment of the Battle of Bannockburn in September. The event costs just under £30,000 to stage and features a cast of hundreds, drawn from battle re-enactment enthusiasts across the country, a re-creation of a fourteenth-century army camp, food and drink, as well as other family entertainment.

In 2002, supported by extremely limited advertising, the event attracted 4000 paying visitors and, despite glorious sunshine, resulted in a loss of £5000 for the Trust.

In 2003, 1576 was tasked with developing a sub-campaign for Bannockburn that would attract a much larger paying audience to the event and help turn around the disappointing performance of the event in the previous year.

The budgets were tight so we needed a high-impact campaign that would generate a greater media value than was actually being paid for. To this end, we developed two executions for local and national press, the first playing on the realistic nature of the battle re-enactment itself, using the line 'The Battle of Bannockburn 2003. Painfully Accurate.' (See Figure 6.)

Perhaps more contentiously, the second press execution tapped in to the lead news story of the time: the 'Most Wanted' playing cards being utilised by the coalition troops in Iraq. Our press execution featured such a playing card, but instead of a senior member of the B'aath Party, the card sported an image of Edward II, Bruce's adversary on that historic day in 1314 (see Figure 7).

We also developed an ambient advertising execution, aimed at generating press coverage, featuring a car in the Bannockburn car park riddled with arrows and spears, with a sign to one side stating 'Cars parked at owners' risk' (see Figure 8).

The campaign gained media coverage consisting of 28 separate articles in local and national press, and was reported on both BBC Scotland and STV evening news.

The event was a massive success, with almost 12,000 paying visitors (a 300% increase on 2002) and the Trust made a profit of £16,000 on the day.

Interestingly, more than 6000 toy swords were sold on the day, providing a clear indication of the profile of those now attending.

In 2004, the campaign was repeated, but the event itself faced a stern test from the weather. On the day of the re-enactment it was pouring with rain. Nevertheless, the impressive attendance and revenue numbers from 2003 were maintained, with another 12,000 paying guests coming along.

NATIONAL TRUST FOR SCOTLAND

THE BATTLE OF BANNOCKBURN 2003.
PAINFULLY ACCURATE.

"Aaaaaargh!" "Aiiiiiiie!" "Gnnnnnng!" Yes, hundreds of re-enactors have been learning their lines. When they recreate one of the bloodiest battles in Scottish history, it won't be pretty, but it'll be spot on. The Scottish and English camps and the tactics will be totally authentic. And all on the original site. If you're a wee bit on the squeamish side, don't worry. There'll be plenty more to see including horseback displays, falconry and archery. The fun – sorry, the savagery – takes place on 20 and 21 September. For tickets, visit Bannockburn Heritage Centre or call 01786 812 664.

The National Trust for Scotland
For you.

Just like the real thing. In association with
real
100-101 fm

All of the money raised at this event goes towards preserving Bannockburn for future generations.

Figure 6: *Bannockburn re-enactment press ad (1)*

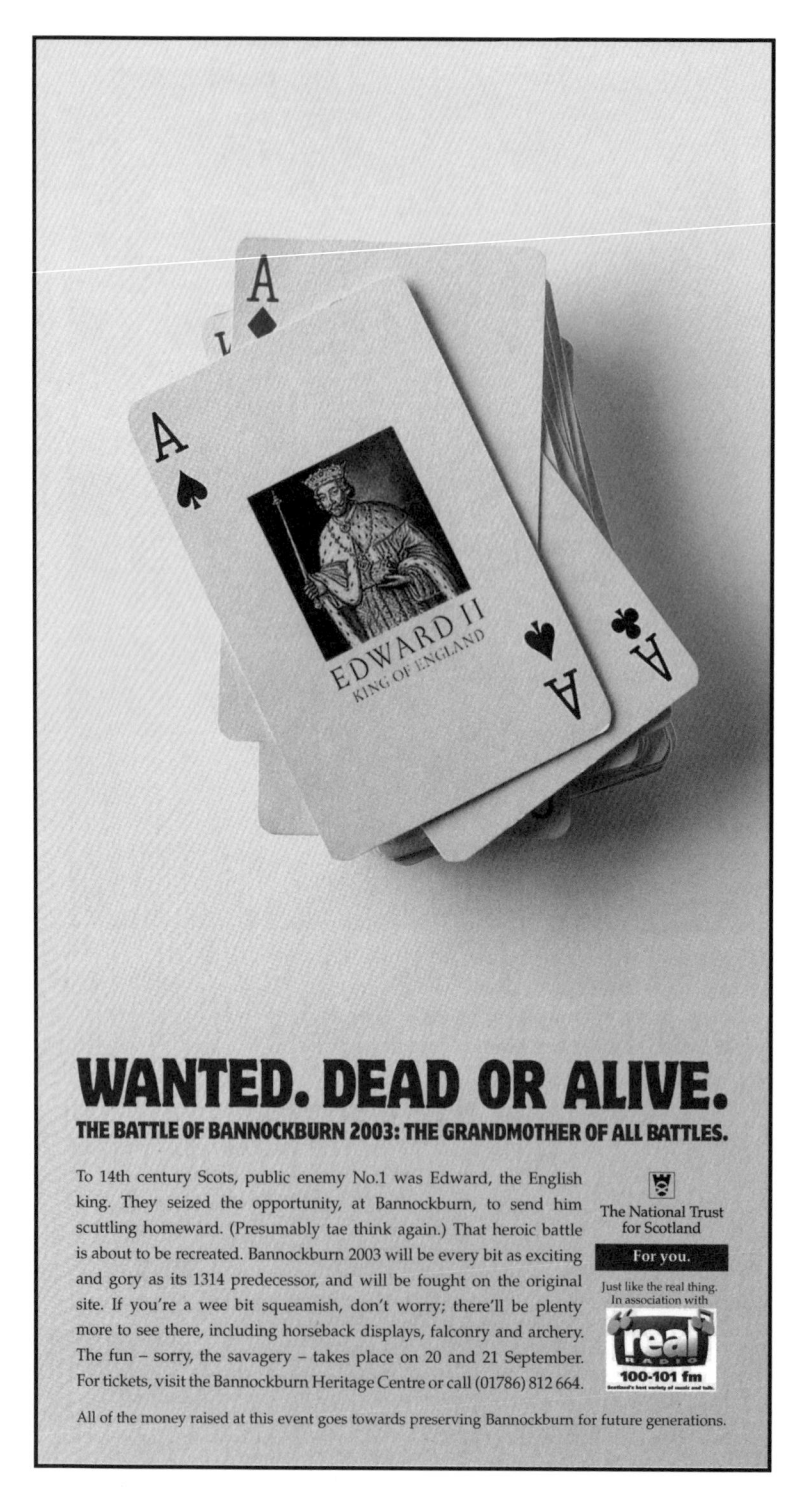

Figure 7: *Bannockburn re-enactment press ad (2)*

NATIONAL TRUST FOR SCOTLAND

Figure 8: *Bannockburn ambient advertising*

WHAT ABOUT THE WIDER CAMPAIGN?

From the launch of the campaign, the impact was obvious. In May 2003, visitor numbers were up 15% on the previous year across all the Trust's properties, while the 'National Invitation' outperformed the previous year's event by 30%.

The broader picture was just as good. At outset, the National Trust for Scotland set 1576 the objective of arresting the decade of decline in visitor numbers. We did more than that. Across all the properties in the Trust's portfolio, visitor numbers were up 6% for 2003 compared to 2002 then up again by 3% in 2004 (see Figure 9).

For the five most important properties in the Trust's portfolio, the increase in visitor numbers was even greater, up 9% for 2003 over 2002 and up again by 12% for 2004.

Our insight guided the Trust towards putting more weight behind events throughout 2003 and 2004 to attract families with young children. There is not

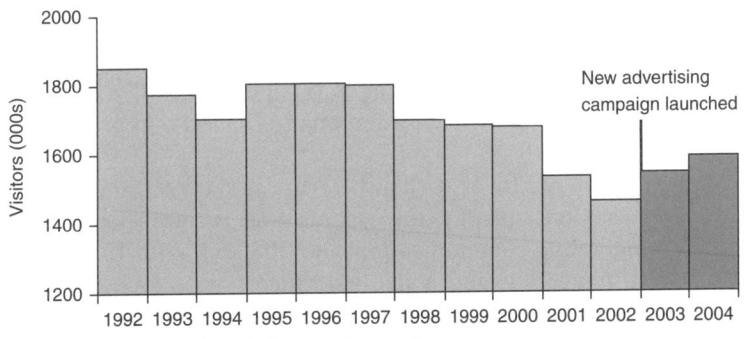

Figure 9: *Turning around the decline in visitor numbers*

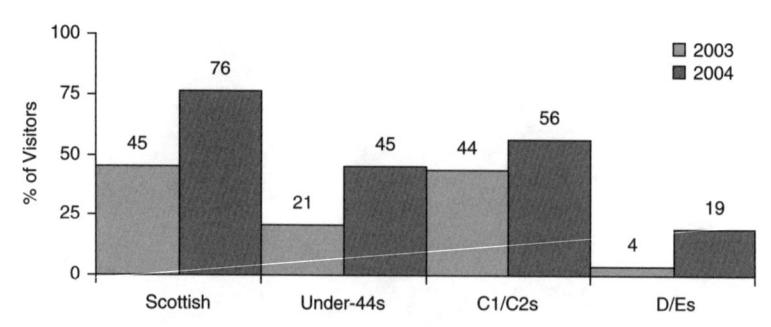

Figure 10: *Changing the profile of visitors to the Trust*

only anecdotal evidence that this is being achieved (such as the pattern of merchandise sales at events – the Bannockburn toy sword phenomenon) but also empirical evidence through independent research.

We were also successfully broadening the appeal of the Trust and helping it engage with more people in Scotland. Independent entry and exit research conducted by Lynn Jones Research at 12 key Trust properties in 2003 and 2004 indicated that a broader mix of consumer types was visiting. Significantly, more Scots, more younger people and a broader mix of social groups were coming along to Trust properties and events (see Figure 10).

So, 1576's advertising communications campaign had delivered a turnaround in visitor numbers and had helped the Trust broaden its appeal among the people of Scotland, not only achieving, but exceeding, the client's initial objectives.

The National Trust for Scotland is a large and multifaceted organisation. Moving the organisation's culture to a more commercial and marketing-orientated focus has been akin to turning around an oil tanker. It takes a while, and initially changes may seem small. However, within the organisation itself, these changes herald a significant cultural shift, and as with an oil tanker, once a change in direction has been achieved, the momentum gathers pace.

THE FUTURE

This is just the start. Commitment to a new advertising communications strategy has quickly delivered results for the National Trust for Scotland. A decade of decline in visitor numbers has been reversed and the brand is beginning to engage with a broader public in Scotland.

The 'For You' proposition has been wholly adopted by the Trust and now underpins all elements of the marketing mix, including all advertising, direct marketing and printed collateral, even extending to PowerPoint presentations given by Trust staff.

There is a new consumer focus within the Trust and a determination to build on these early successes. Consequently, the organisation is significantly increasing its annual spend on marketing communications in 2005 and, with 1576, is developing a major TV advertising campaign for the first time.

The campaign will continue to gain momentum over the coming years. Good news for the Trust, the Scottish public ... and manufacturers of toy swords.

SILVER

6

Oral Cancer Campaign
How Henry helped save lives

Principal author: Margaret Byrnes, The Bridge
Media agency: The Media Shop

EDITOR'S SUMMARY

The Bridge's challenging campaign to raise oral cancer awareness, and prompt timely treatment where necessary, had to be sensitive both to people's contradictory attitudes to their health (overcoming complacency on the one hand and the fear of a bad diagnosis on the other) and to the resource issues facing the NHS. This it did, and the sound argument and admirable focus on proof of effectiveness made this well-written paper a worthy Silver winner. In bringing about a change in understanding and behaviour among a key target group, thus saving lives, this was a heartening story.

Figure 1: *Henry*

WHY ORAL CANCER?

The man pictured in Figure 1 is Henry – a typical west of Scotland middle-aged man – drinks a bit too much, smokes, avoids going to the dentist or doctor, and had never heard of oral cancer, much less the signs or symptoms. Henry had a sore spot in his mouth that wouldn't go away, he ignored it for a while and eventually went to the doctor. He was diagnosed with oral cancer. Because Henry presented late, the cancer was large and deep, his treatment lifesaving but invasive. Nowadays, Henry has difficulty speaking and swallowing, but he owes his life to the doctors. Left untreated any longer Henry would have died.

Each year over 530 people in Scotland are told that they have mouth cancer – only half of them survive for more than five years, often because the cancer has been detected too late. Although it is a debilitating disease, it can be treated successfully if it is detected early and survival rates could improve by up to 30%.

The West of Scotland Cancer Awareness Project (WoSCAP) hypothesised that a successful oral cancer campaign could save the lives of people like Henry.

WoSCAP is a partnership between five west of Scotland NHS Boards and is funded by lottery money. In July 2003, WoSCAP commissioned the Centre for Social Marketing (CSM) at Strathclyde University to conduct research to inform the strategic development of a mouth cancer campaign. The key learnings from this stage of research were as follows.

- Spontaneous awareness of types of cancer focuses most commonly on breast, lung, prostate and skin cancers, with bowel, cervix, throat, pancreas and testicular cancer mentioned less frequently.
- Among the target audience low awareness is equated with low prevalence – so mouth cancer was not on the radar.
- The concept of early detection of cancer, and hence early treatment leading to improved outcomes, is relatively familiar. While the benefits were accepted at a

logical and objective level, at an emotional and personal level cancer-related fears meant there was considerable reluctance to confront the issue.
- While keen to advise 'others' to go forward with symptoms, many would be much more hesitant to do so themselves.

An additional study of 1000 people by MRUK found the following.

- Awareness of mouth cancer was negligible, with only 6% spontaneous awareness and only 45% prompted.
- A high proportion of individuals could not name any symptoms of oral cancer at all (54%).

RISK OF RUNNING AN ADVERTISING CAMPAIGN

At face value, the evidence collected provided a strong case for running an advertising campaign. However, a mass-media communication strategy was not without risk. There was widespread concern among all stakeholders that a poorly devised campaign could cost lives, not save them.

The big worry with this campaign was that we might swamp the health service. The everyday nature of the signs and symptoms risked that large numbers of the 'worried well' would descend upon their GP or dentist, meaning everyone would have to wait that much longer for an initial appointment, then that more cases would be referred to the hospital services where, again, waiting time would be affected. The knock-on effects to diagnosis and treatment times would be terrible.

The creative development and media-planning processes had to address this concern.

DEVELOPING THE ADVERTISING

The advertising objectives were:

- to raise awareness of mouth cancer and the importance of early detection
- to arm people with what signs to look out for and what action to take should they find something.

Five creative routes were developed to explore the appropriate approach, appropriate tone of voice and appropriate language.

1. 'Survival' sought to challenge the fatalism around cancer and help give hope to the people with symptoms. The importance of getting help early was established through testimonials from people who have gone through it.
2. 'Niggling worries' are part of the mindscape when it comes to cancer. We explored a route that examined this and how we play games with ourselves and bury our heads in the sand.
3. 'Humour' explored the language, the excuses we use and how to talk about symptoms. It was explored for its ability to break through the barriers.

4. 'Here comes the science bit'. We tried to use science in a detached and rational way to explore whether detachment could lead to the required change in behaviour.
5. 'Habits' explored the quirks of human nature and the ceremony that some people have when looking at themselves in the mirror. The idea was to show them how easy it can be to self-check as part of what is already a routine.

The research found that survivor testimonies had most impact because they provided a compelling way of linking the symptoms with the health consequences. Cancer is a frightening disease and this campaign was seen as presenting 'new' information about a disease that the target audience had little or no knowledge about. There had been an underlying disbelief that the symptoms, which often appeared trivial, could be cancer. The use of real people added a credibility that helped overcome this underlying disbelief. A 40-second TV commercial and radio ad formed the core of the campaign, with noticeboard posters, leaflets and PR supporting the broadcast work.

The implications of ignoring your symptoms were dramatised by the endline 'If in doubt, get it checked out' (see Figure 2) and in the contrast between the first two survivors, Robert and Harvey, who went to the doctor early and who have had successful treatment, and Henry who left it very late and had most of his jaw and tongue removed, resulting in speech difficulty.

Figure 2: *Endframe of the television ad*

THE RESULTS

The campaign was evaluated using two studies. First, CSM at the University of Strathclyde conducted pre- and post-campaign research. The research took place in the campaign and control areas, and took the form of semi-structured in-home interviews. The sample reflected the age and social class of the key targets for the campaign. A baseline was taken in July–August 2003 before the campaign, with the follow-up in March–April 2004.

To claim success we would need to demonstrate not only that people had seen the advertising, but that they had understood it, that it had made them more aware of the symptoms of oral cancer, and that they had taken some action as a result of that knowledge. This increase in knowledge and understanding would be among those with symptoms but also among the wider at-risk population.

Awareness of the campaign

Were people aware of the advertising? Prompted awareness of the TV commercial in the intervention area reached 83%. Given that those in the research sample were all over 40 years old this is a particularly high awareness figure as advertising awareness notoriously tails off among the 45+ age group as they tend to be less engaged with advertising in general. This compared to 23% prompted awareness in the control area (see Figure 3).

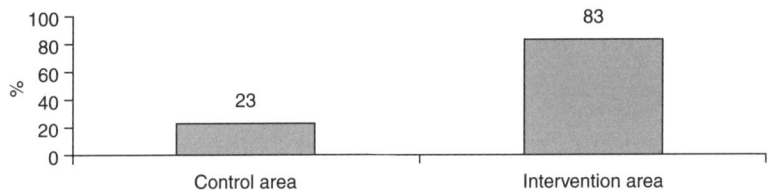

Figure 3: *Prompted advertising awareness*

Understanding of the advertising message

The spontaneous responses in Table 1 suggest that people understand the subject matter: They:

- understand the need to raise awareness of mouth cancer
- feel an emotional involvement with the testimonials
- can relate this back to themselves and their family.

TABLE 1: SPONTANEOUS RESPONSES TO TV AD

Base: (483) all respondents in the campaign area who have seen the TV ad	%
Raises awareness of mouth cancer	50
'Makes you think about mouth cancer'	19
'Get it checked out'	35
'Watch out for changes'	5
Emotional response	35
Sympathy for the people in the ad	18
Relief	2
Shock that the symptoms are so everyday	4
Worried for [Henry]	5
Frightened how serious mouth cancer is	5
Personalisation of the message	32

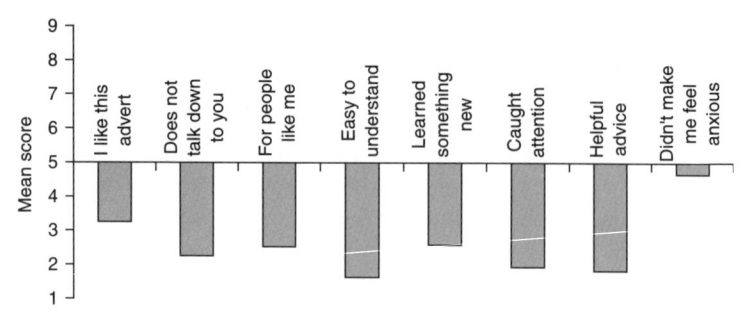

Figure 4: *Prompted responses to TV commercial*

At a prompted level we can also see that respondents understood the content of the advertising. A nine-point semantic differential scale was used to ask respondents to rate the advert, with 1 being 'totally agree' and 9 being 'totally disagree' with a range of statements. Figure 4 shows very positive ratings for all criteria. The bottom half of the chart is positive and, the nearer to 1, the more positive.

We can see that respondents found it likeable, easy to understand, for people like them, and not patronising. They also felt that it caught their attention and that they learned something new.

The anxiety rating of 4.65 is where we would want it to be: well short of panic but enough for people to feel some concern about the message and the need to act.

Knowledge and awareness of mouth cancer

So they had seen the commercial and they thought that it was impactful and easy to understand. But what had happened to their knowledge about oral cancer?

Table 2 shows awareness of cancers. Baseline awareness of mouth cancer was very low. Both spontaneous and prompted levels have increased in the intervention area.

TABLE 2: AWARENESS OF VARIOUS CANCERS

Base: all respondents	Unprompted awareness				Prompted and unprompted awareness			
	Campaign area		Control area		Campaign area		Control area	
	Baseline (571) %	Follow-up (583) %	Baseline (351) %	Follow-up (351) %	Baseline (571) %	Follow-up (583) %	Baseline (351) %	Follow-up (351) %
Lung cancer	68	66	65	62	99	98	100	98
Breast cancer	66	60	61	64	99	99	98	99
Bowel/colorectal cancer	45	36	51	47	96	97	97	98
Skin cancer	27	18	27	21	97	97	97	97
Prostate cancer	25	22	23	32	92	94	93	96
Stomach cancer	20	16	20	23	90	90	87	91
Cervical cancer	20	17	17	18	91	91	89	89
Testicular cancer	17	8	12	12	87	88	88	86
Mouth/oral cancer	12	16	11	12	82	92	80	85
Ovarian cancer	11	9	10	15	84	85	84	83
Bladder cancer	3	3	5	5	61	65	58	65

ORAL CANCER CAMPAIGN

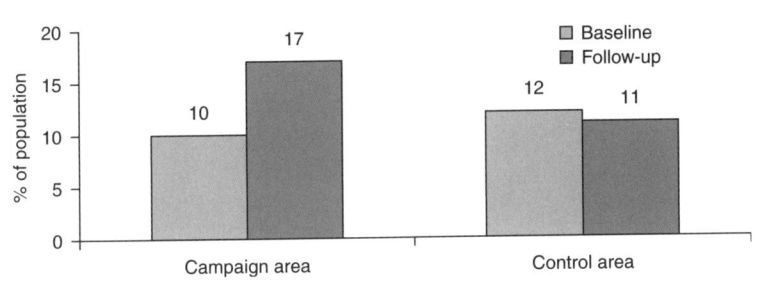

Figure 5: *Saliency of mouth cancer (conversations)*

And, though too complex to show in Table 2, prompted awareness of mouth cancer among those who have seen the TV advert reached an almost universal level of 94%.

Not only were people more aware of mouth cancer, they were more willing to talk about it. After the campaign, almost twice as many people in the intervention area held a conversation about mouth cancer as had done so before the campaign (see Figure 5). In the control area the figure reduced marginally.

What about detailed knowledge of the symptoms? Figure 6 shows that we not only improved awareness of the signs but that the persistence message also penetrated. This was not seen in the control area, where ulcers remained at 34%, sores 11%, any patch 7% and persistence 11%.

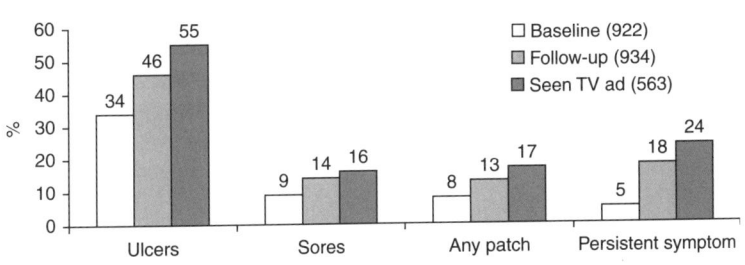

Figure 6: *Awareness of symptoms in campaign area*

Campaign impact on primary and secondary care

A second study of the effects of the campaign was conducted post-campaign among patients attending the 11 secondary care rapid referral clinics across the campaign area. This would be the acid test. The advertising objectives were to raise awareness of mouth cancer and the importance of early detection, and to tell them what action to take should they find something. Quantitative independent research measured the impact of the campaign on primary and secondary care.

The research took the form of a self-completion questionnaire. The results of this study were very encouraging.

- A total of 64% of the sample (583) had heard or seen a campaign about mouth cancer.
- Of the 343 patients who said they had seen a campaign about mouth cancer, 92% reported having seen a TV advert and 7% having heard a radio advert.

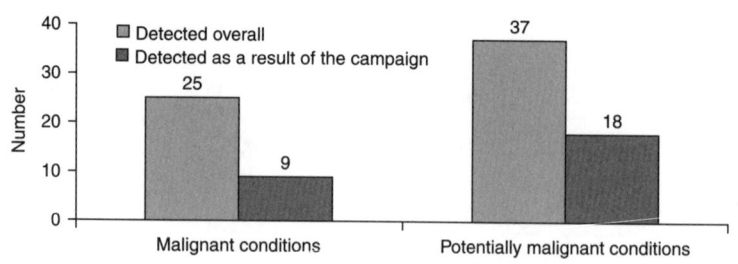

Figure 7: *Analysis of cancers and pre-malignant conditions detected*

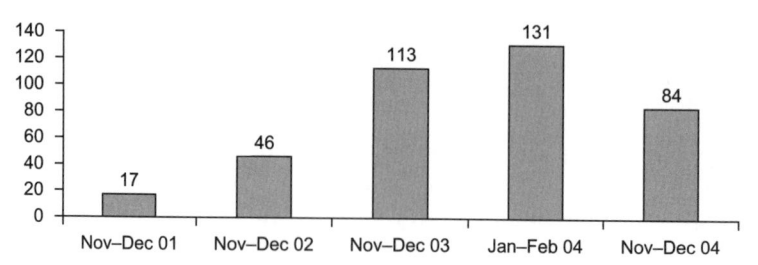

Figure 8: *Referrals to Oral Medicine (Dental School) for suspicious lesions*

- Of those who had seen the campaign, 68% responded that it had encouraged them to seek advice more quickly. Given people's usual tendency to discount the effect of advertising on their behaviour, this figure is very high.
- Critically the campaign had not generated the numbers of 'worried well' that had been feared at the planning stage.

Figure 7 shows the analysis of the cancers and pre-malignant conditions that were presented. Pre-malignant conditions are conditions that can be treated successfully and monitored to prevent cancer developing in the future.

Research suggests that 68% of people presented earlier than they would have done – that's 42 people (68% of 25 plus 37) who are likely to require less expensive, less invasive treatment. It also suggested that 27 (9 plus 18) malignant or potentially malignant conditions would have presented later or not at all had it not been for the campaign.

When compared to previous years we can see the very real impact the campaign has had and continues to make. Figure 8 compares the number of referrals to Oral Medicine (Dental School) for suspicious lesions. The campaign resulted in a 185% increase in numbers and, long after the campaign had ended, numbers remain at almost double.

We would argue that we demonstrated clear success: in awareness, in understanding, in knowledge and in action.

DISCOUNTING OTHER FACTORS

The WoSCAP campaign is the first of its kind in Scotland, and has been carefully examined and analysed with the use of data collected pre- and post-campaign in both the campaign area and the control area.

These data allow us to conclude that the only difference between the two areas was the campaign.

Additionally, we can confirm that no other factors were at play (e.g. storyline about mouth cancer in a TV soap or a famous person being reported as diagnosed with mouth cancer).

RETURN ON INVESTMENT

The real return on investment is to be measured in lives – the lives of people like Henry. However, it is still important to look at this project from a financial perspective.

The total advertising campaign budget was £250,000, which divided by 27 people equals £9259. Treatment costs to the NHS are complex and vary by individual, but the average cost of hospital care and operation alone for a single patient with advanced oral cancer is £25,000 with oncology costing a further £10,000. This does not include costs for diagnosis, radiology, intensive care, ongoing outpatient care, speech therapy, restorative dentistry and the cost of recurring disease. On this basic cost analysis we may have saved 27 (the cases that would not have presented early had it not been for the campaign) multiplied by £25,741 (the average cost of treatment minus the average cost of advertising), which equals a saving of £695,000 – an ROI of 278% in six months. In addition, there are the savings generated by the 41 cases that presented earlier than they would otherwise have done.

We are confident that, given the ongoing reported positive impact of the campaign by service providers, the NHS will see a continued return.

CONCLUSION

Has the campaign been a success? A patient from the Southern General Hospital who presented early and is now doing well, says, 'I saw that man on the telly and I thought I'd better go and see about this sharpish.' True story.

SILVER
BEST NEW CLIENT

7

Seriously Strong Cheddar

How advertising created a seriously big impact on seriously strong cheese

Principal author: Ruth Lees, 1576
Media agency: MediaCom

EDITOR'S SUMMARY

McLelland's powerful performance as one of the fastest-growing grocery brands in the UK has been very impressive. This well-presented argument from 1576 successfully showed how a blend of smart strategic thinking and commitment to creating an appealing 'seriously strong' brand personality stimulated this performance. That the advertising and related promotional activity were effective is undeniable and the judges wished only for clearer and more comprehensive analysis of the scale of that effectiveness and the ROI of the regional campaign in the context of the brand's national success.

INTRODUCTION

This paper will prove how advertising successfully grew a little-known cheddar cheese brand with awareness and perception problems into a 'lighthouse' brand – a brand with 'attitude' that got the competition running scared. We will show how the advertising helped Seriously Strong aggressively steal market share, threatening number-one cheddar brand Cathedral City's position, and build consumer loyalty, the 'holy grail' of the cheddar cheese market. All of this within a period of only one year of advertising in 2003.

We will demonstrate that, against all odds, a brand working within a very traditional, commodity-driven market, if prepared to take risks, can make a huge difference by outsmarting its competitors, broadening its appeal and making itself famous.

First, let's put Seriously Strong into its market context.

THE CHEDDAR CHEESE MARKET

Cheese is a ubiquitous, staple product with enormous consumer penetration – over 98% of all households buy cheese. In the cheddar cheese sector, as in many other commodity/frequent purchase sectors, supermarket own-label pre-packaged cheese has the biggest share of the market with 83%. It is a market driven by promotions, namely BOGOFs, and defined by strength.

However:

> 'The growth in the cheese market has been driven by added value sectors, with consumers becoming more adventurous in their purchasing behaviour. In cheddar, consumers are trading up from mild cheese to stronger flavours, a change driven by brands. Indeed, the branded natural cheese market is a very exciting sector.'
>
> *Dairy Crest Cheese Report, 2001*

So, while own-label dominated and was relatively static in volume terms, there was a rise in the much smaller but lucrative branded cheddar market, which enjoyed a 17% price premium over the commodity sector (see Figure 1).

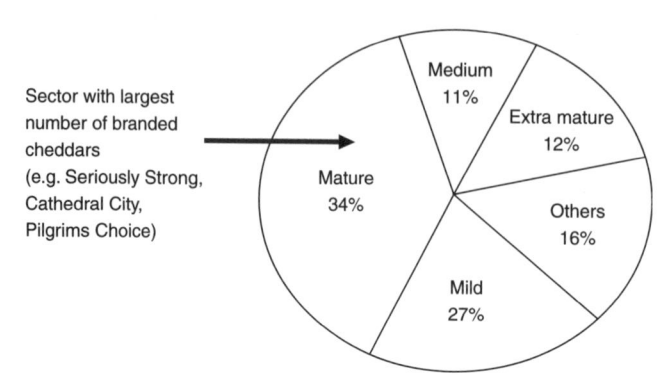

Figure 1: *Profile of the cheddar cheese market*
Source: Dairy Crest Cheese Report, 2001

SERIOUSLY STRONG CHEDDAR

This branded cheddar sector contains only a cluster of brands led by Cathedral City, owned by Dairy Crest, but it held great potential for all the players, including the new kid on the block, Seriously Strong.

The key aim of the cheddar brands is to steal share from each other and get consumers to trade up from own-label, becoming loyal to their brand – or as loyal as possible in a hugely promiscuous market – by getting into consumers' repertoires.

'Building loyalty among customers is key to sustained growth and competitive advantage.'

TNS Cheese Report, February 2002

HOW DID SERIOUSLY STRONG FIT IN?

At the time of our story, Seriously Strong was owned and created by McLelland, the third largest producer of cheddar cheese in the UK. Trading since 1849, McLelland was a privately owned Scottish family business based in Glasgow, with an impressive track record of powerful sales growth, from a turnover of £28 million in 1995 to £136 million at the beginning of 2003.

McLelland's vision was to always maintain a balance between tradition and young entrepreneurial drive and innovation, combining the great traditions of Scottish cheese-making with a distinctive taste for adventure and fun, as our story will demonstrate.

As the brand-orientated 1990s progressed, McLelland already had a highly successful portfolio of brands (Galloway, McLelland Mature, Orkney, Arran, Isle of Bute, Mull of Kintyre and Highland) but wanted to create a new brand – something 'entirely different' for the market.

McLelland had developed the product and brought it to market in 1996. Seriously Strong was a very full, rich, sweet cheddar with hint of caramel, which delivered a real flavour punch – more like an extra mature cheddar but at a mature cheddar price point. The product would go on to win many accolades from the trade: 'Best Cheddar' at the British Cheese Awards and 'Gold' at the World Cheese Awards in 2001 among them.

Around this high-quality product, McLelland created a very distinctive name and pack, and launched it initially in Scotland, rolling out to the rest of the UK rapidly (see Figure 2).

Figure 2: *McLelland's Seriously Strong Cheddar pack*

The client stated that:

'We knew we had created a genuinely strong cheddar of great quality and fantastic taste but we wanted to bring it to the market in a way that reflected our generation of cheese-makers – in a younger, more contemporary way that would capture the imagination of the trade and create a point of difference in the market. We wanted to create a cheddar cheese brand that would be famous for being different, to shake things up a bit while not compromising one iota on quality.'

Alistair Irvine, joint MD, 2002

McLelland only really began to invest marketing money in the brand in 1999 with an initial print campaign directed at the trade (appearing in FHO), with the title 'Safe Sex, Dangerous Cheese' (see Figure 3).

Figure 3: McLelland's 1999 print campaign

SERIOUSLY STRONG CHEDDAR

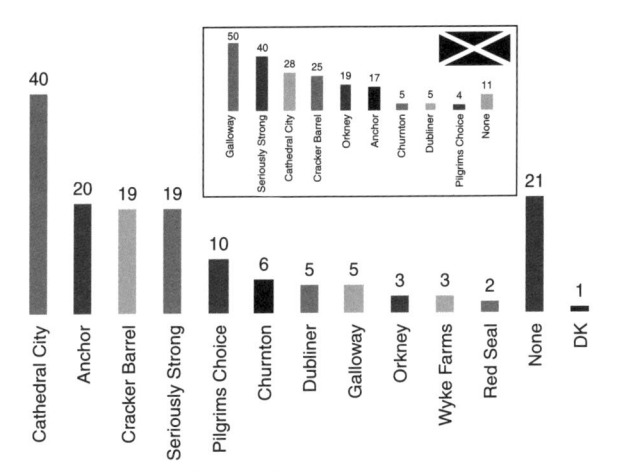

Figure 4: *Brands of cheese ever bought*
Base: all principal shoppers
Source: TNS Cheese Monitor, 2002

An old adage has it that cheese is an aphrodisiac, and the idea was that Seriously Strong must be even more so! The trade absolutely loved it – it was like a breath of fresh air blowing away decades of conventional cheddar cheese marketing.

McLelland now had sufficient stock, trade support and distribution, being in all the major multiples, to develop the brand for the consumer market and needed outside help. 1576 was appointed in spring 2002.

So, as an agency, we started with the Seriously Strong brand name, its distinctive packaging, extremely good distribution, healthy sales and a directive to make the brand 'famous'.

Seriously Strong itself had experienced positive levels of overall growth since its launch in 1996 – it was particularly strong in its homeland of Scotland where it was number two, and it was joint number three nationally (see Figure 4).

However, Cathedral City dominated, Anchor and Cracker Barrel were well established and Pilgrims Choice was up and coming. All these brands were battling it out for the same customers, with little to choose between them.

Our job was to help Seriously Strong stand out from the crowd and to create a step-change in sales during the course of one year, 2003.

SERIOUSLY STRONG BRAND DEVELOPMENT

During 2002, 1576 conducted a series of research projects to fully understand the cheddar cheese market, its brands and Seriously Strong.

Where would brand growth come from?

First, we segmented the cheddar cheese market to understand better who our core target market for the campaign should be and where the real opportunity for growth lay. The cheddar market broadly segments as shown in Figure 5.

Clearly, our core focus would be the 'Experimenters' who made up nearly half of the cheddar market – they were open to new brands and new ways of talking

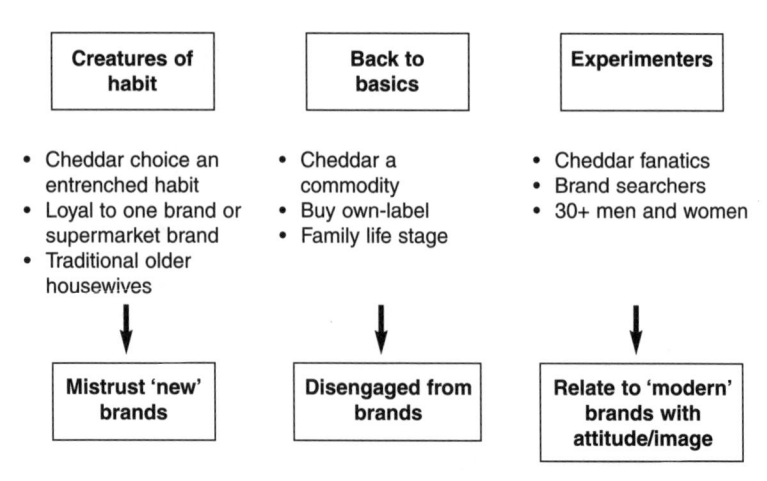

```
┌─────────────┐     ┌─────────────┐     ┌─────────────┐
│ Creatures of│     │   Back to   │     │ Experimenters│
│    habit    │     │   basics    │     │             │
└─────────────┘     └─────────────┘     └─────────────┘
```

- Cheddar choice an entrenched habit
- Loyal to one brand or supermarket brand
- Traditional older housewives

- Cheddar a commodity
- Buy own-label
- Family life stage

- Cheddar fanatics
- Brand searchers
- 30+ men and women

```
┌─────────────┐     ┌─────────────┐     ┌─────────────┐
│ Mistrust 'new'│   │ Disengaged from│  │ Relate to 'modern'│
│    brands   │     │    brands   │     │  brands with    │
│             │     │             │     │ attitude/image  │
└─────────────┘     └─────────────┘     └─────────────┘
```

Figure 5: *Segmenting the cheddar cheese market*
Source: 1576 brand development research

```
┌─────────────┐           ┌─────────────┐
│  Functional │           │   Emotional │
└─────────────┘           └─────────────┘
```

'Replenishers'
- Own-label
- BOGOF brands
- Convenience
- Volume

'Active Choice Makers'
- Brands
- Provenance/brand story
- Appealing identity
- Value

```
                          ┌─────────────────┐
                          │ Seriously Strong│
                          └─────────────────┘
```

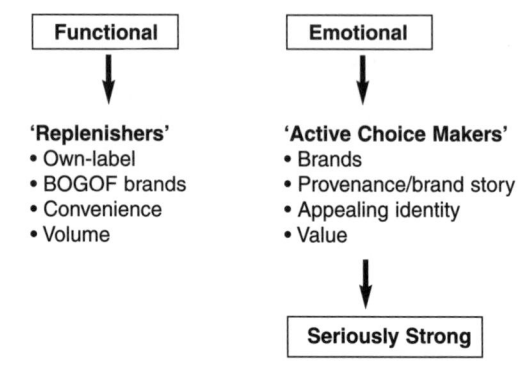

Figure 6: *How do people buy cheddar cheese?*

about cheddar cheese. We also looked at how consumers bought cheddar cheese, and saw that it split between 'functional' and 'emotional' need states (see Figure 6).

Again, Seriously Strong was clearly a more 'emotional' choice for people prepared to pay a bit more for brands that they liked, that stood for something.

Since we were inheriting a brand that had existed for several years without any consumer advertising, we also had to understand how the brand was perceived.

THE PROBLEM

Based on 1576 brand development research, we realised fairly quickly that the Seriously Strong brand, prior to advertising, was sending out mixed signals:

> 'Apart from price promotions, strength and pack appearance are the two main criteria which consumers use to help them choose – the appearance of the packaging is used by consumers to guide them as they often have nothing else to go on.'
>
> *Dairy Crest Cheese Report, 2001*

SERIOUSLY STRONG CHEDDAR

BRAND IMAGE AND STRENGTH PERCEPTIONS (PRE-ADVERTISING)

Using semiotic analysis to understand the key signifiers of the packaging and name alone, the brand signified the following.

- A top-strength cheddar – tangy, rich, salty with a bite. This really appealed to men, who told us 'SS is particularly easy to choose – it is immediately clear what you are getting.'
- The Seriously Strong name was considered modern, different and clever by most – somewhere between Ronseal ('Does what it says on the tin') and Pepperami ('If you're hard enough') – novel territory for a cheddar cheese. This down-to-earth, no-frills, tongue-in-cheek, humorous and quirky brand appealed strongly to men and younger women.
- However, this could also be a disadvantage. The name signifies that it is potentially too strong for some women (older, with families) who anticipated an overpowering, pungent, 'blow your head off' taste – the equivalent of the vindaloo in curry terminology. There were no clear signals that it was, in fact, strong, but flavoursome, creamy and smooth.
- Potentially, it could be seen exclusively as a youthful bloke's brand (a John Smith's).
- However, certain elements of the packaging (namely the rosette) suggested a very good-quality cheddar with a strong, confident personality and credentials.

Overall, Seriously Strong was a brand giving off mixed signals, created by entrepreneurial flair rather than conventional brand development. Importantly, however, it came across as a very different and distinctive brand – one that really stood out on the shelf. It simply lacked cohesion. The brand persona 'glue' that advertising could bring with a clear tone of voice was desperately needed in the mix for balance.

So most of the brand perceptions were very positive but the incorrect strength perception was worrying and would need addressing: Cathedral City was regularly on offer and positioned itself as 'mature yet mellow' cheddar, an easier option for a lot of women to go for.

The big finding was that we knew that once consumers had tried Seriously Strong, they all loved it! It is strong but wonderfully so and not at all 'vindalooish', so encouraging trial was critical.

LACK OF AWARENESS (PRE-ADVERTISING)

Since there had been no consumer advertising, Seriously Strong also had very minimal spontaneous brand awareness (see Figure 7). However, when prompted, awareness jumped up (see Figure 8).

Clearly, Seriously Strong had very little top-of-mind presence but quite a lot of residual awareness. Advertising was needed to convert and build top-of-mind awareness – crucial in the brand loyalty war.

While loyalty is hard in this market, it's not impossible. We needed an increase in loyalty to Seriously Strong by getting consumers to add it to their repertoire.

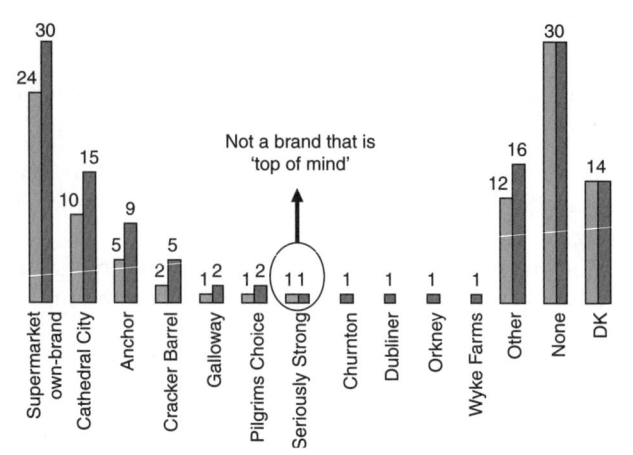

Figure 7: *Spontaneous awareness of cheddar brands*
Base: all principal shoppers
Source: TNS Cheese Report, 2002

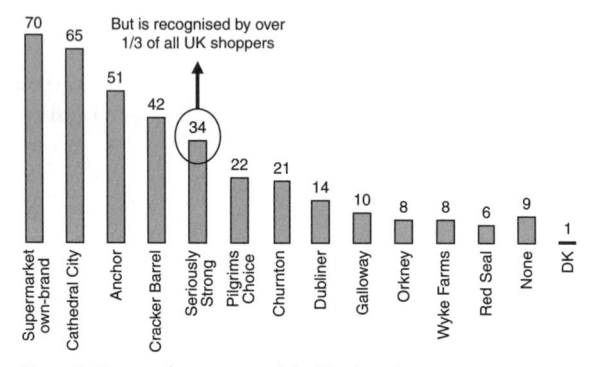

Figure 8: *Prompted awareness of cheddar brands*
Base: all principal shoppers
Source: TNS Cheese Report, 2002

THE COMMUNICATION STRATEGY

It was not an option to change the pack or the name – the brand was a success already and we did not want to throw the baby out with the bath water.

Also, our client wanted to continue its pioneering work in creating a new and different 'lighthouse' brand for the cheese market, and therefore wanted to develop a brand persona and campaign that also broke 'conventions'. It did not want to show cheese, people eating cheese, cheese boards or cheese sandwiches – unlike the competition (see Figure 9).

It wanted a strategy that positioned Seriously Strong well away from the key competitors in the branded cheddar market.

Therefore the strategy was to create a compelling brand persona via advertising (PR and promotions) for Seriously Strong, which 'softened' the brand image, appealing more to women purchasers without alienating the loyal male consumer, while remained distinctly different for the category.

SERIOUSLY STRONG CHEDDAR

Figure 9: *Cheese advertising from two of Seriously Strong's competitors*

The role for advertising was:

- to create a compelling brand persona that reflected the true strength and taste of Seriously Strong cheddar cheese, and prepared expectations correctly and positively
- to build awareness and to stand out from other cheese brands
- to generate sales, trial and loyalty by stealing share from other brands primarily, but also own-label cheddars.

BRAND AND CAMPAIGN DEVELOPMENT

'I thought it was going to be really, really strong but it's lovely – I could eat that all the time. Can I have some more please.'

1576 creative development research, 2002

Advertising clearly had to take the product truth – that Seriously Strong is a strong cheese – and take some of the rougher edges off it to appeal to the 'Experimenters', but also more specifically to women (the core purchasers of cheese) and men (the core consumers of strong cheese), and to tell all cheese lovers that Seriously Strong is a highly desirable strong cheddar cheese.

We wanted to create a 'lighthouse' brand that:

- had a clear, compelling persona that was very different from other cheddar cheese brands (and that would reposition them as being old, traditional and fusty)

- had a great deal of confidence with a very real sense of who it was
- was an intrusive, highly noticeable character
- had the potential to develop an emotional- rather than rational-based relationship with consumers
- had the ability to change consumers' emotional relationship with the category.

Basically, the aim was to reposition Seriously Strong and, in doing so, to reposition the competition, as illustrated in Figure 10.

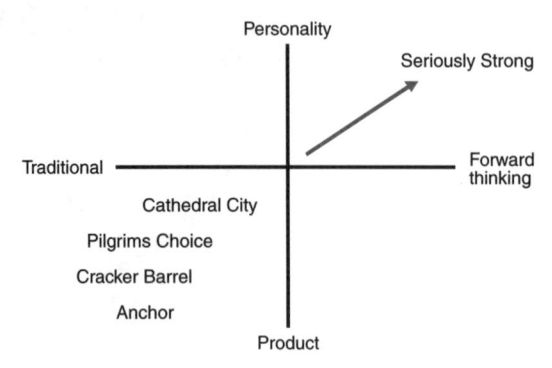

Figure 10: *Repositioning the competition*

The core brand proposition

'Seriously Strong – deliciously strong cheddar that is impossible to resist.'

Tone of voice

To be a beacon in a sea of traditional blandness – contemporary, populist, tongue in cheek.

THE CAMPAIGN IDEA

The campaign idea was very simple: to create a sophisticated, smooth, 'James Bond'-type character, a ladies' man, who would do anything to get his hands on Seriously Strong cheese. Our character was a human mouse (a man with an animated mouse's head), who masterminds Seriously Strong cheese heists while relaxing on his yacht in the Mediterranean (see Figure 11).

Considering most consumer perceptions of cheddar cheese imagery were rural – pastoral scenes, cows, villages, older gentlemen in tweed jackets and cheese boards – this campaign was going to shake things up a bit.

1576 created two ads: a 40-second ad to establish the idea ('Heist') and a 20-second ad ('Yacht') to begin to develop the character and storyline. We advertised in Scotland and the Midlands – the former being Seriously Strong heartland with huge potential still for growth and the latter being Cathedral City heartland territory and a crucial cheddar market to break into in the UK.

SERIOUSLY STRONG CHEDDAR

Figure 11: *Seriously Strong's 'mouse mastermind'*

The advertising consisted of two key bursts in both regions in March/April 2003, as well as June/July in Central and August/September in Scotland.

We also ran a wholly synergistic promotional campaign in major multiples to support the campaign, which the trade loved (see Figure 12).

Figure 12: *Promotional campaign*

RESULTS

Our results are drawn from the TNS Cheese Monitor Survey in 2003/04, a qualitative brand assessment project by Frontiers Research, in-store research by McLelland and 1576 creative development research.

First, the advertising clearly had a marked and strong impact (see Figures 13 and 14).

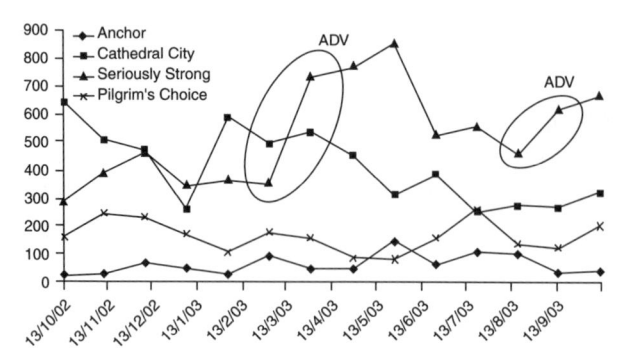

Figure 13: *TV impact, Scotland*
Source: TNS Cheese Monitor, 2003

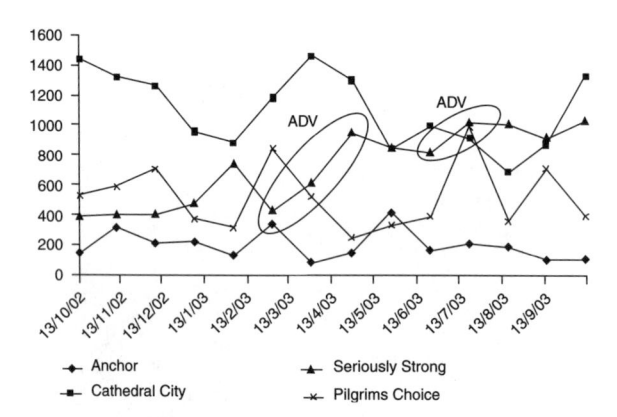

Figure 14: *TV impact, Central*
Source: TNS Cheese Monitor, 2003

Awareness of Seriously Strong also built impressively in advertised versus non-advertised regions. It still went up in non-advertised regions due to ongoing promotions (we were unable to create a control area) but not nearly to the same degree, demonstrating the specific impact of the advertising (see Figure 15).

In-store research by McLelland backed this up (see Figure 16).

During the advertising, Seriously Strong sales grew by a staggering 45% year on year. We had created the 'step-change' in sales demanded by our client (see Figure 17).

SERIOUSLY STRONG CHEDDAR

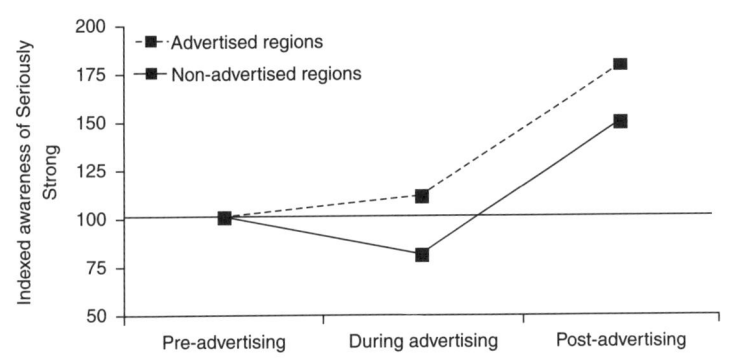

Figure 15: *Awareness of Seriously Strong in advertised vs non-advertised regions, 2003*
Source: TNS £net

- 81% of people have seen the TV advertising

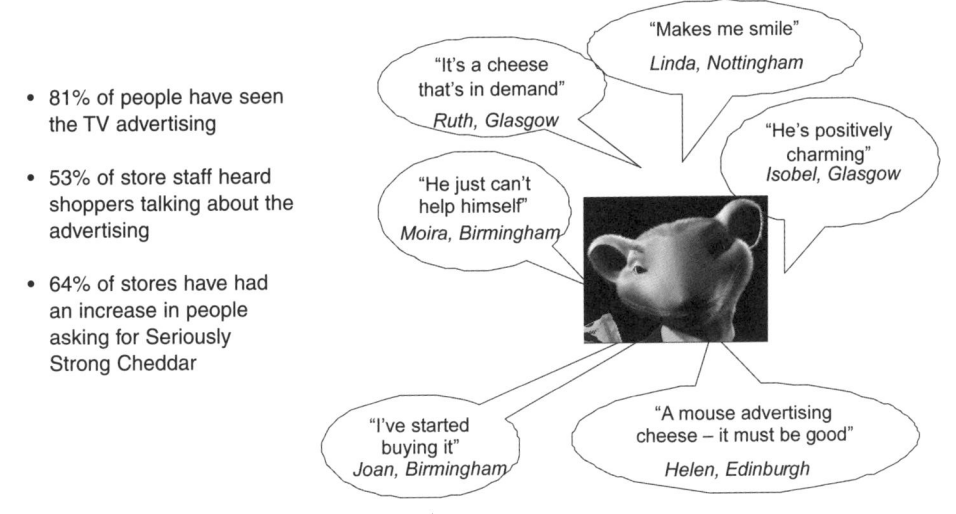

- 53% of store staff heard shoppers talking about the advertising

- 64% of stores have had an increase in people asking for Seriously Strong Cheddar

"It's a cheese that's in demand"
Ruth, Glasgow

"Makes me smile"
Linda, Nottingham

"He just can't help himself"
Moira, Birmingham

"He's positively charming"
Isobel, Glasgow

"I've started buying it"
Joan, Birmingham

"A mouse advertising cheese – it must be good"
Helen, Edinburgh

Figure 16: *In-store awareness of campaign*
Source: McLelland in-store research, 2003

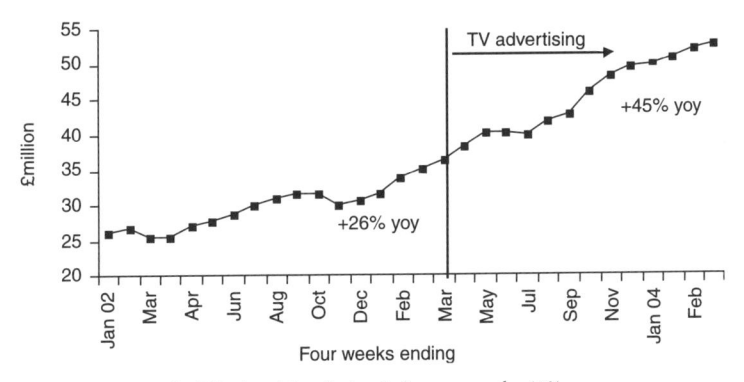

Figure 17: *During the TV advertising, Seriously Strong grew by 45%*
Source: TNS £net, January 2004

SCOTTISH ADVERTISING WORKS 4

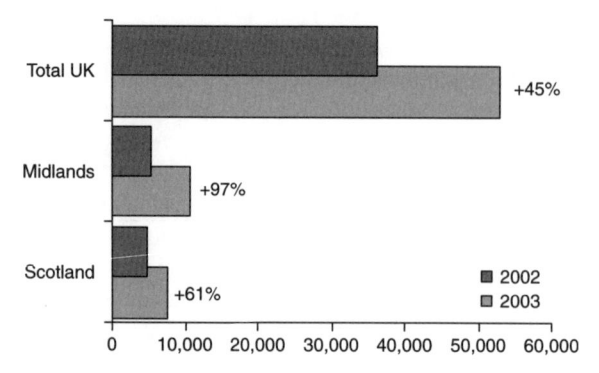

Figure 18: *Seriously Strong: a national brand*
Source: TNS £net, January 2004

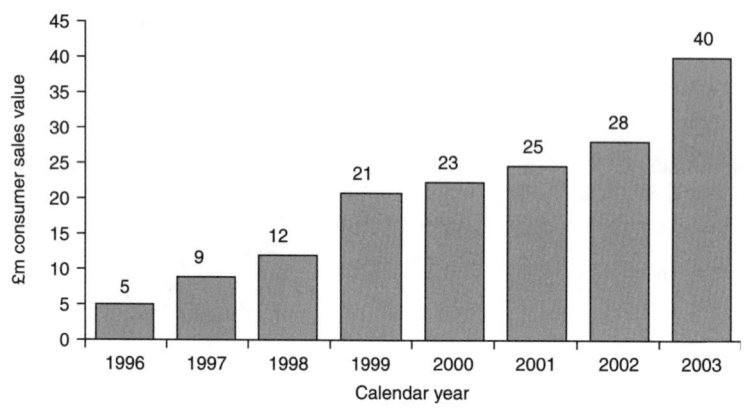

Figure 19: *By the end of 2003, Seriously Strong was a £40 million brand*
Source: TNS £net

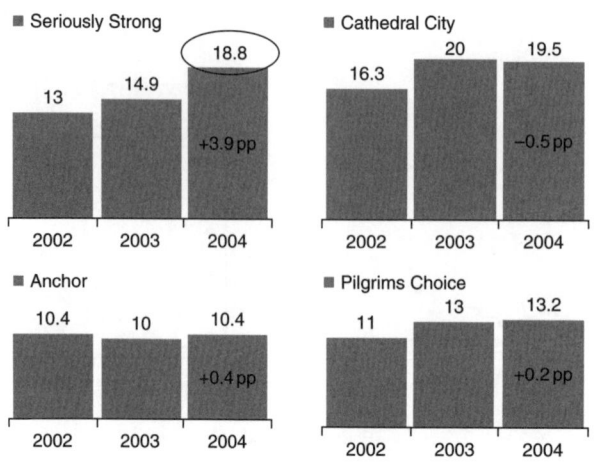

Figure 20: *Residual impact on brand loyalty in 2003/2004*
Source: TNS £net, January 2004

SERIOUSLY STRONG CHEDDAR

By creating such lifts in the two regions we had turned Seriously Strong into a national rather than regional brand (see Figure 18).

By the end of 2003, Seriously Strong was a £40 million brand (see Figure 19).

Against all odds, we began to build brand loyalty in 2003 and saw this come to fruition in 2004 with a significant leap for Seriously Strong at the expense of the other key brands (see Figure 20).

If you look at where sales were coming from, you can see why this is happening. The advertising actively encouraged switching from private label and Pilgrims Choice in the Midlands, and private label and Cathedral City in Scotland (see Figures 21 and 22).

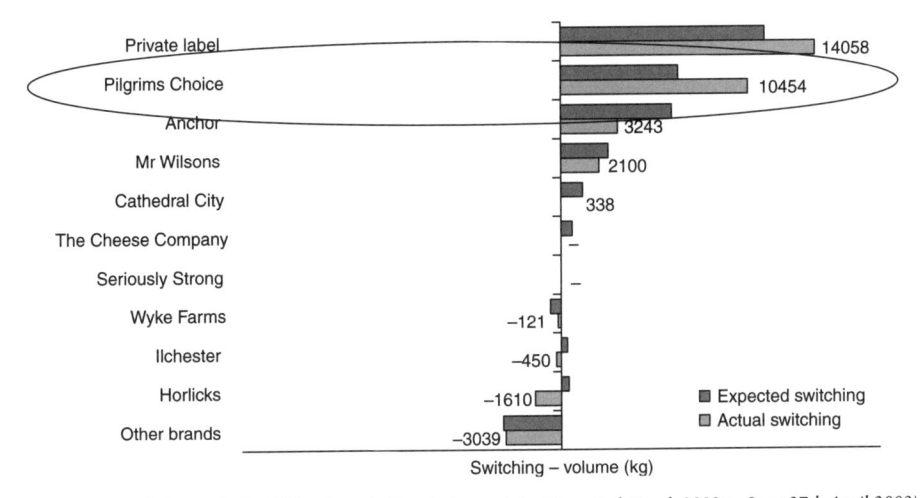

Figure 21: *Seriously Strong in the Midlands: switching during vs prior (8 we 2nd March 2003 vs 8 we 27th April 2003)*

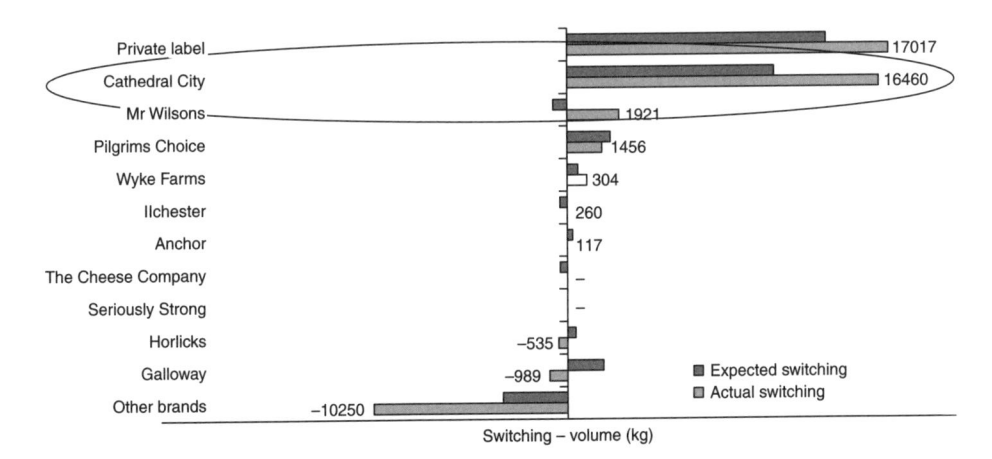

Figure 22: *Seriously Strong in Scotland: switching prior vs post (8 we 2nd March 2003 vs 8 we 22nd June 2003)*

The advertising also clearly helped Seriously Strong to close the gap between itself and the market leader Cathedral City (see Figure 23).

Qualitative research after the campaign ran reassured us that the advertising had indeed built on the positives of the pack and name, adding new elements that helped to address the taste perception problems, while building a stronger brand image for Seriously Strong (see Figure 24).

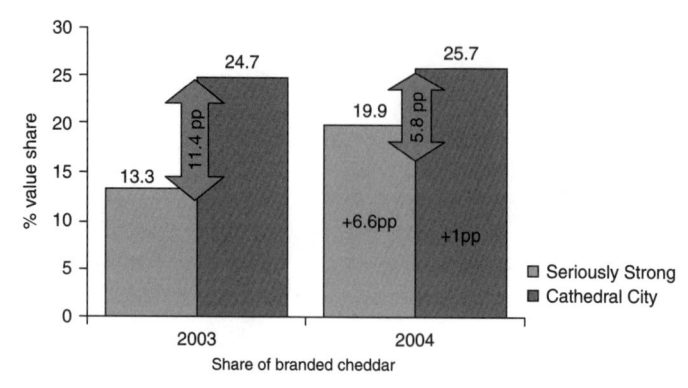

Figure 23: *Closing the gap on the market leader*
Source: TNS £net, February 2004

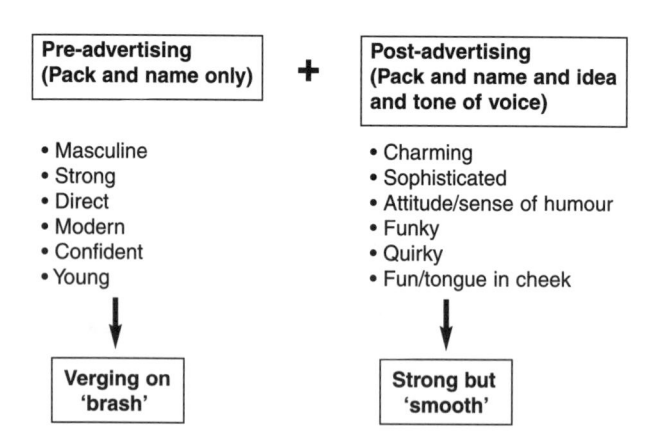

Pre-advertising (Pack and name only)	+	Post-advertising (Pack and name and idea and tone of voice)
• Masculine • Strong • Direct • Modern • Confident • Young		• Charming • Sophisticated • Attitude/sense of humour • Funky • Quirky • Fun/tongue in cheek
↓		↓
Verging on 'brash'		Strong but 'smooth'

Figure 24: *Developing Seriously Strong's brand image through advertising*
Source: Frontiers Research

In addition to this, the advertising successfully repositioned the core competition, Cathedral City and Pilgrims Choice, very effectively – Pilgrims Choice in particular suffering from this process (see Table 1).

SERIOUSLY STRONG CHEDDAR

TABLE 1: REPOSITIONING THE COMPETITION

	Seriously Strong	Cathedral City	Pilgrims Choice
As a car:	BMW Audi TT Aston Martin	Jag Land Rover	Escort Skoda Horse and cart
As an animal:	Lion Tiger	Poodle Cat (Homely)	Donkey Camel
As music:	Heavy metal	Classical/choir	Val Doonican

Source: Frontiers Research

In focus groups, cheese consumers were genuinely impressed with Seriously Strong's approach:

'It's a new, dynamic brand, one of the market leaders, a big brand because it is advertised on TV.'

Male, Midlands

'I thought it was going to be too strong for me, but the advertising suggests that it is quite classy, quite moreish so it must be easy to eat – I'd certainly want to give it a go.'

Female, Scotland

'I know he's just a man with an animated mouse head but he's quite sexy – a bit like James Bond or maybe more like George Clooney in *Ocean's Eleven* – sophisticated and stylish but a bit of a rogue. It is very different for cheese advertising.'

Female, Midlands

'Well I'd do anything for that taste – like the mouse man!'

Male, Scotland

Impressively, Seriously Strong emerged as one of the fastest-growing brands of 2003, a significant feat indeed for a brand that had virtually no consumer top-of-mind awareness prior to the advertising (see Figure 25).

Finally, and crucially, the advertising helped Seriously Strong achieve a fantastic ROI: £15 for every £1 spent.

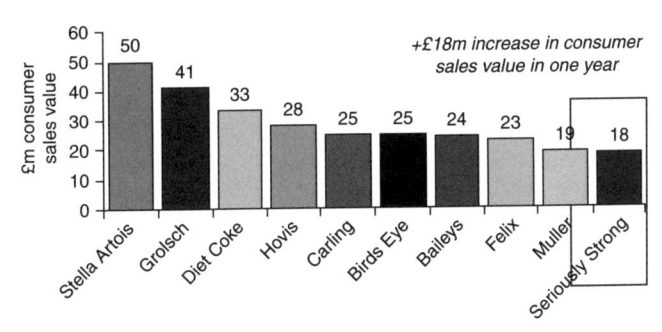

Figure 25: *Seriously Strong was one of the fastest-growing brands in 2003*
Source: TNS £net, January 2004

CONCLUSIONS

This paper has clearly demonstrated that a new TV campaign for Seriously Strong cheese built a compelling brand persona, which addressed strength issues that were creating barriers to purchase. It helped to create a step-change in sales, and broadened the appeal of Seriously Strong. But more than that, this story is a celebration of an entrepreneurial company prepared to stick its neck out and take risks in a very traditional market by creating its own ground rules and remaining true to them.

8

University of Dundee
Academic brand creation

Principal author: George Cumming, Frame C
Media agency: MediaCom

EDITOR'S SUMMARY

Dundee University deserves full credit for giving its backing to a challenging but very successful campaign from Frame C, stimulating both the quantity and quality of undergraduate applications. The momentum recorded in this team's previous IPA paper gathered pace as the whole university organisation took the campaign theme on board and the Dundee brand gained competitive strength. A clear return on investment sealed the argument for Dundee's second Silver award.

OVERVIEW

The initial phase of the University of Dundee's foray into advertising resulted in the reversal of a worrying downward spiral in consumer demand (applications). It is now, in tandem with the agency, producing a category-busting focus on brand building – brand building of a scale that is significantly shifting consumer opinion and changing internal behaviour and attitudes within the university.

This is an important case study as it demonstrates the following learning:

- the value of understanding young people
- the value of a compelling and differentiating positioning
- a creative idea that cuts across all promotional activity
- a unique insight into the potency of brand rather than communications strategy, changing opinion and behaviour.

From the outset, the agency has carefully followed consumer research findings, demonstrating a close understanding of the opinions and expectations of school leavers and indeed undergraduate students as well. The first campaign in 2000 was extremely controversial, creating national press and media coverage as a result of its social culture undertones. 'Serious Fun' as a proposition was an immediate success. Consumer demand rose rapidly, allowing the university a greater choice of more qualified applicants, thus reducing entrants through the UCAS clearing system.

Consumer demand to date (February 2005) shows a staggering 83% increase in applications, UCAS clearing students are down to a nominal 3% of total entrants and 97% of graduates take up employment within three months of graduation. The university has also been voted top Scottish University in the 2004 *Sunday Times Good University Guide*, moving from 42nd to 28th in the 2004 UK league table in *The Times Good University Guide*.

The evidence of brand emergence is clear – strange, in a place like Dundee, known more for 'dour and dreich' than 'serious and fun'.

SCALE OF THE CHALLENGE

The main obstacles worthy of comment in this sector are as follows.

1. Advertising and marketing activity is low as a result of an over risk-averse market standpoint.
2. Understanding the target audience of young people over a period of time can be very difficult to gauge.
3. Academic brands do exist, but one could argue that they have been established over centuries, rather than decades (e.g. the iconic institutions such as Oxford, Cambridge and St Andrews). Establishing a strong brand from a low base is very difficult.
4. The sustainability of results over a long period of time (beyond a campaign or two) is extremely rare in this sector.

UNIVERSITY OF DUNDEE

THE BRIEF

The initial brief in 2000 – to arrest the decline in applications and reduce clearing entrants – was answered comprehensively by 2002. The client (Director of Admissions) posed the next challenge: magnify the differentiation of the university from the market, and build a brand position that is sustainable in the long run.

Naturally, the level of applications had to be maintained, but of paramount importance was the quality of applications, which could play an influential role in advancing the overall reputation of the university. Reputation is a key currency in the academic market.

UNDERSTANDING THE MARKET

Overview

In the period 2000–2005, market demand for university places in Scotland increased by 24%, primarily led by the ever increasing popularity and accessibility of a university education.

Three market segments exist: the established high-quality universities, the middle market and the new converted colleges at the more readily accessible end of the market. Figure 1 presents the market segmentation and shows the university's change of position.

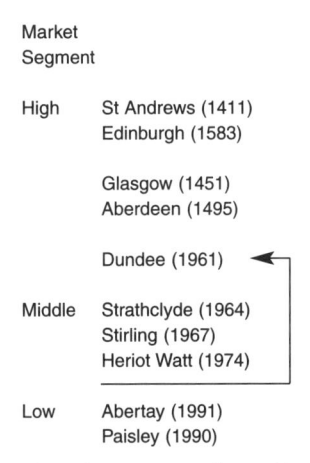

Market Segment	
High	St Andrews (1411)
	Edinburgh (1583)
	Glasgow (1451)
	Aberdeen (1495)
	Dundee (1961) ◄─┐
Middle	Strathclyde (1964)
	Stirling (1967)
	Heriot Watt (1974) ─┘
Low	Abertay (1991)
	Paisley (1990)

Figure 1: *Scottish university market positioning*
Note: university market (not all institutions) by university and year of Royal Charter, using *Sunday Times Good University Guide* to determine latest positioning

Consumer insight

Key insights through research proved that this media-savvy, computer games generation requires to be stimulated by clear and meaningful messages. The notion that it can be pigeonholed as 'youth culture' is wrong. According to the Scottish Executive, around 52% of all young people are now at university; they are the

ABC1 consumers of the future and, as such, require and tolerate less patronising communications.

In order to find the most motivating communication triggers and get closer to the target audience, a variety of research was conducted in and around Dundee, Glasgow and Edinburgh. By means of qualitative groups, in-depth interviews and small group discussions held in cinema foyers, clubs and fast-food outlets, with prospective students and current undergraduates, the key insights were as follows.

- School leavers are much more media attuned than they are given credit for, resulting in a requirement for messages to be refreshed regularly.
- Dundee students have to work harder to enjoy themselves than those at other universities, resulting in a strong 'esprit de corps'.
- The work ethic and maturity towards a work hard/play hard belief was much stronger than anticipated.
- School leavers had a deep-seated belief that a good university education was a stepping-stone to lifetime success.

BRAND STRATEGY: A DEEPER UNDERSTANDING OF THE CLIENT

Focus was now on long-term brand building. The agency analysed the whole university experience, the people involved and its pressure points from a business perspective.

In order to formulate a brand strategy, it was essential to recognise the division of responsibilities between agency and client. Figure 2 surveys the input to output scope of the business (the brand experience). Within this model it was apparent that the agency could directly influence consumer attraction, the conversion process and staff buy-in, but clearly had no direct control over the university's own management of resources.

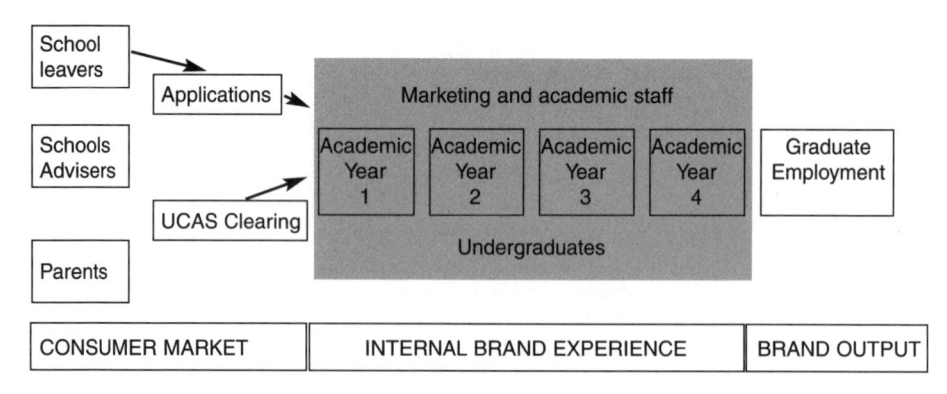

Figure 2: *Simplified university model*

Key groups include the consumer market (influencers and participants), the internal process (education and fun) and the interface with the outside world (employment).

The strategy split into three main thrusts, as follows.

UNIVERSITY OF DUNDEE

1. Spreading consumer awareness in the 'hot' areas of Dundee, Tayside, Fife and Strathclyde.
2. Using the brand proposition to cut through all communications activities, especially the conversion points (e.g. open days, visitor days, prospectuses, freshers' magazines).
3. Persuading and coercing the university into adopting a 'Serious Fun' approach, penetrating through to staff.

BRAND DEVELOPMENT

So much initial emphasis was spent on jumpstarting consumer demand that it took three full years to get to the point where confidence in the longevity of the 'Serious Fun' proposition was truly established. It can be said that a brand is a thousand small expressions and, with this thought in mind, the agency sought to maximise these expressions at every point of contact with the target audience, staff and outside world in general.

The agency recognised that by expanding brand awareness the university's competitive power in the market would be driven in four areas: consumer market (all influencers and prospective undergraduates); undergraduates; all staff; and ultimate employment. Albeit that the university would strongly influence the level of degree results in the latter case.

Consumer market: growing opinion

As part of the annual research process, agency staff and a researcher had gone out on the hoof to student unions, cinemas and fast-food restaurants around Dundee, Glasgow and Edinburgh.

Their remit was twofold:

1. to track opinion
2. to track awareness of the campaigns.

Tracking in 2001–2004 revealed the data shown in Table 1, based on sample sizes of 450 young people.

TABLE 1: INDEX TRACKING OF YOUNG PEOPLE'S OPINION 2001–2004 (TEN-POINT SCALE)

	2001	2002	2003	2004
Quality of Dundee University in market	5.2	5.5	6.4	6.8
Likelihood to recommend to family and friends	4.2	5.1	6.5	7.1

Source: D. Hicks

Within these figures, awareness among young people in Glasgow 2003–2004 showed the most marked opinion shift. In terms of campaign awareness, the 'Epitaph' TV campaign proved to be the most significant recollection with 74%. Opinions are still, nevertheless, clouded by bias towards Dundee as a place to live.

Undergraduates: delivering promise

The agency fostered close ties with undergraduate students, through involvement in focus groups and as student ambassadors on open days. Using them as a sounding board to gauge opinion on how the proposition is developed and refined, this collaborative approach has helped the agency compose its thoughts. As part of this embrace, campaigns were very much part of campus communications, thus maintaining the internal brand experience. Undergraduates are a key secondary audience.

Staff: brand involvement

A key agency success was its achievement, through the Admissions Department, in reformatting open days, so important in the conversion process. They were given a 'Serious Fun' look, with everything from 'Serious Fun' disposable cameras to the deliberate positioning of 'in tune' academic staff, whose communication skills would promote the university in a much more engaging manner. Figure 3 shows the growing significant numbers attending open days.

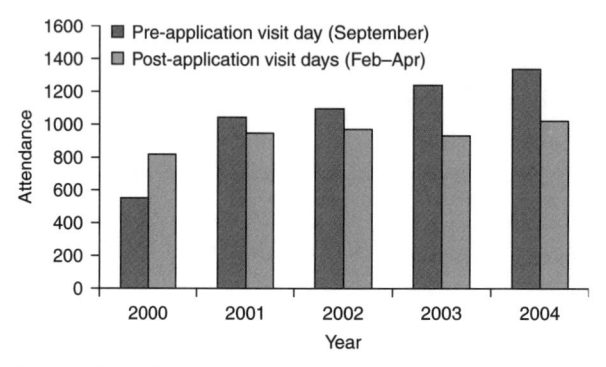

Figure 3: *Conversion process activity*

A similar approach was adopted by differentiating the university's presentations at student fairs provided for school leavers. The mix of serious and fun was communicated through branded exhibition systems, gifts, takeaways and postcard communications.

CHANGING CREATIVE

From a controversial opening campaign with a limited use of communication channels, further campaigns were refined to fit the ongoing research findings. By 2003 the consumer insight, as discussed, had moved on. Communicating the allure of the stepping-stone (conduit) to success was now the key creative challenge.

In autumn 2003 the 'Epitaph' campaign asked, 'What do you want yours to say?' in reference to what graduates' epitaphs on headstones might say. Projected in a fun tone, the serious consideration of future success was posed.

UNIVERSITY OF DUNDEE

Figure 4: *Examples from the TV campaigns*

Not only did this campaign hit the mark with the school leavers, but it went on to win the award for Best 30-second TV Ad at the 2004 Scottish Advertising Awards.

The success of 'Epitaph' led to the 2004 campaign message, 'Discovery'. This was communicated by playing on the intrigue of discovering the rest of your life, which could lead to the realisation of success.

Figure 4 shows examples from the TV campaigns executed to date, and their evolution from graphic images to more sophisticated messages.

Media

In recognition of previously successful media campaigns using 20-second TV executions in Grampian, Central Scotland and Ulster, no additional coverage was required on terrestrial channels. However, in 2004, for the first time, the TV campaign extended to SkyTV to target the youth market channels of E4 and MTV. The results of this innovative move are awaited with optimism.

The use of radio was also an integral part of the campaigns, again with the 'Serious Fun' proposition running through their execution. Unlike the TV campaigns, the radio focus was primarily on Tay FM and Wave 102, providing coverage in Tayside and Perth.

COMMUNICATIONS

The 'Serious Fun' brand has now extended through all university communications, TV, radio, outdoor, and through the communications and materials used in the

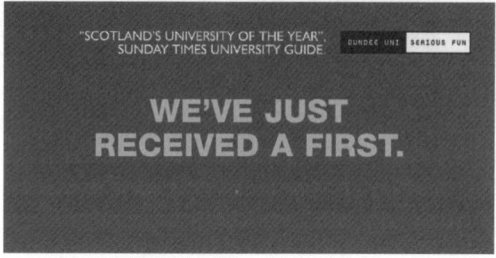

Figure 5: *Examples of communication materials*

conversion process (the open days, the prospectuses and freshers' magazines). Figure 5 provides some examples of the variety of communications used.

In 2004 an outdoor site in the city centre of Dundee was booked for the full year, hence being a central source of brand awareness, through campaign images, messages and general information (including the 48-sheet which proclaimed the *Sunday Times Good University Guide* 2004 award).

RESULTS

Reflecting back on the brief, we are looking for evidence of three main outcomes:

1. maintenance of consumer demand (applications)
2. an improvement in the quality of applications
3. proof of a significant growth in awareness and confidence in the university, driven by the advertising campaigns.

Consumer demand (up)

In its core market (Scotland), no other university can match Dundee University's growth rate in consumer demand. Table 2 puts this growth into perspective by highlighting the huge success in building profile and demand.

UNIVERSITY OF DUNDEE

TABLE 2: DEGREE APPLICATIONS

Inst code	Institution name	2000	2001	2002	2003	2004	2005	% change 2005/2000
D65	University of Dundee	6,190	6,653	8,360	8,847	9,638	11,302	+82.6%
S36	University of St Andrews	6,019	8,720	7,867	7,144	8,337	10,064	+67.2%
E56	University of Edinburgh	26,006	27,261	28,740	28,063	32,134	36,359	+39.8%
A20	University of Aberdeen	8,936	10,574	11,410	10,906	10,913	11,403	+27.6%
P20	University of Paisley	4,482	4,228	5,473	5,637	5,859	5,503	+22.8%
Q25	Queen Margaret University College	4,971	5,461	4,985	4,961	4,978	6,057	+21.8%
G28	University of Glasgow	20,804	21,631	23,887	23,107	22,628	24,193	+16.3%
S78	University of Strathclyde	14,345	15,117	15,898	16,147	16,185	16,348	+14.0%
S75	University of Stirling	7,998	9,059	9,134	8,908	8,335	9,045	+13.1%
H24	Heriot-Watt University Edinburgh	5,822	6,426	7,365	6,665	6,769	6,413	+10.2%
G42	Glasgow Caledonian University	12,821	13,087	13,345	13,345	14,136	13,896	+8.4%
R36	Robert Gordon University	5,472	5,464	5,309	5,232	5,512	5,696	+4.1%
A30	University of Abertay Dundee	3,703	4,009	4,933	4,429	3,798	3,806	+2.8%
N07	Napier University	5,998	5,716	7,023	7,085	6,722	6,025	+0.5%
	Scottish degree application totals	133,567	143,406	153,729	150,476	155,944	166,110	+24.4%

Source: UCAS

Putting the scale of this growth in demand into a UK context, Table 3 presents an insight into not only the percentage growth but also the actual hard numbers in applications growth.

TABLE 3: GROWTH IN APPLICATIONS FOR UK UNIVERSITIES

Movement in applications numbers, 2001–04

University	2004	2001	Movement	% move
University of Dundee	10,779	7,063	3,716	53%
Queen Mary	16,624	10,888	3,736	34%
Surrey	7,348	5,479	1,869	34%
Newcastle	25,824	19,583	6,241	32%
East Anglia	12,876	9,973	2,903	29%
Manchester	49,501	38,400	11,101	29%
Liverpool	26,869	21,037	5,832	28%
Sussex	12,107	9,563	2,544	27%
SOAS	2,489	1,968	521	26%
Cambridge	11,597	9,177	2,420	26%
Oxford	10,361	8,240	2,121	26%
Kent	11,982	9,777	2,205	23%
Royal Holloway	7,955	6,596	1,359	21%
Essex	8,850	7,418	1,432	19%
Swansea	10,691	9,025	1,666	18%
York	17,617	14,873	2,744	18%
King's College London	20,602	17,418	3,184	18%
Durham	23,229	19,815	3,414	17%
Reading	19,954	17,058	2,896	17%
Leeds	48,206	41,214	6,992	17%
Exeter	20,231	17,486	2,745	16%

Source: UCAS statistics

Quality (up)

Key quality indicators in this market are UCAS clearing numbers and level of entry requirements.

UCAS clearing entrants (down)

Figure 6 quite clearly shows the dramatic drop in school leavers entering with sub-standard higher qualifications. Reducing the number of entrants who are not qualified to join the courses significantly reduces the risk of drop-outs and enhances the possibility of improved degree pass rates.

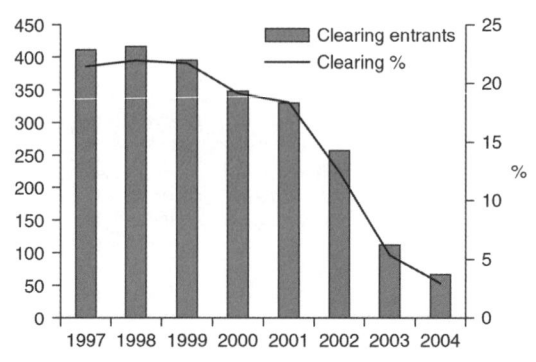

Figure 6: *UCAS clearing entrants*
Source: University of Dundee Admissions Statistics, 2004

Entry requirements (up)

Table 4 shows a general increase in the standards of entry into the university, based on the points-scoring system.

TABLE 4: ENTRY REQUIREMENTS, 2002–06

	2002	2003	2004	2005	2006
Accountancy	240	240	240	240	240
Arts and Social Sciences	220	220	220	240	240
Engineering	200	220	220	240	240
Law	264–300	264–300	264–300	264–312	264–312
Life Sciences	200	200	200	220	240
Physical Sciences	200–240	200–240	200–240	220–240	220–240

Source: University of Dundee Admissions Statistics, 2004

While courses such as Accountancy remain unchanged, other courses have ramped up their requirements. Applying the principle of basic economic theory, where supply is limited and demand is high, 'price' can be driven up. This is a very important point, as Dundee is, in effect, increasing the worth of its courses while continuing to increase demand (a prime example of brand value and repositioning in the market).

Such a shift in the university's positioning again serves to reduce the gap at the top end of the market.

Awareness and opinion shift (up)

Primary evidence of brand awareness is found explicitly through applications, and secondarily, though the research findings conducted to track opinion, confidence and awareness.

UNIVERSITY OF DUNDEE

Market share (up)

We can see from Table 5 that the university's overall market share can be considered to have moved in 2000–05 by two percentage points, from 5% to 7%, or from 6% to 9% using the middle- and upper-market segments.

TABLE 5: UPPER QUALITY SEGMENT OF SCOTTISH UNIVERSITY MARKET, APPLICATION TREND 2000–05

Established university market

Inst code	Institution name	2000	2001	2002	2003	2004	2005	% change 2005/2000
D65	University of Dundee	6,190	6,653	8,360	8,847	9,638	11,302	83%
S36	University of St Andrews	6,019	8,720	7,867	7,144	8,337	10,064	67%
E56	University of Edinburgh	26,006	27,261	28,740	28,063	32,134	36,359	40%
A20	University of Aberdeen	8,936	10,574	11,410	10,906	10,913	11,403	28%
G28	University of Glasgow	20,804	21,631	23,887	23,107	22,628	24,193	16%
S78	University of Strathclyde	14,345	15,117	15,898	16,147	16,185	16,348	14%
S75	University of Stirling	7,998	9,059	9,134	8,908	8,335	9,045	13%
H24	Heriot-Watt University Edinburgh	5,822	6,426	7,365	6,665	6,769	6,413	10%
	Scottish degree application totals	96,120	105,441	112,661	109,787	114,939	125,127	30%
	University of Dundee share	6%	6%	7%	8%	8%	9%	

Source: UCAS

GEOGRAPHICAL GROWTH

It is interesting to note that the source of applications has predominantly originated from the Tayside and Fife regions, but with growing demand in Strathclyde.

At present, 88% of applications arise from Scotland, which is unsurprising in the sense that English and Welsh applicants are faced with tuition fees, never mind the expense of accommodation and travel.

Figure 7 shows the demand growth and the brand reaching out further, but not far from home.

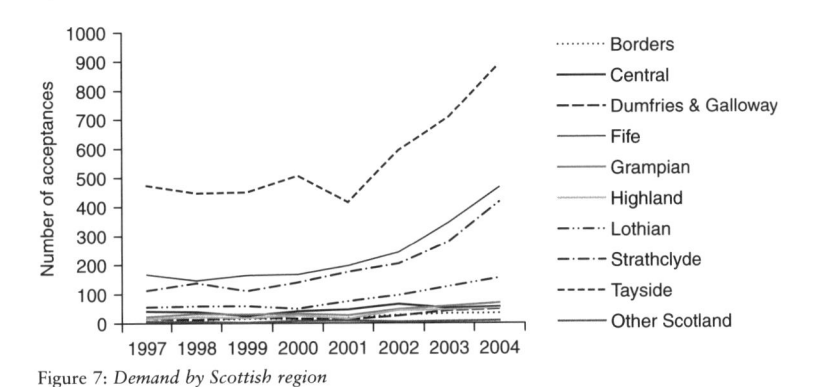

Figure 7: *Demand by Scottish region*
Source: University of Dundee Admissions Department

RETURN ON INVESTMENT

Table 6 details the figures behind the minimum claimed return on the five advertising campaigns. We can calculate that the net additional income would be

£11 million against an advertising cost (including media) of £1.04 million. This is an elevenfold return on advertising investment. Impressive!

TABLE 6: RATIONALE BEHIND ROI ESTIMATE (£000s)

	2000	2001	2002	2003	2004	Total
Entrants	1817	1796	2069	1975	2199	9856
Targets	1697	1703	1776	1850	2050	9076
Over/(under)	120	93	293	125	149	780
Income/head (£k)	4	4	4	5	5	
Incremental income	480	372	1172	625	745	3394
Average course length (yrs)	3.5	3.5	3.5	3.5	3.5	17.5
Total income	1680	1302	4102	2188	2608	11879
Advertising spend	80	89	100	104	122	495
Media spend	60	73	101	151	166	551
Total marketing spend	140	162	201	255	288	1046
Return on investment (number of items)	12.0	8.0	20.4	8.6	9.1	11.4

OTHER IMPEDIMENTS

The university continues to rely on the advertising agency as its only source of external marketing.

Clearly, the agency could claim some of the benefits of the indirect effects of its work, including the impact of the fall in drop-out rates or the impact of the additional research investment; however, these remain a grey area.

CONCLUSION

Amid some fantastic results, the University of Dundee has been building a unique brand, one which has an internal essence in harmony with the promise it makes to its existing and prospective consumers.

The commercial reality is that the university has managed to put up its price (entry requirements), drive up its sales demand (applications) and improve its quality, resulting in a more commanding market positioning. This is all financially justified by the fantastic return on investment over five campaigns. Great in anyone's language!

Let's be quite clear, the advertising has had a stunning effect, but the university has been more than capable of leveraging the benefits to establish high-quality courses and high-fill employment rates. However, the effects of the advertising and the way in which the agency has integrated the communications strategy, translating through the conversion points and staff behaviour, is remarkable.

Section 3

Bronze Winners

BRONZE
CHAIRMAN'S AWARD

9

Anderson Strathern Solicitors
'From this day forward, we leave our green wellies at home'

Principal author: Helen Hourston, Citigate SMARTS
Media agency: Spiritmedia Scotland

EDITOR'S SUMMARY

A winner with a difference. Anderson Strathern used Citigate SMARTS to good effect in repositioning and re-presenting the firm through a cultural change programme. The agency went well beyond conventional advertising to improve its client's internal and external reputation, engaging its staff to change attitude and behaviour with positive business results. The advertising was a relatively modest element of the overall activity, but acted as a catalyst to the organisational change that spurred Anderson Strathern's growth, especially through new client acquisitions.

INTRODUCTION

This paper describes how a simple brief to update a corporate identity turned into a march on the enemy gates.

Advertising is about communication in all its guises, and the success of this paper comes from communication in its simplest form. It may be unlike others in the *Advertising Works* series – not because there has been no effect, because clearly there has. We have added to the brand equity and will prove it. But, like many advertising case studies, the real success of this story is intangible.

This is a different kind of success story. It tells how Citigate SMARTS worked with the partners and employees of an old, established Edinburgh law firm to help them throw off their traditional image, challenge perceptions of themselves in the market and compete head on with the cream of the Scottish law industry. It's a story as much about the instilling of pride and confidence in a workforce as it is about commercial success. But, as we'll show, with one surely comes the other.

LET'S TAKE A LOOK BACK

At the end of 2003 Anderson Strathern, if defined by the number of partners, was a top-ten Scottish law firm. It had been around for over 200 years, was respected by its clients as 'a safe pair of hands', but knew that this heritage alone was not enough to maintain a secure market positioning.

The foundations of Anderson Strathern, and indeed its perceived strengths, were with wealthy private clients and rural landowners, rather than in the corporate business sector. Over the years the firm had built up a strong, well-established, primarily east-coast client base – individuals whose families, generation after generation, had used its services.

Perceptions of the firm in the market mirrored those of its clients. And, despite retaining teams of lawyers in just about every legal specialism, the firm was still seen as a private-client specialist. Research carried out by the firm at the end of 2003 confirmed this and the results left little room for doubt.

'They're a rural and private client firm, they don't do anything else.'

Existing private client

'Not cutting edge; stuffy. They need to let their hair down a bit.'

Corporate client

'I didn't even consider applying to them. They're a bit old school and green wellies – definitely not dealmakers.'

Legal trainee, top-ten firm

Despite this, private clients were clearly happy with the services they were receiving. They associated strong values with the business: 'reliable, traditional, professional'. However, the much larger, corporate market perceived that the firm lacked a commercial approach to business and cited it as being 'more reactive than proactive' and 'not hungry for business'.

ANDERSON STRATHERN SOLICITORS

THE BEGINNINGS OF CHANGE

In reality Anderson Strathern had begun the process of re-engineering internally to become more commercially focused. It had employed marketers to sit on its board, and introduced state-of-the-art IT systems. Despite these radical changes the right message was not getting out.

Aggressive middle-market competition was catching up with Anderson Strathern. And, unless a more positive picture of its strengths and expertise could be projected, the firm was in serious danger of losing both its market position and, potentially, even some of its clients.

Rather than abandon its traditional client base, as many firms had done, Anderson Strathern set itself a more difficult task. It wanted to retain and improve its services to the traditional client base while expanding its commercial offering.

TIME FOR A CHANGE

The partners of the firm recognised that something had to be done and with an office move looming, the time was right for a review of its brand identity.

The brief received by Citigate SMARTS outlined the following objectives.

- Challenge existing perceptions of Anderson Strathern as an old-fashioned and traditional firm of generalists by projecting a more modern, commercially focused and forward-thinking image of the firm.
- Communicate the individual services offered by its 12 specialist divisions, without undermining the parent brand.
- Grow business by cross-selling a wider range of services to the existing client base, and expand that client base by raising awareness of the commercial services offered.

THE REAL CHALLENGE

The brief was clear. We could easily have responded with a new identity and positioning campaign for the firm, but we recognised that a vital link was missing. Without it the brand wouldn't have meaning and our communications wouldn't add up. The missing link was the staff of Anderson Strathern.

For years, agencies have asked companies to pour money into building their external brand while largely neglecting to consult with the employees about what that brand is or the critical role they are expected to play in delivering it.

We didn't just want to slap a shiny veneer on the surface of Anderson Strathern. Over the years the firm had invested a huge amount in its staff. If they were the key to the company's reputation, our money would be wasted if we failed to get them on board. We needed to build the brand from the inside. If we could do this, we believed the firm's brand values and identity would be communicated in a much more powerful way.

Although it would take longer and cost more money, the management team recognised the value of what we were saying.

People own what they create

Our strategy was simple: 'people own what they create'. If the brand was to have meaning for the employees, and in turn for customers, then the firm's staff needed to be active participants in its definition. We wanted the staff to discover the brand for themselves.

If we got this right the development of external branding would be more powerful and, critically, the new image would be much closer to reality.

Face to face: the best media choice

The communications process started when we invited staff and partners to a series of six workshops. This meant that at least 50% of the firm's staff would be directly involved in the brand development process.

The workshops were a success. The staff and partners were positive about their inclusion. The outcomes were consistent. There was a common vision: *for the firm to get the recognition that it deserved; to be seen as offering diverse and specialist services, but as one joined-up company not individual specialists; they wanted to be recognised as more than the sum of the individual parts – as one of the best full-service practices in Scotland. A modern, progressive and respected firm.*

In support of this vision, the following values were agreed, all using existing attributes as foundations.

- Specialist
- Forward thinking
- Business minded
- Client focused
- Professional
- Solution driven
- High quality
- Bespoke advice
- Investor in people
- Approachable

But we didn't just want our well-articulated vision and values to be framed and put on a wall. We wanted the staff to translate them into real-life experiences and live their lives by them every day. So, for each value, a set of practical service initiatives was proposed that would ensure the brand was brought to life.

THE CREATIVE PROCESS

The outcome of the workshops also defined the creative brief. The firm's vision (to ultimately be seen as the best full service firm in Scotland – one joined-up company of specialists) was distilled down to a single proposition:

'More than the sum of the individual specialists'

With complete buy-in both from partners and staff the creative process was easy. We created a fresh, strong and more streamlined identity, but one that respected the heritage of the company. In order to allow the 12 specialisms to work both individually and as part of the whole, photographic icons and a colour-coded scheme were used to distinguish them. Each colour and image was carefully selected with the specialism in mind, considering its function, personality and area of expertise (see Figure 1).

ANDERSON STRATHERN SOLICITORS

Figure 1: *The 12 'specialisms' brochures*

The press advertising creative was distinctive, building on the styling of the brand identity and reflecting the values of the firm. It used a series of bold questioning headlines to reinforce the collective specialisms of Anderson Strathern (see Figure 2).

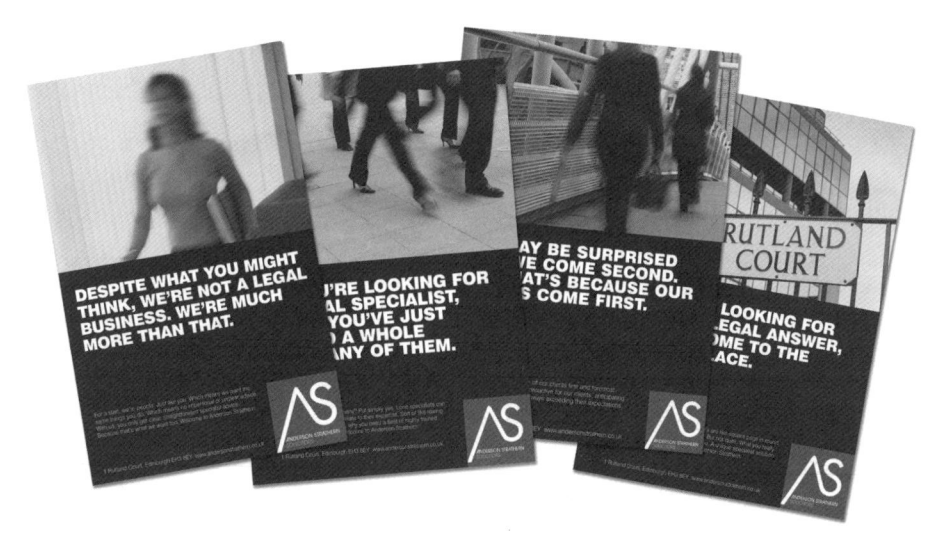

Figure 2: *Press advertising creative*

THE INTERNAL CHANGE

The physical manifestation of the brand internally took many forms: brand identity guidelines, the internet, signage, corporate stationery and other support materials. We reviewed every possible piece of communication. Everything had to reflect the values of the new brand and be delivered in a language and tone that was consistent with it.

THE LAUNCH AND TURNING-POINT

The most important channel to deliver the brand message to the world needed to be the staff themselves. But the support of an external campaign and the unveiling of the new identity to make the business world sit up and take notice would add impact.

They did. Our advertising launched into the Scottish business press at the same time as the new brand was unveiled. This was a truly integrated piece of communication. Every ad, every piece of corporate literature, every bit of digital marketing, every newsletter, every bit of signage and every member of staff were saying the same thing, in the same tone and at the same time.

'From this day forward we leave our green wellies at home.'

Not your usual battle cry, but it was a critical turning-point in the organisation's future; the one that started the march on the enemy gates.

WHAT EFFECT HAS OUR COMMUNICATION HAD?

First, it's important to state that the brand development process was generally welcomed by the clients. They wanted their advisers to be known to be at the cutting edge of legal advice. However, although the risk was small, there was a chance that the more traditional private clients might be alienated by the change; in the event, this was not the case. In the competitive and hard-nosed legal world, this has to be seen as a success factor.

Moreover, there has been a positive and unprompted response from clients in the form of commending letters. These demonstrate that the positive effect of the branding is very definitely taking place.

'The company has moved from a traditional and long-established company to a company that is more forward-thinking and reactive, whilst retaining its professionalism.'

Finance manager, existing third-sector client

'The firm has changed from the traditional image of a solicitor in offices full of paperwork to one of a modern firm with IT systems – not only more up to date but more efficient. The new-look Anderson Strathern can be described in exactly the same terms as the service I receive by the company – professional, modern and effective.'

Chief executive, corporate client

ANDERSON STRATHERN SOLICITORS

THE BEST RESULTS THE FIRM HAS EVER SEEN

The most objective source of feedback for the legal sector is the annual *Legal 500 Directory*. It publishes results on achievements over the year, based on peer and client opinion.

In results recently published, Anderson Strathern saw its ratings go up in five categories and saw new entries in two categories. This is an outstanding achievement to have taken place in less than a year and the best results the firm has ever seen by this measure.

> 'There's definitely something going on at Anderson Strathern, they've always been there – big and quiet – now they're poaching our best people.'
>
> *Partner, competitive firm*

> 'The firm is capable of going head to head with anyone now.'
>
> *Competitor,* Chambers and Partners Directory, *2005*

Clients and competitors alike are sitting up and taking notice. If traffic to its website is any indication of this fact then things are looking good. Website usage was up 47% for the 12 weeks following the launch, compared to the same period in 2003.

AWARDED FOR TEAMWORK

Additionally, the firm entered the annual Cuthbert Scottish Legal Awards at the beginning of 2005. In 2004 two individuals from the firm had received top awards. However, in 2005, for the first time ever, the firm was rewarded with nominations for teamwork – four in total, including best firm. It came away with two top prizes on the night, including best website and best support team. Internally the firm had seen significant changes take place; but to have these recognised through external awards was absolute testament.

A SHARED VISION

We know that the branding campaign was well received internally. But we also now know that the staff better understand what the firm stands for, and are more optimistic about its future. Research recently undertaken by the firm supports this (see Figure 3).

WHAT ABOUT THE BUSINESS EFFECT?

Most papers look at business growth as the primary measurement of success. In this case it is secondary. We were confident that if we could define and harness the brand internally, then support this with external marketing, the more tangible results would come over time; and they did. In the six months following the launch of the brand externally, Anderson Strathern has seen a 17% increase in new clients across the whole firm – a result that far exceeded short-term expectations.

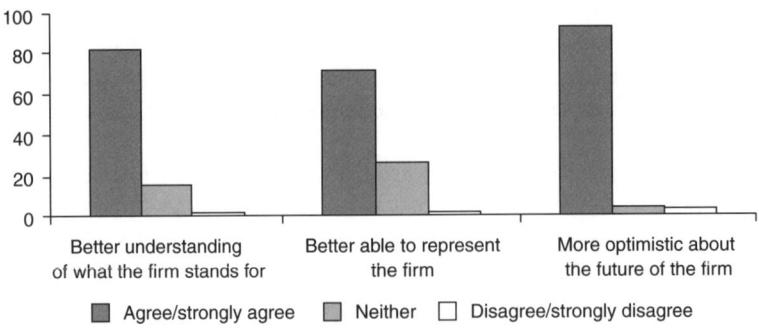

Figure 3: *Understanding of the firm (%)*
Base: 38 respondents

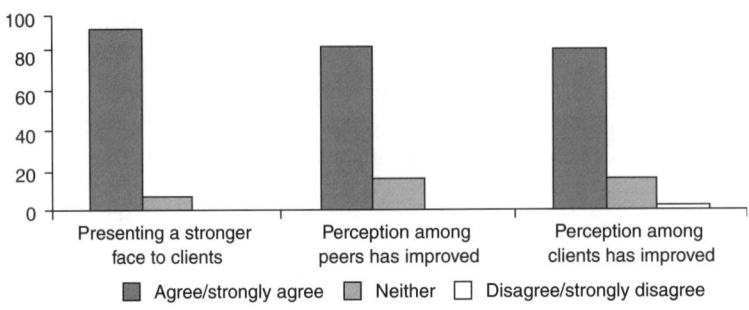

Figure 4: *Perceptions of the firm (%)*
Base: 38 respondents

And, they weren't just any clients:

'We are attracting a new calibre of corporate client that is reflective of the modern, commercially focused company that we now are, as well as retaining and improving our service to our long-standing clients to whom we owe our continued reputation.'

Steve Jackson, Marketing Manager, Anderson Strathern

A SOUND INVESTMENT

Can we measure the payback on the investment made by Anderson Strathern over the course of the year?

The total budget including production was £140,000, a figure that has easily paid for itself, and more, with work from new clients alone. Yet this doesn't take into account the less tangible value of a committed and united team of people who share the vision for the company ... and the long-term value that will bring.

'It's difficult to put the value of this exercise into financial terms. Our staff are key to the firm's reputation, and the brand reflects the values they have established over many years. We are confident going forward they'll manage that reputation well. I think that's worth a lot.'

Robin Stimpson, Managing Partner, Anderson Strathern

WHAT ELSE COULD HAVE DRIVEN THE EFFECT?

Although the firm had invested in internal change in the years prior to the review, the pre-branding research shows that this had no real external effect on perceptions.

The firm saw no changes in management during the course of the year and no new specialist services were added. The market in Scotland saw no significant shift – the only growth was fuelled by the London operations of the larger firms.[1]

Neither did Anderson Strathern spend more on external advertising in 2004 (£24,586) than it did in 2003 (£27,318).[2]

However, to coincide with the branding, the firm did move offices to new, more modern premises during the year. While we recognise that this fact must have had an effect on perceptions, on its own it could not have accounted for the significant change that took place.

CONCLUSION

This paper has demonstrated how our 'inside-out' communications strategy has seen the turning of the tide for Anderson Strathern. How it galvanised the staff to take ownership of the brand they helped create. How it encouraged a culture of 'unbeatable togetherness' that was recognised in awards. How it dramatically changed perception, making the market sit up and take notice. And, ultimately, how it led to a 17% increase in new clients across the business in just a six-month period.

---

1. Source: *The Lawyer*, November 2004.
2. Source: NMR.

BRONZE
BEST INTEGRATION

10

Broadband Registration Drive
The HIE road to broadband

Principal authors: Philip Jones, Spiritmedia Scotland,
and Roddy Ritchie, Arrow Creative Marketing Solutions
Media agency: Spiritmedia Scotland

EDITOR'S SUMMARY

The judges were impressed by the geographical challenge inherent in promoting broadband to the scattered communities of the Highlands and Islands. In this complex case, success depended on the detailed project management of Spiritmedia and Arrow Creative, which showed how an ingenious collaborative effort and skilled integration of media led to results that exceeded expectations. As with other Bronze papers, the judges would have appreciated greater clarity on the ROI involved, here in terms of the commercial and societal benefits flowing from the region's adoption of broadband.

BIG COUNTRY

The Highlands and Islands of Scotland make up a truly unique area in terms of environment – diverse with a rich heritage – and community. The land area covers some 39,000 square kilometres and has a population of just over 400,000; the 640 km from Shetland in the north to Campbeltown in the south supports many fragile communities – communities that have evolved and grown on the traditional industries of agriculture and fishing. New areas of economic development are typified by small- to medium-sized enterprises in the manufacturing, IT and tourism industries, to name but a few. Effective communication within the area and to reach the rest of the world is crucial for sustainability and future development. This campaign shows without doubt that the people and communities of the Highlands and Islands were prepared to stand up and 'speak up for broadband'.

BROAD WHAT?

In 2002 Highlands and Islands Enterprises (HIE) identified the need to stimulate demand for broadband services to a level where the HIE network and partner local government networks could justify the significant investment required to convert exchanges.

The task was to inform the business community of why broadband was crucial as a utility service, while also informing the wider population of its benefits and, most importantly, to stimulate registration of interest.

The starting-point was zero: no triggered exchanges and a handful (168) of registrations.

WHAT WAS REQUIRED?

Initially, exchanges were identified by BT and set a registration target. This target reflected the people served by each exchange, and varied from 100 to 500 registrations needed. An individual or business counted as one registration. When this registration level was reached it would trigger, at some time in the future, the conversion of the exchange to broadband.

The market was still in a low state of 'buyer awareness' and in many cases was confused by mixed messages of what broadband is, and what it can do.

The tender was issued by HIE with objectives identified as:

- to raise awareness of broadband as a utility and stimulate registrations of intent over a specified time period (2003–04)
- to acquire qualitative and quantitative information on new registrations to develop a sound management/intelligence system
- where appropriate (and allowed), to introduce those seeking advice on the use of broadband to educators/champions for regional development, etc.

Phase 1 of the campaign was to start in January 2003 and run until March 2003. It was envisaged that an additional two or three campaign phases would be conducted later in the year, dependent on the success of phase 1.

BROADBAND REGISTRATION DRIVE

Targets were based on business registrations to date – at that time, over a three-month period there had been 168 registrations. The target was to more than double this number, with 500 additional business registrations (January–March). The initial budget was estimated at £500,000 for all services required, for the first phase of the campaign.

THE GATHERING

In response to the brief a collaborative group was assembled. From the start, real collaboration and integration of effort were mandatory requirements. Members of the collaborative group knew each other's strengths and shared a common desire to make the campaign as successful as possible.

The collaborative group members' locations and contributions were as follows:

- Highlands and Islands Enterprise, Inverness – client
- Navertech, Thurso – web development, systems coordination
- Key Commercial Services, Bonar Bridge – fulfilment, data cleaning
- Sea Bridge, Orkney – focus group research
- ITP Solutions, Inverness – contact centre, data management
- Arrow Creative Marketing Solutions, Muir of Ord – creative development
- Atlantic Marketing, Thurso – project coordination
- Spiritmedia, Edinburgh – media planning/buying, information distribution.

For details of the collaborative team in a geographic context, see Figure 1.

A core steering group was established – Alistair Murray (Atlantic Marketing), Roddy Ritchie (Arrow) and Philip Jones (Spiritmedia) – identified as the main drivers of the project. After appointment Calum Davidson and Alison Wilson from HIE made the core group five. In short the plan was hatched.

VIRTUALLY UNITED

With the group appointed, the first meeting with HIE took place on 7 January 2003. The launch date was agreed to be 27 January for all activity, and phase 1 had to finish before the end of March due to the pending Scottish Parliament elections.

With the collaboration spread from Orkney to Edinburgh an efficient communication and reporting system needed to be established immediately. In addition, the inventory of accountability and reporting requirements was growing:

- 10 Local Enterprise Companies (LECs) needed to be collaborative partners, and 'see' what activity was taking place in their area.

For each of the 10 this was to include:

- creative, on-the-ground media activity and spend
- results of registrations by postcode, and any specific requirements from businesses in their LEC area
- registrations must be logged as business or personal use
- registrations attributed by media
- registration hot or cold spots, by postcode.

SCOTTISH ADVERTISING WORKS 4

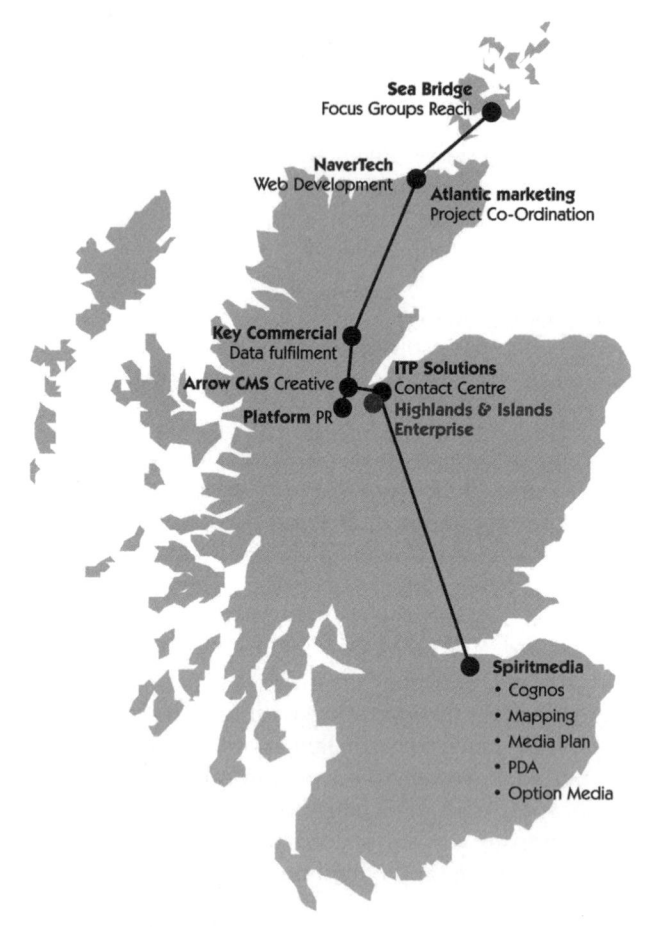

Figure 1: *The collaborative team in a geographic context*

To address these issues, two data systems were brought into play. ITP solutions developed a web-based contact centre data management system, developing a contact centre script to include logging of comments good or bad. This provided the main source of registrant feedback data.

Spiritmedia introduced a browser-based data warehouse that showed registrations linked to media attribution, by LEC area and broken down by business and personal use (see Figures 2 and 3).

BROADBAND REGISTRATION DRIVE

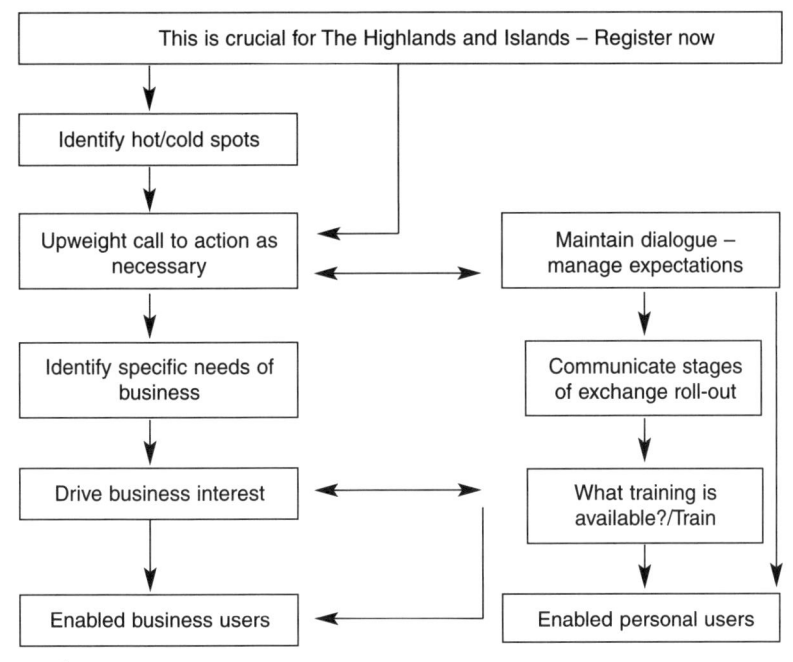

Figure 2: *Actual campaign strategy*

Within the same portal, each LEC area was identified on a four-level mapping system showing adult population, number of registrations, penetration, and location by postcode. All the data were updated twice weekly to track the effectiveness of the campaign as it happened (see Figure 4).

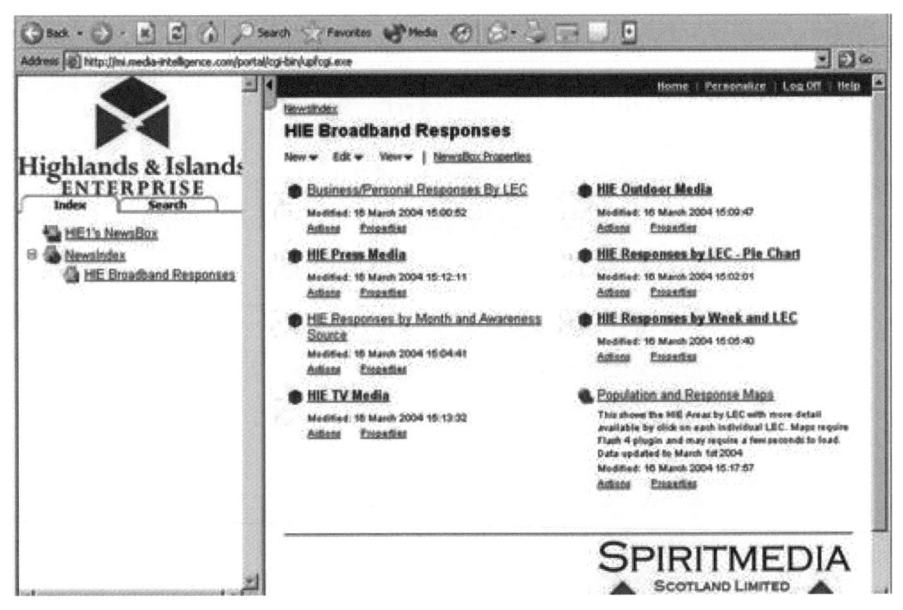

Figure 3: *Spiritmedia's browser-based data warehouse*

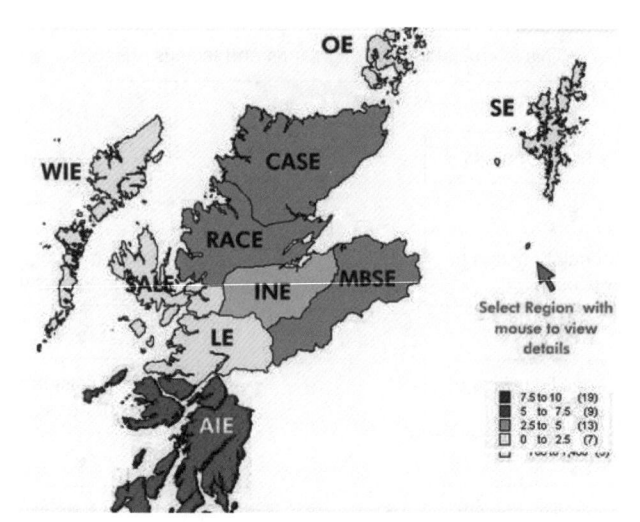

(a) *Broadband Scotland*

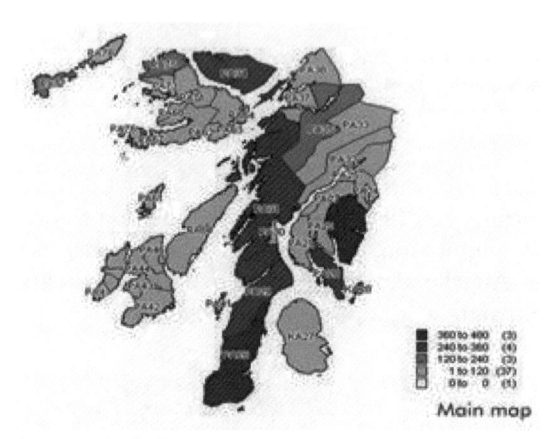

(b) *AIE individual responses*

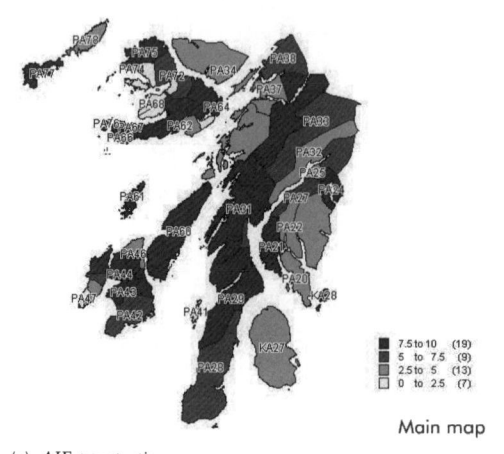

(c) *AIE penetration*

Figure 4: *Mapping screen grabs*

BROADBAND REGISTRATION DRIVE

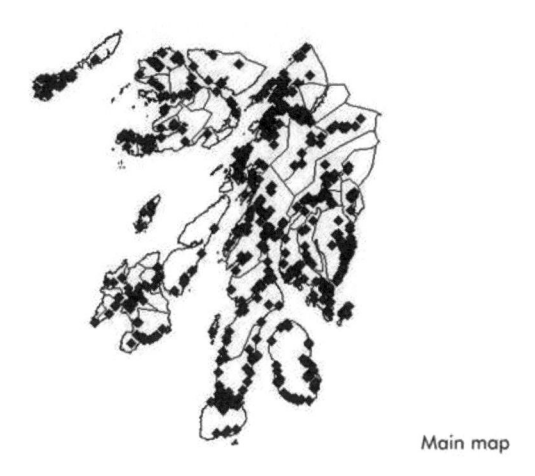

(d) *AIE postcode response*

Figure 4 (continued)

Navertech, Atlantic Marketing and Key Commercial Services developed reporting and backroom processes to keep the data flowing to these two systems. All of this was achieved and completed in the 10 days prior to launch. It worked as shown in Figure 5.

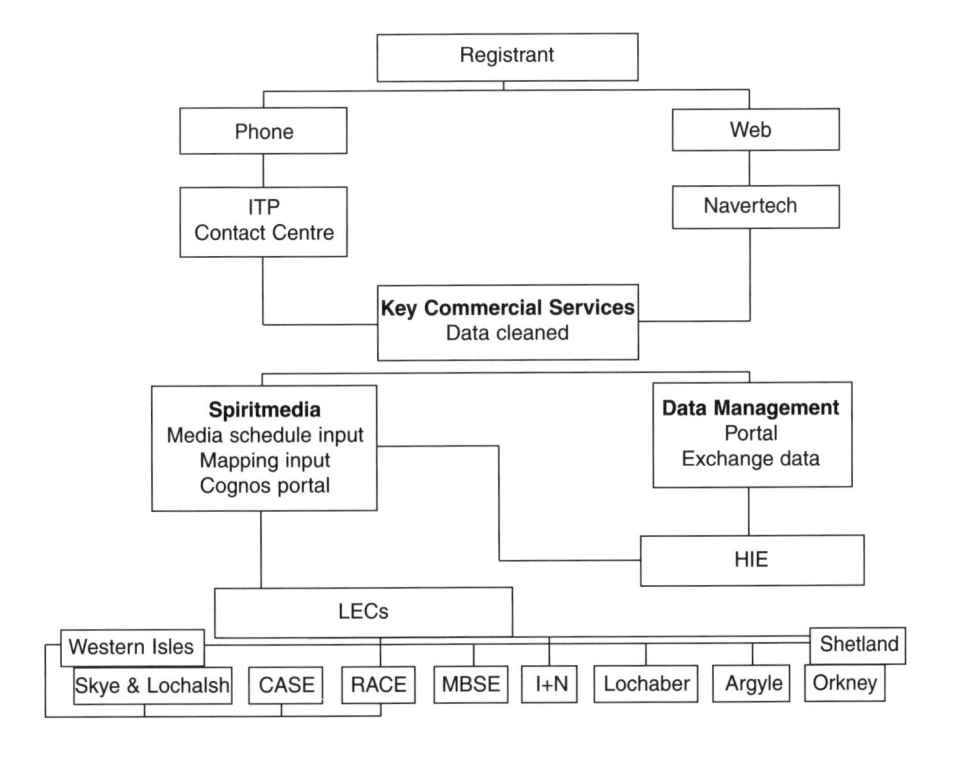

Figure 5: *Path of the data flow to the two systems*

A FOUR-PHASE PROCESS

The campaign ran as four distinct phases, as described in Table 1.

TABLE 1: PHASES OF THE CAMPAIGN

Phase	Timing	Objective
Phase 1	Jan–Mar 03	Stimulate registration Drive awareness
Phase 2	Jun–Jul 03	Identify 'cold' spots Communicate with registrant
Phase 3	Oct–Nov 03	Business-specific activity
Phase 4	Feb–Mar 04	Final push to trigger exchanges

Throughout the period, more exchanges were being given target registrations by BT. Ultimately some 153 exchanges were triggered by the activity.

WE WERE ON THE RIGHT TRACK BUT WE WANTED TO DIG DEEPER

How the focus groups informed the campaign

A series of focus groups and one-to-ones took place. These were spread over time and the geography of the HIE area. The main findings are shown in Table 2.

TABLE 2: FOCUS GROUP FINDINGS

General attitudes
- Non-users perceived broadband as expensive
- Speed was well understood
- Users wouldn't be without it
- Concern that broadband was being positioned as an end in itself rather than a means to an end

Benefits
Business
- Reduced cost
- Marketing channel
- Speed
- An enabling technology that will increase opportunity

Personal/home
- Entertainment (game play, music, video)
- Phone line not tied up
- Social inclusion
- Community survival; global connection overcomes geographic remoteness

Barriers
- Perceived cost
- Reluctance to be an early adopter
- Still some confusion, even resentment, at being asked to register; if it is that important why isn't it being provided like a utility?
- A lack of immediate personal benefit

The points made in Table 2 fed back to the campaign strategy, creative development and media planning as follows:

- focus on benefits and costs
- simplicity and consistency of message across multiple formats
- use of local community business champions would increase credibility and require media to suit
- continue to press the case for action
- give reassurance that something will happen.

HIGHLANDERS GET IT

It was a big country – and, creatively, a big challenge. We had utilised the 'choosing process' marketing pattern of: 'Is this product, service or idea good for me, my family, my business, my community/friends and the world?'. This question was used as the main focus for finding an appropriate creative vehicle and language management strategy, and for fixing in the collaborative team's mind's eye that broadband is a true utility and not a product. An important point for all.

Therefore, finding something that would exclusively 'chime' with the people of the big country was of paramount importance for the success of the campaign. Interestingly, another utility that has had a profound positive effect on the people of the Highlands and Islands is the development of hydroelectric power – a true utility power revolution in the Highlands and Islands. The positive changes that came about thanks to the hydro revolution have been fundamental to the stability and development of the Highlands and Islands for the last three decades.

The collaborative team felt that this very important comparison was the perfect creative vehicle for the process of explaining what broadband was and, importantly, asking the people of the big country to support the idea of 'speaking up for' and ultimately getting the broadband utility. Stimulating and driving the power of the collective good with creative language, we felt, was the best way of promoting broadband – and getting high registration figures.

Four creative phases of the campaign were developed. Phase 1 introduced the combined importance of broadband as a utility for individuals, the region, families, business, education, and so on, plus the start of the registration scheme (see Figure 6).

Phase 2 increased the stakes on registration and the importance of registering interest (see Figure 7).

Phase 3 developed business and community champions as indicated in the focus group research (see Figure 8).

Phase 4 was designed to bring it home to the villages, towns and communities for the final push on registrations (see Figure 9).

The consistent creative thread and the importance of the original message (hydro experience) was kept throughout the creative/media campaign. This consistency and exclusive comparison (hydro) was fundamental to the people of the big country 'getting it'.

Figure 6: *Phase 1 graphic*

Figure 7: *Phase 2 graphic*

BROADBAND REGISTRATION DRIVE

Figure 8: *Phase 3 graphics*

Figure 9: *Phase 4 graphic*

MEDIA WILDERNESS

Phase 1 activity had to establish the campaign. Getting the message across about broadband in order to stimulate registrations needed a powerful broadcast delivery channel, television being the initial choice. But the HIE area doesn't fall neatly into any one broadcaster's footprint, as shown in Figure 10.

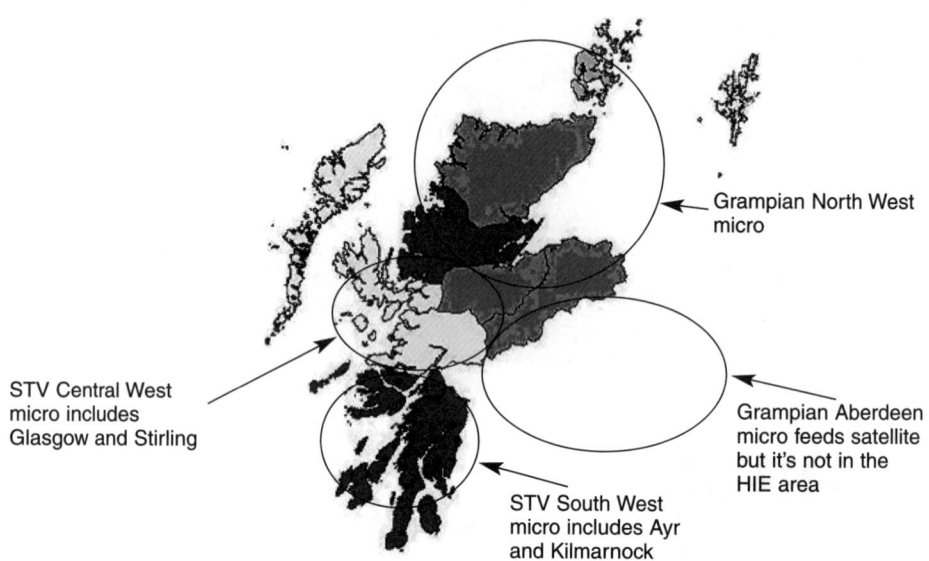

Figure 10: *Broadcasters in HIE area*

It was clear that the Grampian North West micro would form the foundation of the TV activity, but the importance of satellite delivery of Grampian TV to the Western Seaboard and to island communities could not be ignored. The signal for this is fed from the Grampian TV Aberdeen micro, but does not broadcast its terrestrial signal to the HIE area. Ultimately it was decided to use the Aberdeen micro area in this crucial first phase.

Equally complex media availability issues were seen with radio and outdoor. Plenty of great opportunities in and around Inverness – not much elsewhere.

Where TV couldn't be used effectively – namely the southern part of the Western Seaboard, Argyle, the Isles and Campbeltown, in particular – the broadband message was placed on ad trailers, then on lorries operating out of Oban and Campbeltown (see Figure 11).

This proved to be innovative and effective media thinking, achieving good visibility and the call to action.

TAKE IT TO THE PEOPLE

From the start, the importance of 'collaborative' community was identified as the cornerstone of getting the message across, and media that were part of the community infrastructure were used.

BROADBAND REGISTRATION DRIVE

Figure 11: *Ad trailer and lorry*

- Community press and radio took the message to the Isles and remote areas.
- Ferry terminals and the ferries themselves carried advertising, where islanders were in many ways a captive audience.
- All island airports carried light box posters (see Figure 12).
- Cinema was included in the form of the 'screen machine', a 40-ton mobile film projection unit that travels to remote areas with the latest releases, parking in ports and townships on the islands.

As results on media awareness and focus group feedback became available, the media mix was amended to reflect the findings.

Clear unambiguous leaflets were produced that directly reflected the focus group findings (see Figure 13).

Figure 12: *Airport and ferry terminals*

Figure 13: *Local campaign leaflet*

As the campaign progressed into phases 2 and 3, identification of hot and cold spots enabled media platforms to be added or removed on a regional basis.

- Campbeltown, Argyle and the Isles needed special attention, so the Scottish Television Southwest micro was used, and supported by pinpoint precise local press using 'post-it note' inserts targeting specific postcode sectors – a first for these titles (see Figure 14).
- The advertising was driving registrations and awareness, the process was iterative and flexibility was essential.

In phase 4, 10 identified exchanges needed attention to reach their trigger level. The media needed to be 'in your face', literally, and relevant to the village, town or community. This was not a job for commodity media buying. Field forces were put on the street, early registrants were emailed using opt-in email to spread the word, utilising tailored messages that were date-specific and had a degree of inter-

BROADBAND REGISTRATION DRIVE

Figure 14: 'Post-it notes' used in local press

community competition in the copy. The emails were tracked in real time and fed back to the data management portal, and subsequently back to the field force (see Figure 15).

PDAs (personal digital assistants) were used to make registration easy and, again, fed directly into the data management portal (see Figure 16). This minimised wastage of effort: when the registration level was reached it was time to move on.

Backlit ad vans supported the field teams in the 10 villages, towns and communities, with relevant creative messages targeted at the individual villages, towns and communities (see Figure 17).

PR was integrated with this above-the-line activity in phase 4, to maximise community involvement and awareness (see Figure 18).

The total media spend for the four phases, covering 15 months, was £419,806.

WHAT HAPPENED IN THE BIG COUNTRY?

The best planning and reporting system would mean nothing if the desired objective was not reached.

To recap, the task was to stimulate awareness of broadband and generate registrations with an initial target of 500 business registrations. Data needed to be collected, analysed and channelled to appropriate areas for use. It is safe to say that we achieved this ... and some.

Highlands & Islands ENTERPRISE Registration Drive

Dear ,

As you may know the Keith exchange has been given a trigger level of 500 registrations by BT. This means that if the trigger level is reached then BT will enable your exchange for ADSL Broadband.

Currently there are 426 registrations on the exchange, including your own, but you still need a further 74 people to register to achieve the target. Other communities in our area have managed to secure this level of registrations, and we're confident that Keith can do so too.

I would urge you to encourage any of your family or neighbours who have not yet registered their interest to do so now and help your community to get Broadband. If everyone found just one other person to register then the target would practically be achieved.

As you already know there is no financial commitment to registration and many other areas in the Highlands and Islands such as Dufftown have already reached their triggers. They will soon have ADSL Broadband showing that results are very achievable.

In order to help your community reach its trigger level we will be sending a team of people to Keith Saturday 20th March to assist in taking registrations. Look out also for our adverts in the local press and on Grampian Television.

Further details are available on our web site at www.hie.co.uk/broadband where you should encourage people to register or get them to call our broadband hotline on 0800 0272327.

With your support your community has the power to bring fast Internet access to Keith – please take this opportunity to spread the word!

Thanks for your help.

Stuart Robertson

Highlands & Islands ENTERPRISE

Speak up for Broadband

Forward this email | Unsubscribe

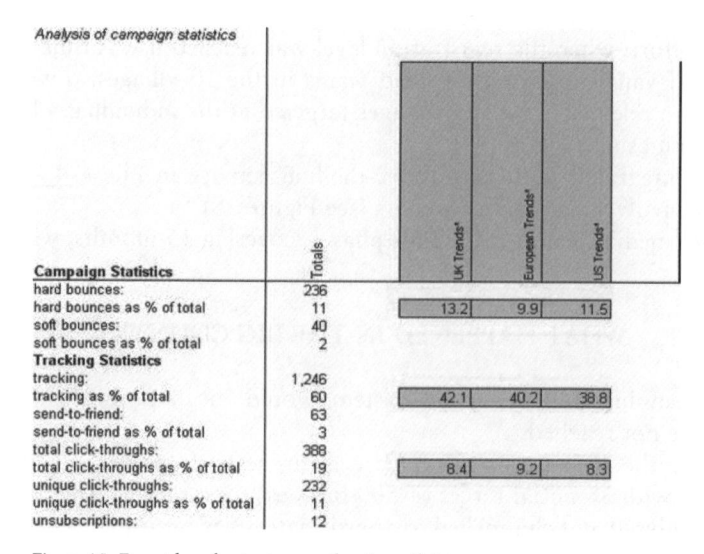

Analysis of campaign statistics

Campaign Statistics	Totals	UK Trends*	European Trends*	US Trends*
hard bounces:	236			
hard bounces as % of total	11	13.2	9.9	11.5
soft bounces:	40			
soft bounces as % of total	2			
Tracking Statistics				
tracking:	1,246			
tracking as % of total	60	42.1	40.2	38.8
send-to-friend:	63			
send-to-friend as % of total	3			
total click-throughs:	388			
total click-throughs as % of total	19	8.4	9.2	8.3
unique click-throughs:	232			
unique click-throughs as % of total	11			
unsubscriptions:	12			

Figure 15: *Examples of outgoing email and email data vs stats*

BROADBAND REGISTRATION DRIVE

Making registration easy

Address data
Address details can either be typed in or can be found electronically by selecting the target icon.
Telephone number and email address (where available) will allow for ongoing correspondence.

Registration
The two key questions will confirm the request for registration and also allow for ongoing correspondence.
Drop-down boxes are used in both fields.

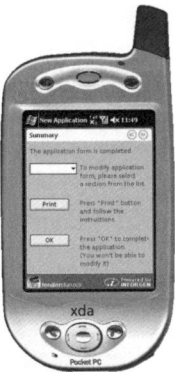

Registration
The registration is now completed.
By selecting the 'OK' button, the information is sent electronically to the secure server.

Figure 16: *PDAs*

Figure 17: *Field force support*

Figure 18: *Examples of PR*

BROADBAND REGISTRATION DRIVE

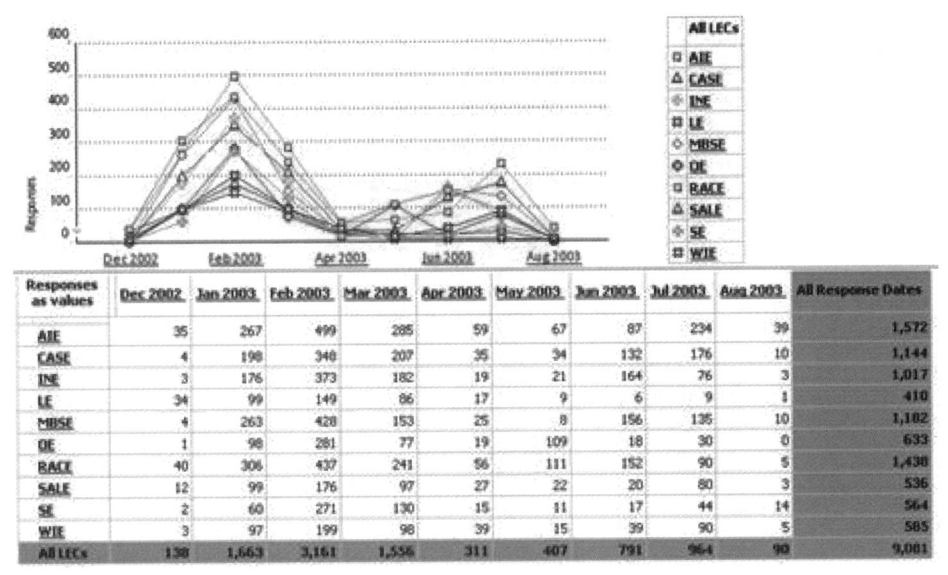

Responses as values	Dec 2002	Jan 2003	Feb 2003	Mar 2003	Apr 2003	May 2003	Jun 2003	Jul 2003	Aug 2003	All Response Dates
AIE	35	267	499	285	59	67	87	234	39	1,572
CASE	4	198	348	207	35	34	132	176	10	1,144
INE	3	176	373	182	19	21	164	76	3	1,017
LE	34	99	149	86	17	9	6	9	1	410
MBSE	4	263	428	153	25	8	156	135	10	1,182
OE	1	98	281	77	19	109	18	30	0	633
RACE	40	306	437	241	56	111	152	90	5	1,438
SALE	12	99	176	97	27	22	20	80	3	536
SE	2	60	271	130	15	11	17	44	14	564
WIE	3	97	199	98	39	15	39	90	5	585
All LECs	138	1,663	3,161	1,556	311	407	791	964	90	9,081

Figure 19: *Phase 1 and 2 registrations by LEC*
Note: time lag data not included

In phase 1 the total number of registrants was 6524, of which 1370 were identified as business registrations: 174% above target. By August and the end of phase 2, the total number of registrants had risen to 9443 with business registrants at 1936: 287% above the initial target (see Figures 19 and 20).

Media placement/strategy and creative/strategy were reflecting focus group findings with endorsement of the choice of lorries to cover the Western Seaboard, and so on. Hot and cold spots had been identified by LEC and postcode (see Figures 21 and 22).

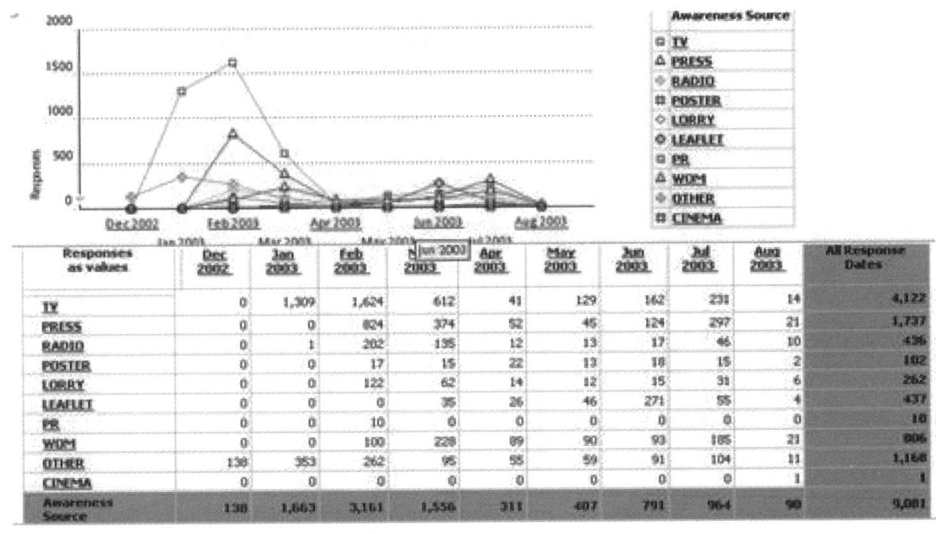

Responses as values	Dec 2002	Jan 2003	Feb 2003	Mar 2003	Apr 2003	May 2003	Jun 2003	Jul 2003	Aug 2003	All Response Dates
TV	0	1,309	1,624	612	41	129	162	231	14	4,122
PRESS	0	0	824	374	52	45	124	297	21	1,737
RADIO	0	1	202	135	12	13	17	46	10	436
POSTER	0	0	17	15	22	13	18	15	2	102
LORRY	0	0	122	62	14	12	15	31	6	262
LEAFLET	0	0	0	35	26	46	271	55	4	437
PR	0	0	10	0	0	0	0	0	0	10
WOM	0	0	100	228	89	90	93	185	21	806
OTHER	138	353	262	95	55	59	91	104	11	1,168
CINEMA	0	0	0	0	0	0	0	0	1	1
Awareness Source	138	1,663	3,161	1,556	311	407	791	964	90	9,081

Figure 20: *Phase 1 and 2 registrations by media*
Note: time lag data not included

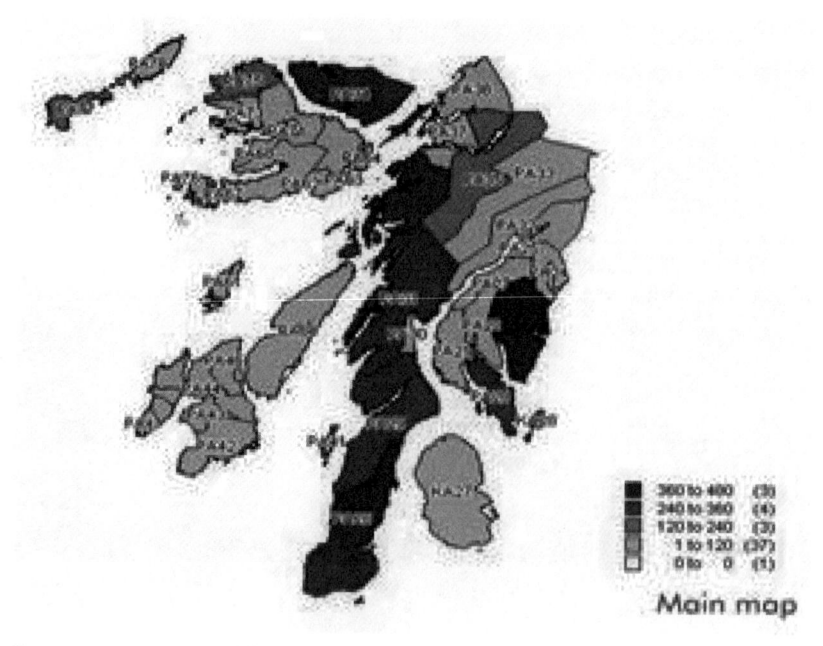

Figure 21: *Responses mapped by postcode and LEC*

By the end of phase 3, total registrations stood at 13,122, with business registrations of 3505. With phase 4 hitting the streets in February and March 2004, coordination between the above-the-line media campaign and the field force was at its peak. In three months an additional 12,844 registrants were completed, 3361 being businesses. In total: 26,134 registrations, 6839 of which were business registrations – 15 months from start to finish and 1268% above original expectations (see Figure 23).

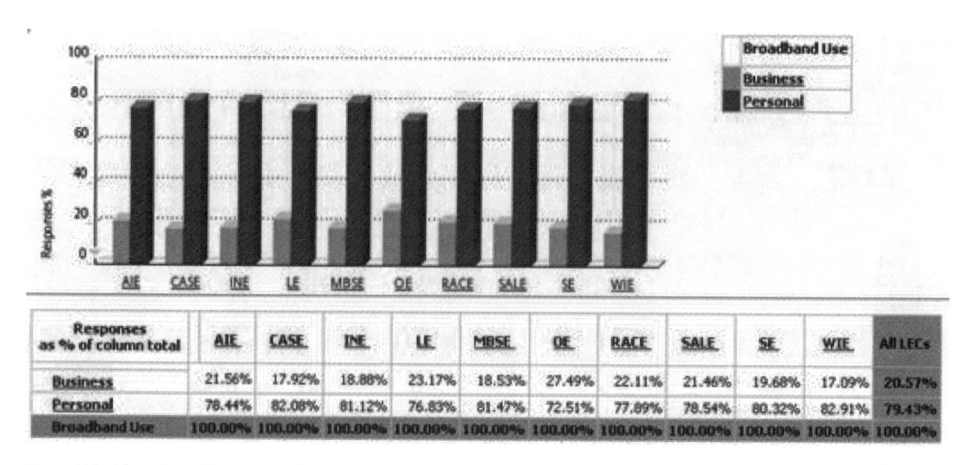

Responses as % of column total	AIE	CASE	INE	LE	MBSE	OE	RACE	SALE	SE	WIE	All LECs
Business	21.56%	17.92%	18.88%	23.17%	18.53%	27.49%	22.11%	21.46%	19.68%	17.09%	20.57%
Personal	78.44%	82.08%	81.12%	76.83%	81.47%	72.51%	77.89%	78.54%	80.32%	82.91%	79.43%
Broadband Use	100.00%	100.00%	100.00%	100.00%	100.00%	100.00%	100.00%	100.00%	100.00%	100.00%	100.00%

Figure 22: *Phase 1 and 2 response by user type*

BROADBAND REGISTRATION DRIVE

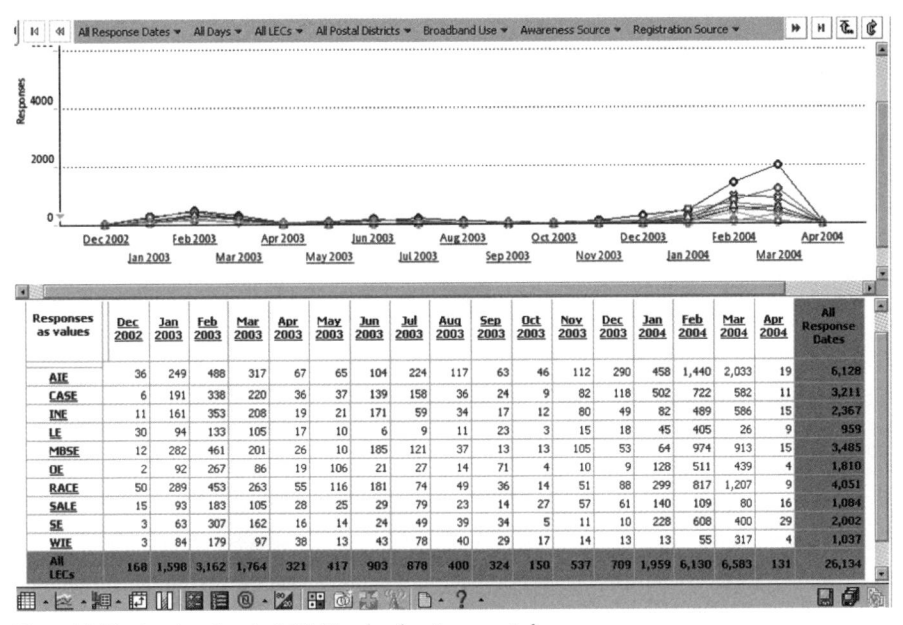

Figure 23: *Total registrations by LEC (time lag data incorporated)*

HOW THE CAMPAIGN COMPARES WITH THE REST OF SCOTLAND AND THE UK

There is little doubt that the campaign in itself was a phenomenal success. It is even more impressive when it is compared to UK and all-Scotland data. To say the HIE area was punching above its weight would be an understatement. The HIE population represents 0.67% of the UK population (see Figure 24).

Registrations in the HIE area accounted for 2.87% of all registrations throughout the UK (see Figure 25).

A total of 1.53% of the entire UK population registered, whereas 6.5% of the HIE population registered: a fourfold increase (see Figure 26).

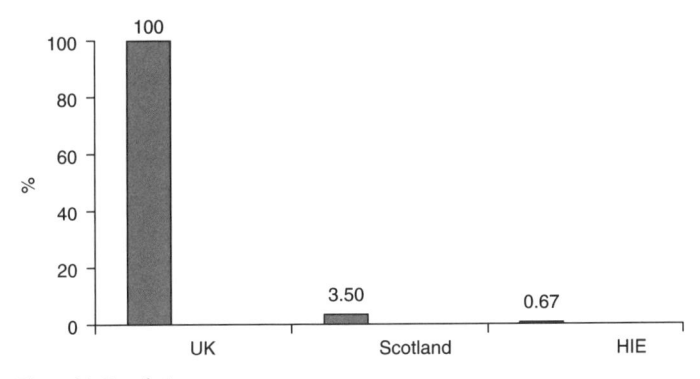

Figure 24: *Population*
Source: Broadband Resource

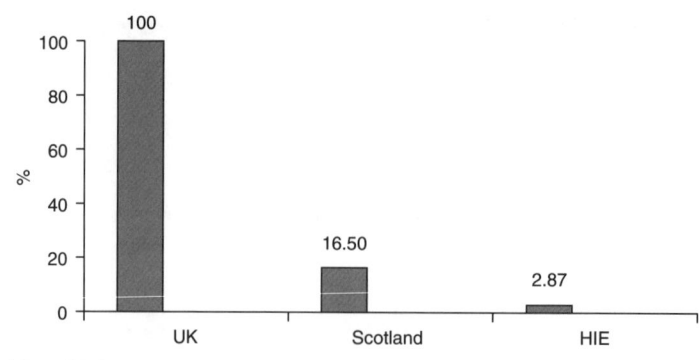

Figure 25: *Pre-registrations*
Source: Broadband Resource

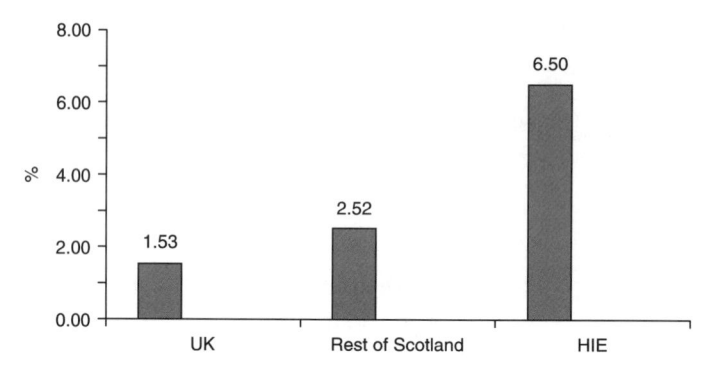

Figure 26: *Percentage of registrations vs population*
Source: Broadband Resource

The only difference between the HIE area and the rest of Scotland and the UK was this campaign.

AND FINALLY ...

The nature and characteristics of the people of the big country, both indigenous and relocated, are: pioneering, optimistic, realistic and, above all, intelligent. They got it ... broadband is important to them for connecting to the world – and what benefits them benefits their family, business and fragile communities.

They were the winning collaborative force and voice of broadband in the big country: the people of the Highlands and Islands of Scotland.

Finally, respect and admiration must be given to the client and team at Highlands and Islands Enterprise. Trusting to a truly collaborative team, delivering what seemed to be on the surface a very difficult job, a result that surpassed all expectations. Best practice had been shared not only within the group but also externally to organisations such as BT, the CBI and the Federation of Small Businesses.

BRONZE

11

Grolsch

You can't rush these things

Principal author: Thea McGovern, The Leith Agency
Collaborating author: James Cobb, Coors Brewers UK
Media agency: Vizeum

EDITOR'S SUMMARY

Building on The Leith Agency's already proven campaign, this paper showed the benefits of long-term commitment to a strategy, and to learning how to develop it creatively and in terms of media efficiency. Continued brand growth and good payback resulted. More thorough isolation of the effect of the advertising on the brand's excellent performance and on the media spend's ROI might have prompted a higher award. An interesting detail was the correlation drawn between high advertising production values and high product quality perceptions.

INTRODUCTION

Irving Berlin once said, 'The toughest thing about success is that you've got to keep on being a success.' It's a feeling you come to share when you work on the Grolsch brand.

In 2003 we told the story of how successful brand-building advertising reinvigorated a brand that looked to have peaked in the early 1980s.

This paper brings the story of Grolsch's achievements up to date. It demonstrates how a series of significant changes to the advertising and media approach have further strengthened the brand. In doing so, the campaign has contributed to making the brand the fastest-growing lager in the take-home market and helped Coors become the number one on-trade brewer in the UK.

QUICK RECAP

Our 2003 Scottish IPA paper told the story of Grolsch's UK performance between 1999 and early 2003. It told how Bass (now Coors) was under pressure to strengthen its portfolio with a credible premium continental lager and signed a joint venture with Grolsch in 1994. It showed how Grolsch had gone from boom to bust in the late 1980s and early 1990s and, consequently, what an uphill struggle Coors faced to turn the brand around in the UK.

The challenge presented to The Leith Agency in 1999 was to communicate the product truth that Grolsch is brewed slowly, in a way that would engage the target audience of young, male lager drinkers. Drawing on the brand's Dutch origins the agency identified a cool, laid-back Dutch attitude to life that appealed to the target audience. In the advertising, a Dutch hero showed that, as with Grolsch, things are better for not being rushed.

The advertising helped resurrect the brand. By 2003 Grolsch had exceeded its gargantuan target of 500,000 barrels a year and witnessed its rate of sale increase threefold. Against the odds, Grolsch became a top-ten premium lager again.[1]

WHERE NEXT?

Simply maintaining Grolsch's 500,000 annual barrel volume would have been a worthy challenge. However, Coors Brewers had publicly stated its ambition to become the UK's number-one brewer by 2010 and, before you could say 'resting on our laurels', Coors issued Grolsch with a new set of ambitious targets for the period 2003–06.

Target 1: number two in take-home by 2004

Grolsch's meteoric rise (back) to fame between 1999 and 2003 was achieved against relatively low levels of on-trade distribution[2] (see Table 1).

---

1. *Scottish Advertising Works 3*, 'The Revitalisation of Grolsch'.
2. Source: ACNielsen On-Trade Audit 2004.

GROLSCH

TABLE 1:

	Dec 2002	Dec 2003
Grolsch	8%	8%
Kronenbourg 1664	18%	19%
Stella Artois	35%	39%

The complex factors involved meant Grolsch's on-trade distribution situation would take time to resolve. Fortunately, the off-trade was a different story. Here Grolsch had everything to play for and on a much more level playing field[3] (see Table 2).

TABLE 2:

	Nov/Dec 2002	Nov/Dec 2003
Grolsch	94	95
Kronenbourg 1664	96	96
Stella Artois	100	100

Coors decided the off-trade would be the core battleground for Grolsch and set the brand the target of overtaking Kronenbourg 1664 to become the clear number two premium lager in the sector by the end of 2004.

Target 2: outperform the premium lager market

Coors' lager portfolio is made up of Carling (the UK's biggest-selling beer), Grolsch (a 5% ABV premium continental lager) and Coors Fine Light Beer (an American-style lager launched in late 2003). Demonstrating that Grolsch was able to outperform the premium lager market was important to Coors so that it couldn't be accused of over-reliance on the huge success of Carling.

Target 3: double volumes by 2006

Grolsch was set the long-term target of doubling volumes to reach 1 million barrels by 2006 – a truly massive challenge.

IMPLICATIONS FOR ADVERTISING

By mid-2003, Grolsch and The Leith Agency had analysed the results of five 'Schtop!' TV ads. This gave us a bank of learning, both qualitative and quantitative, with which to decide how to go forward. Working closely with Millward Brown, we examined how the campaign might contribute to the new targets.

---

3. Source: ACNielsen Off-Trade Audit 2004.

SCOTTISH ADVERTISING WORKS 4

Advertising efficiency – all-time high

Millward Brown calculates advertising efficiency, based on the percentage by which 100 GRPs raise ad awareness, with campaigns receiving an AI (advertising index) score accordingly. Grolsch's AI had been increasing with each new TV ad (see Table 3).

TABLE 3: AI SCORES FOR GROLSCH ADS

Grolsch ad	Launch date	Advertising index (AI) score
Bank	May 2000	4
Bank & Blue Movie	Nov 2000	6
Monkey Wedding	June 2001	6
Interrogation	March 2002	7
Avenger	Nov 2002	9

Increased branding

Branding was also building over time, with 88% now correctly linking the adverts and brand[4] (see Figure 1).

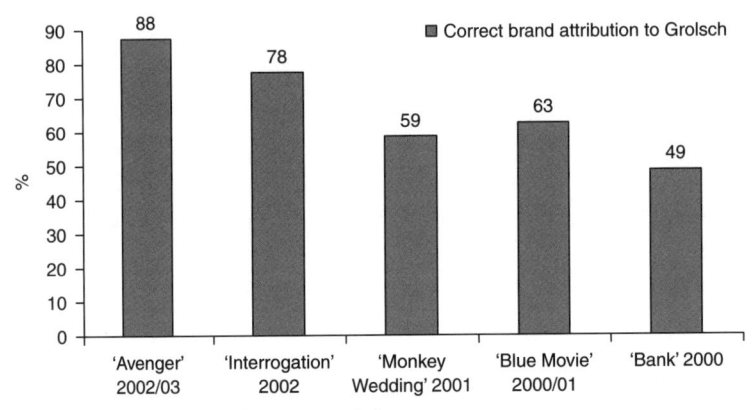

Figure 1: *Level of brand attribution to Grolsch*

Enjoyment and involvement

But was our target audience growing tired of more executions from the same campaign idea? The evidence suggested not. Our 2002 TV ad, 'Avenger', achieved similar ratings of 'enjoyment' and 'involvement' as previous ads in the Grolsch campaign and still outperformed the Millward Brown study average[5] (see Figure 2).

Millward Brown summed up the situation when it said:

> 'Consistent structure and message is driving the success of the campaign (and) paying off in what is a very inconsistent market (Budweiser, Fosters, K1664). [It is a] powerful tool for future executions.'

---

4. Source: Millward Brown.
5. Source: Millward Brown.

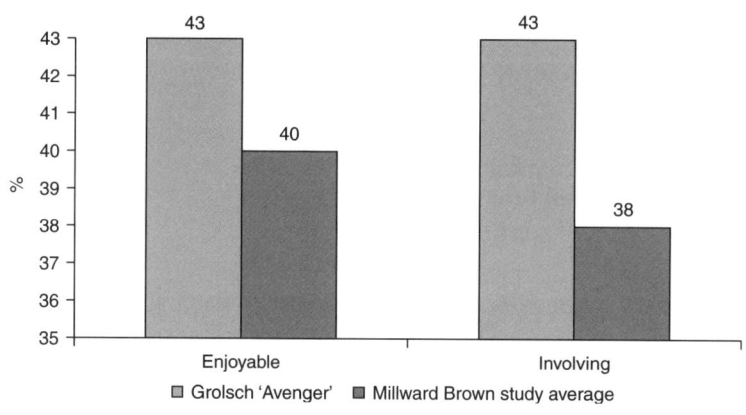

Figure 2: *Grolsch's performance vs the Millward Brown study average*

Having agreed to continue with the 'Schtop!' campaign, the challenge was to see how we could make it work even harder than it had to date. We reviewed our advertising targets.

With such high-profile, well-liked advertising, the only factor we could really amplify in the advertising was the quality perceptions. In other words, we needed to increase people's desire for the brand based on a belief in its quality.

We set two fundamental advertising targets:

1. maintain current high awareness and enjoyment of Grolsch advertising
2. build Grolsch's high-quality, premium lager perceptions.

Qualitative research had raised an important consideration. Grolsch's advertising risked falling between two stools. It lacked the belly-laugh humour of mainstream beer ads (e.g. Peter Kay's work for John Smith's) but also lacked the epic 'wow factor' of Stella Artois or Guinness advertising. To reinforce the brand's quality credentials, we needed to escape this no-man's-land and place our stake firmly in the ground.

Grolsch is a premium lager and laddish humour, more traditionally the domain of standard-strength lagers, was not a place the Grolsch brand owners wanted to go.

After much deliberation, a decision was taken at Grolsch to increase the amount of production money available for TV commercials with the clear objective of being seen to compete with the big boys. However, in recognition of this, there was a strong desire to extract every last bit of efficiency out of the campaign. Three changes were put in place:

1. putting the product at the heart of the creative idea
2. changing the media from a 'burst' to 'drip' strategy
3. creating alternative endings to prolong the life of new TV executions.

The following is a summary of the main advertising activity that incorporated these changes, after which we will describe in more detail the strategy behind the changes.

ACTIVITY SUMMARY

In the period 2002–04 Grolsch ran the following key communications.

2002   'Avenger' TV
2003   'First Date' TV (see Figure 3)
          Tactical glass rack promotion TV
2004   'Aliens' TV (see Figure 4)

Figure 3: *'First Date'*

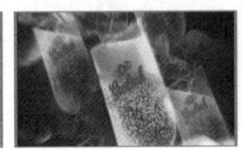

Figure 4: *'Aliens'*

Product at the heart

In previous TV ads, the Dutch hero had carried a Grolsch and used it as an analogy for not rushing; however, going forward we took a decision to make the product more central to the action of the story. Creative ideas where the brand was peripheral to the action were rejected.

We also took a tactical approach within a brand campaign, taking the well-loved ingredients of 'Schtop!' but deliberately placing them in a home-drinking occasion[6] – reflecting the brand's off-trade battle plan.

Product reverence and appetite appeal became mandatory for the brief. We introduced a 'thumb swipe' across the frosted bottle and a lingering drinking shot – elements never used before. These went on to become recurring quality cues in future TV ads.

Media strategy

To date, Grolsch had employed a 'burst' strategy with several periods of high-intensity activity during the year. Moving forward, a decision was taken with media partners Vizeum to adopt a 'drip' strategy. In effect, this meant sacrificing quantity of ratings to quality of programming. The media planners and buyers were no longer restricted to placing Grolsch ads over a short, intense period and could instead cherry-pick programming across the whole year.

---

6. 'First Date' commercial, where we see our hero drinking in his own home for the first time.

GROLSCH

Alternative endings

'First Date' (2003) and 'Aliens' (2004) were designed to run over 12 months, with 'Aliens' being the first to follow the 'drip' media strategy. To maximise the ads' potential over this relatively long period of time, each was filmed with a series of alternative endings that were introduced and rotated over time to keep them fresh in people's minds.

THE RESULTS

TV advertising performance 2003–05

The TV advertising objectives have been met – in some style. In 2003, on the back of the 'First Date' commercial, Grolsch's advertising awareness hit an all-time high of 46%. However, the overall pattern was one of peaks and troughs, reflecting very closely the 'burst' strategy of the media. Since 2004 and the introduction of a 'drip' media strategy, Grolsch's awareness has commanded a sustained lead over number one premium lager Stella Artois.[7] The change in strategy means that at point of purchase there is greater potential for ad memories to be top of mind all year round.

Recent Grolsch advertisements have risen to the challenge of keeping an existing campaign fresh. The 2004 commercial, 'Aliens', not only equals the appeal of previous executions, but also noticeably outperforms on key measures of 'enjoyable', 'distinctive' and 'clever' (see Figure 5).[8]

Consumers have noted and appreciated the higher production values of the 'Aliens' ad and this is contributing to a greater all-round sense of brand and product quality (see Figure 6).[9] Grolsch is no longer at risk of inhabiting the no-man's-land between belly laughs and wow-factor advertising.

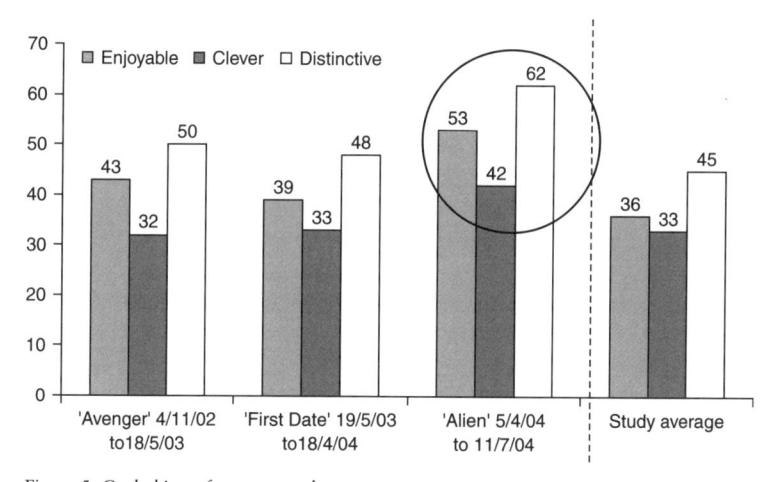

Figure 5: Grolsch's performance on key measures

---

7. Source: Millward Brown.
8. Source: Millward Brown.
9. Source: Millward Brown.

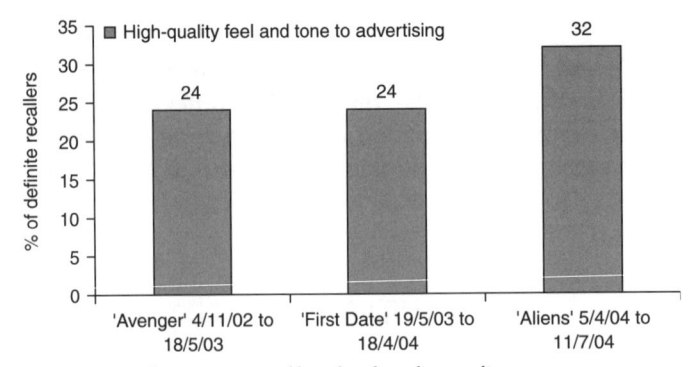

Figure 6: *Growth in perception of brand and product quality*

Qualitative research among our target audience backs this up:[10]

'["Aliens"] is more successful for a number of reasons. Crucially, it is more cinematic in style. Consumers recognise the film allusions and like these, but also praise the sense of budget and quality of filming that is evident here relative to earlier ads.'

In terms of Grolsch's distinct positioning and personality, the key measures 'is a good quality lager', 'is brewed for a long time' and 'becoming more popular' have all shown consistent growth since 2002, and are now at their highest levels in the brand's UK history. Again, we can clearly see a more consistent pattern of growth since the changes in media and creative strategy for 2003 and 2004 (see Figures 7–9).[11]

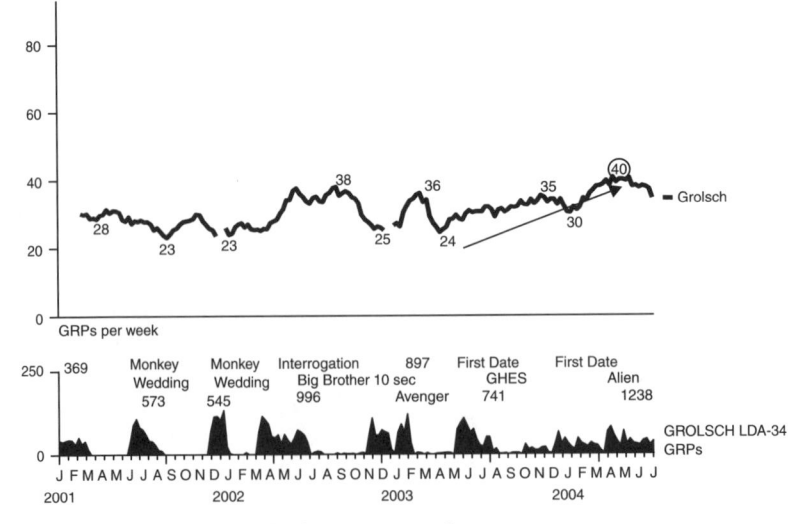

Figure 7: *'Grolsch is a high-quality beer': agree strongly*

---

10. Brand audit, 2004, Chris Barnham Research.
11. Source: Millward Brown, England and Wales, men, 18–34.

GROLSCH

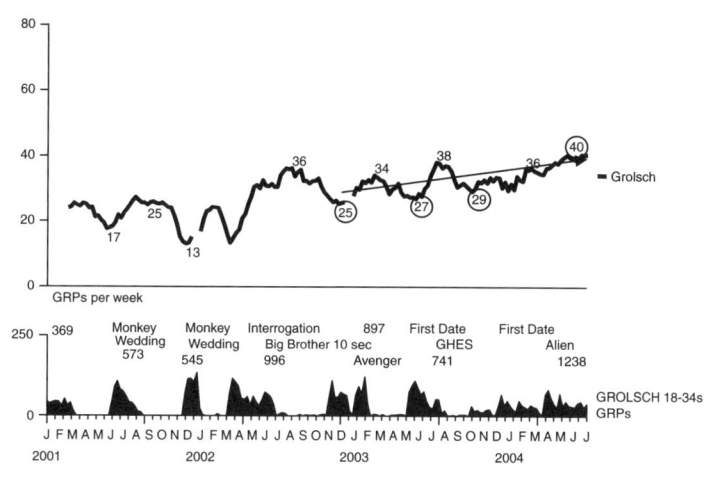

Figure 8: 'Grolsch takes longer to brew': agree strongly

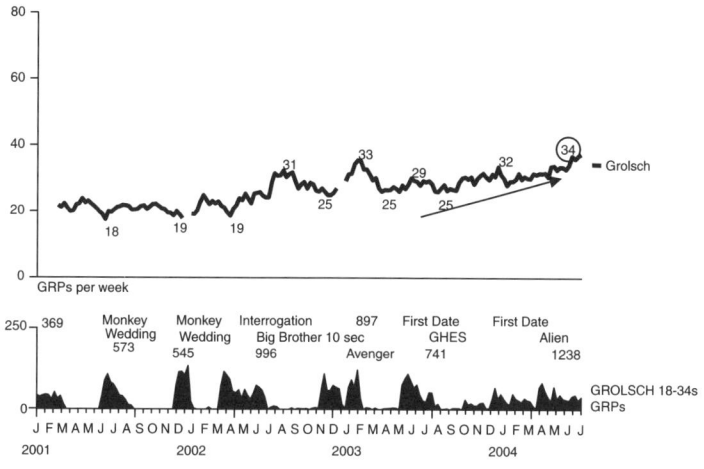

Figure 9: 'Grolsch is becoming more popular': agree strongly

ADVERTISING EFFECT ON BRAND PERCEPTIONS

'Brand health' measures are notoriously difficult to change and tend to require ongoing, consistent commitment to produce significant change.

In the period 2002–04, Grolsch has shown its most significant change to date. Stella Artois still emerges from this study as the dominant leading brand, but comparing percentage changes over time, we see evidence of a changing landscape where Stella appears to be reaching a peak and Grolsch shows signs of being the brand that's 'on the up'.

Spontaneous brand awareness has shown consistent growth between 2000 and 2004, while awareness of key competitors has fallen away in the last two years (see Figure 10).[12]

---

12. Source: Brand Track (also applies to Figures 11 and 12).

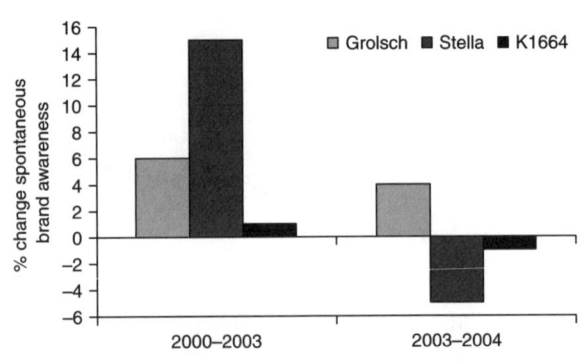

Figure 10: *Grolsch awareness grows as competitors' declines*

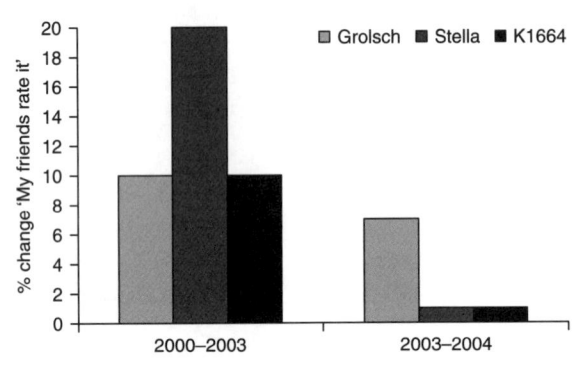

Figure 11: *Grolsch seen as 'on the up'*

Tracking perceptions of 'my friends rate it' suggests that Stella Artois' huge sense of popularity may have reached a peak. Only Grolsch is showing consistent growth, suggesting it's a brand that young men see as 'on the up' (see Figure 11).

Stella Artois has traditionally held a strong lead on the measure 'worth paying more for', reflecting it's 'Reassuringly Expensive' positioning; however, in today's world of discounting and promotion, this is not always strictly the case. The last two years have seen more young men beginning to cast Grolsch in this high-value role – further evidence that the brand has increased its sense of worth and quality in the eyes of consumers (see Figure 12).

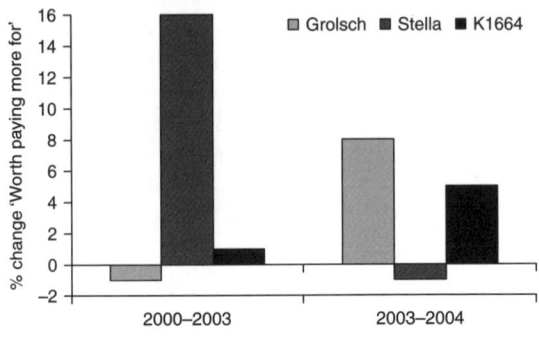

Figure 12: *Grolsch seen in a more high-value role*

GROLSCH

TIME FOR THE SALES EFFECTS

From where our last IPA paper left off in 2002, Grolsch has racked up an impressive new set of headline results.

- Grolsch now sells over one million hectolitres a year (686,000 barrels in 2004). This is already an increase of almost 200,000 barrels on Grolsch's 2002 target and therefore a strong step forward towards the goal of becoming a million-barrel brand by 2006.
- Grolsch has achieved its target to grow ahead of the premium lager market. Between November 2002 and November 2004, Grolsch's total trade MAT volume increased +22.3% while the premium lager market increased volume by just +0.7%.[13]

As mentioned at the outset, Grolsch's on-trade distribution still lags behind key competitors, but we only have to look at the off-trade to see what happens when Grolsch is placed side by side with its competitors and consumers have a free choice. In the off-trade, results have gone through the roof.

In 2003, Grolsch became the fastest-growing top-ten lager in the take-home sector. In 2004 it continued to increase volume at a faster rate than key competitors Stella Artois and Kronenbourg 1664.[14]

In 2003, Grolsch met its target of reaching the number two premium lager position in the off-trade. Though positions did fluctuate in the interim, Grolsch regained the position at the end of 2004.

Grolsch now commands 5.4% volume share of the off-trade premium lager market (5.8% value share), showing sustained growth over time[15] (see Figure 13).

Christmas is a key trading time for premium lagers in the off-trade. Sales performance data for GB multiple grocers over Christmas 2004 show that Grolsch was the best-performing premium brand in the four weeks to 25 December 2004. This helped assist Grolsch's MAT position further into growth (volume +13.3%, value +7.9%). Interestingly, Stella Artois had a poor period, with volumes down

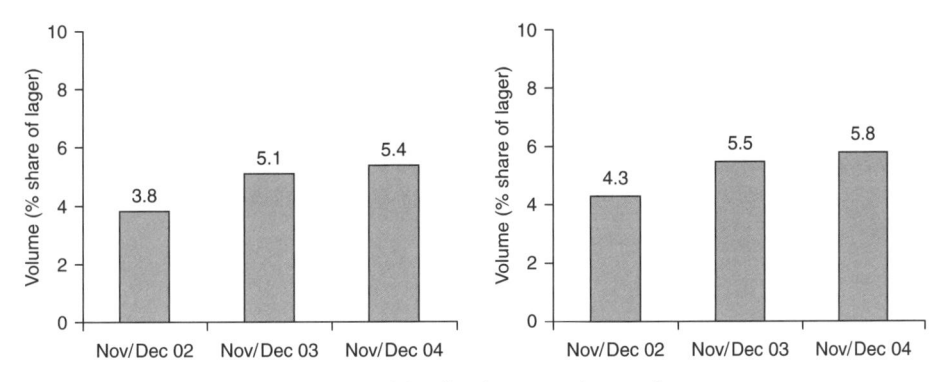

Figure 13: *Grolsch's volume and value shares of the off-trade premium lager market*

---

13. ACNielsen.
14. ACNielsen.
15. ACNielsen.

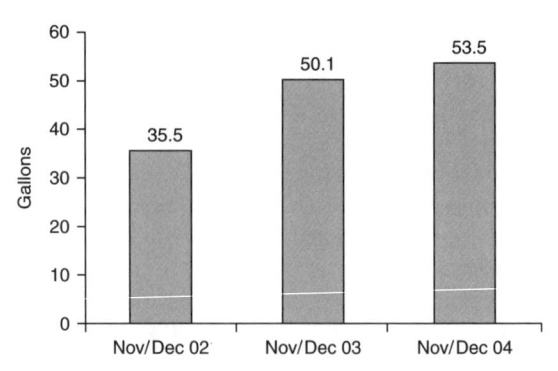

Figure 14: *Grolsch's rate of sale*

−9.9%, and is the only major lager brand in MAT decline (volume −0.7% and value -0.7%).[16]

In our 2003 paper, we drew upon rate of sale as the true indicator of consumer demand, showing how off-trade rate of purchase doubled between 2000 and 2002. Since then, rate of sale has increased by a further 50% over the two-year period[17] (see Figure 14).

Results for Coors

In November 2004, annual data showed that Coors became the number one on-trade brewer in Great Britain.[18]

DISCOUNTING OTHER FACTORS

Over the campaign period, distribution has been relatively stable, particularly in the off-trade, where key business successes have been returned. In the competitive off-trade environment, the top three premium lagers all saw prices fall across the campaign period,[19] leading us to conclude that price is not the critical factor in Grolsch's sustained success.

According to MMS data, Stella Artois' total advertising spend between January 2003 and December 2004 was almost double that of Grolsch.[20] In the period of analysis, Kronenbourg 1664 was between advertising campaigns and largely off air; however, the fact that Grolsch's brand health measures show percentage gains versus Stella as well as Kronenbourg 1664 suggests that Grolsch is doing more than filling Kronenbourg's void.

In summer 2003, Grolsch ran a large promotion in the off-trade offering a rack to chill glasses in the fridge. This was a great success, delivering 50,000 units

---

16. Source: ACNielsen.
17. Source: ACNielsen Off Trade Audit, November/December 2004.
18. Source: ACNielsen On Trade, MAT volume share. Coors Brewers' annual lager volume share: 28.7% (up 2.3pp on 2003) overtaking ScotCo at 27.9% (down −1.1pp on last year).
19. ACNielsen Off Trade Audit, November/December 2004.
20. Source: MMS, Stella Artois total advertising media, January 2003 to December 2004 £20,936981; Grolsch £11,512748.

through key partner Tesco, and a further 50,000 across the off-trade. Getting chilled, branded glassware into homes is an important way of increasing quality perceptions but is not, in itself, responsible for the long-term, sustained growth the brand has experienced.

RETURN ON INVESTMENT

We do not currently have econometric modelling to isolate and precisely quantify the value of Grolsch's advertising. However, in its absence we can put forward a hypothesis. It is not unreasonable to suggest that, without advertising support, Grolsch might have continued to see volume growth in line with the premium lager market over the period 2003–04. According to the latest ACNielsen total trade MAT volume data,[21] had Grolsch grown in line with the premium lager market[22] it would have grown to 447,000 barrels. In fact it grew by over 30 times the market rate[23] and reached approximately 543,000 barrels.

To put this in perspective, the incremental 96,000 barrels are equivalent to a brand the size of Heineken, which ACNielsen is currently tracking at 96,000 barrels, or 1.4% of the total premium lager market.

CONCLUSION

This paper demonstrates how small but significant changes to Grolsch's advertising and media approach have helped it to be a success – and, more importantly, helped it keep on being a success. Irving Berlin said that staying successful was the toughest challenge and he was right – but it's a challenge Grolsch has risen to with aplomb.

---

21. On-trade to November 2004; off-trade to November/December 2004.
22. +0.7% between November 2002 and November 2004.
23. +22.3% between November 2002 and November 2004.

BRONZE

12

My First Bed
A media strategy you can trust

Principal author: Gary Wise, Feather Brooksbank
Creative agency: MWO

EDITOR'S SUMMARY

Even hard-nosed IPA judges can be charmed by an engaging presentation, and that's how most of the panel felt about this story from Feather Brooksbank. Innovative 'media' choice, including product placement in cinema foyers, supporting a well-constructed strategy of presenting My First Bed as a toy, resulted in a 50% market share. This was a solid case, which would have been stronger had it included convincing ROI data to demonstrate payback.

I'm going to explain the media strategy devised by Feather Brooksbank to launch Silentnight's My First Bed range. To do this, I won't be using any jargon or marketing clichés. Instead, I'll be explaining the impact of the campaign through the eyes of our core consumers, parents and children, and highlighting how trust was the key to our success. The My First Bed product was launched two years ago. This paper tells the story of its success from launch to present day.

My First Bed was a new direction for Silentnight. The core strength of the brand prior to the launch was among older purchasers who bought in to the brand attributes of comfort, support, relaxation and home. Silentnight recognised that younger consumers were beginning to favour more fashion-orientated purchases – particularly bedsteads – largely as a result of the interior-design boom with TV programmes like *Property Ladder*, *DIY SOS* and *Changing Rooms*. It decided that it would need to innovate in order to remain the leading player in the bed market.

An in-depth research programme was undertaken among mothers of children aged one to eight, and the My First Bed product was created.

My First Bed is a unique product, with a unique mix-and-match concept (explained later). The challenge for the advertising was to introduce this unique product to a long-established bed marketing environment where the traditional values of support, relaxation, and so on, had always been prominent, and media strategies had focused on direct response (daytime TV/national press). The media for this project would need to be innovative and exciting to reflect the nature of the product, but would also need to tap in to the key motivators for parents to go out and buy a new bed for their children. We needed to launch this product and to lay the foundations for future growth within a new lifestyle, branded bed market. We also needed to make sure that the shift of budget towards this new product would not be to the detriment of the core Silentnight brand.

The objectives of the advertising were as follows.

- Generate awareness of My First Bed as a Silentnight product.
- Maintain core brand awareness, even though budget would now be shifted to the My First Bed product.
- Drive sales of My First Bed.

Our consumers will now take over …

Simon, aged 7 and a ¼

Someone asked me to rite, about why I love My First Bed so much wich is weerd coz I'm not that good at riting. Anyway my first bed is harry hippo. He has a hippo head, and hippo feet and its made by Silentnight and he looks like this (I look much oalder now!) [see Figure 1].

The reeson why I love my hippo bed much is coz I got to choose every bit of him. I chose the colour of my headboard I chose the colour of the base I chose the stripey matress I chose the hippo head (and I could have chose a duck or football or heart and other stuff) and I chose the hippo feet (coz it would be stewpid for a hippo to have duck feet or something) and I chose all of it on the intrenet where I put all the bits together myself. I also love my hippo bed coz, its got a secret storage bit and im not telling you where it is

MY FIRST BED

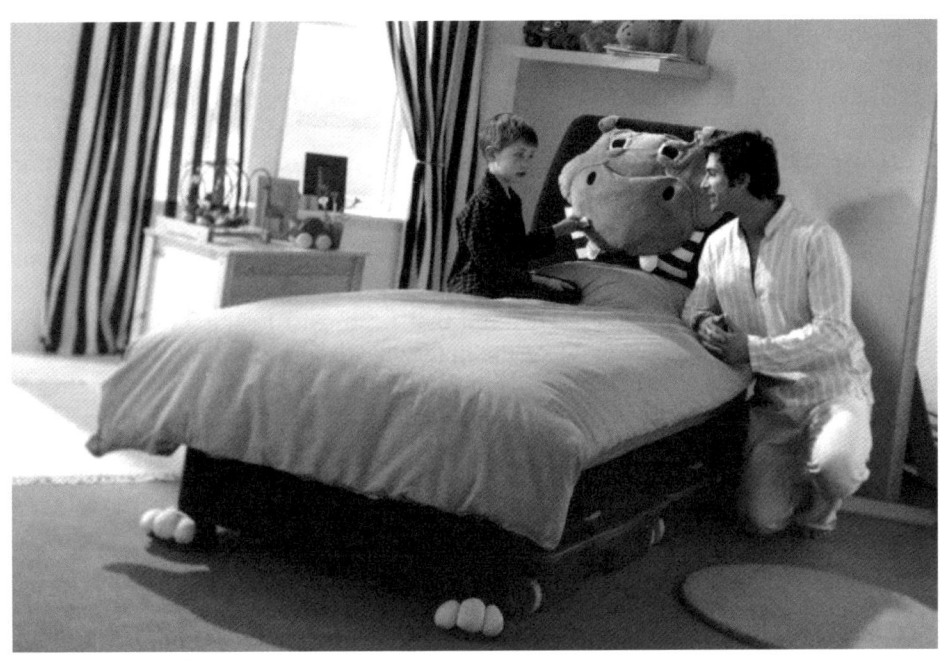

Figure 1: *Simon and his 'Harry Hippo' bed*

Before I got my hippo bed I had a boring bed that had horrybal springs that stuck in my back. then me and my mum went to the cinema and saw a duck bed in the entrence and I got to play with it and my mum rote on a booklet and sent it off and entered a competishen. She said that it ment that they would be able to have our details and then ring us to ask questons about advatising and stuff. Then we went in the cinema and saw Shrek. which was reelly funny and before it came on there was a advert for My First Bed wich was a cartoon with hippos in it and it made me want one more so I said to my mum that I reelly wanted one and we should buy the one in the entrence but she said that she had picked up a brosher and it would be ok and I might be able to get one one day.

Simon's mum, Lorraine

When choosing a bed for my kids, I need to choose a brand that I can trust. Being an ever-worrying parent, I have read all sorts of things about the importance of kids' sleep and how moving them from a cot to their first bed can have disruptive effects. The fact that Silentnight consulted a child psychologist (Dr Dorothy Einon) to examine its My First Bed product was certainly encouraging. The psychologist said that the Hippo and Duck Play Pals would be almost 'guardian-like', watching over children as they fall asleep or wake up. She also noted that the secret storage pockets were ideal for children, who crave places to keep their belongings and like to keep 'secrets' away from siblings (like Simon hiding his Lego Knights from his little sister!). It is also encouraging that Silentnight has its beds tested to British Standards (passing the threshold for domestic flammability risk etc.), it has consulted back-care experts and uses a Miracoil spring system to guarantee support during growing years.

Silentnight has asked me to write a bit on the advertising for My First Bed. I don't know a great deal about advertising, but I do know what works for me and what doesn't! As Simon has already told you, we saw the bed in the foyer of a cinema, which sparked Simon's interest (even though it wasn't actually his 'first' bed!). We love going to the cinema together to see the latest kids' films and it was a bit of fun for the kids to play with the different characters and things that you can choose when putting the bed together.

Before that, I had already seen the advert in my favourite magazine (they tell me it was called a bound-in insert!). I really trust *Living etc* to choose advertisers who sell products that will be good quality and that I can trust for my family. The way the leaflet stood out from the rest of the magazine also grabbed my attention and suggested that this was a quality product. The leaflet showed all of the benefits of the product and the range of options for the beds, which was interesting. Then, when I saw the same leaflet in *Practical Parenting* (I told you I was ever-worrying – I'm always looking in there for tips!), I definitely began to think that this must be a decent product, because I know they wouldn't allow anything but the best kids' products in the magazine.

After all this and the cinema experience, we saw My First Bed advertising on TV. The kids loved the ad because it included the same Hippo and Duck characters that they'd seen before. It also made me think that they must have invested in the beds a lot to be able to put them on TV. Simon was obviously very excited, as he'll tell you now ...

I saw My First Bed on the televishen and got reely exited becoz it ment that mum and dad mite buy me one becoz when people go on televishen it means that they are good. So when I saw it I told my dad about when me and mum had seen it in the cinema and that it looked reely good and was reely comfotabal, and that I reely reely wanted one. and I had done for ages.

So then me and my dad went on to the intrenet and went to see the bit about beds where they had the Hippo bed an the Duck bed and all the other beds on there. It was reely cool coz I got to put all the bits together and ...

He's really cute when he's excited, but he does tend to repeat himself! Pete (my husband) is pretty cynical when it comes to advertising, but he does trust me when I've done my research and is a bit of a sucker for the kids' excitement. So, when Pete and Simon had finished creating the Hippo on the internet and given him a name, it seemed like Harry would soon become part of the family.

And now back to us ...

We came to the conclusion that we would need to have fun with the brand in order to excite kids and showcase the unique aspects of the product. The mix-and-match feature led us to think about the product as a toy, so we knew that interactivity would be important. We also needed national coverage to lay solid foundations for the product. However, none of this would be successful if we couldn't persuade our key purchasing audience (parents) to trust the brand.

The theme of trust was utilised throughout the media schedule, both in terms of media selection (magazines that are trusted, TV that gives status and 'big brand' values) and timing (bound-in inserts followed by cinema and then TV). This timing strategy was designed to grow trust in a very specific way; the bound-in inserts would act as a catalogue to show range and product benefits, the cinema would add a fun element and excite kids, then the TV would re-enforce brand equity and provide the necessary brand status that is important for building trust. It was vitally important in this trust-building operation that parents were reached both on their own in a trusted environment (magazines) and together with their kids (cinema) – the former to generate interest in the product and the latter to exploit pester power. The interactivity of the cinema foyer display would be invaluable in openly displaying the product to our audience and letting them test it for themselves without the pressured sales environment of a showroom.

RESULTS

Did we achieve our first objective: to raise awareness of My First Bed?

As highlighted above, we handed out competition leaflets in the cinema foyers where the bed display stunts were happening, so that we could call our audience and ask them what they thought. A total of 194 five-minute interviews took place in September 2003 (Solihull and Huddersfield). The results were undeniably encouraging. Here are some findings:

- Silentnight top in unprompted brand awareness of bed manufacturers with 51%
- Silentnight top for bed manufacturers who make beds for children at 50% vs nearest competitor Slumberland at 8% (see Figure 2)
- 70% of interviewees had heard of My First Bed (see Figure 3)
- 78% recalled seeing the cinema advertising
- Silentnight top for unprompted cinema advertising recall (followed by Peugeot, Frosties and Vauxhall)
- 85% thought that cinema was the right environment for the My First Bed message (see Figure 4)
- it did the job very well and evoked trust – it was 'for' our target audience, they 'enjoyed watching it' and it made Silentnight 'more appealing' to them; creative work, from MWO, had engaged well with the audience through continued use of the popular Hippo and Duck cartoon characters
- 87% of respondents with kids aged three to eight remembered seeing the foyer stunt (84% of all interviewed)

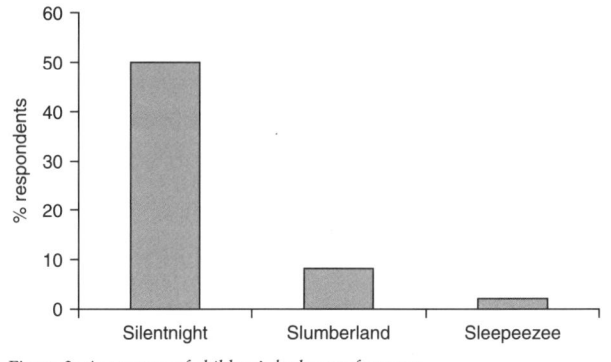

Figure 2: *Awareness of children's bed manufacturers*
Source: Dipsticks Research, September 2003

SCOTTISH ADVERTISING WORKS 4

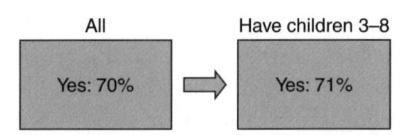

Figure 3: *How many had heard of My First Bed?*
Source: Dipsticks Research, September 2003

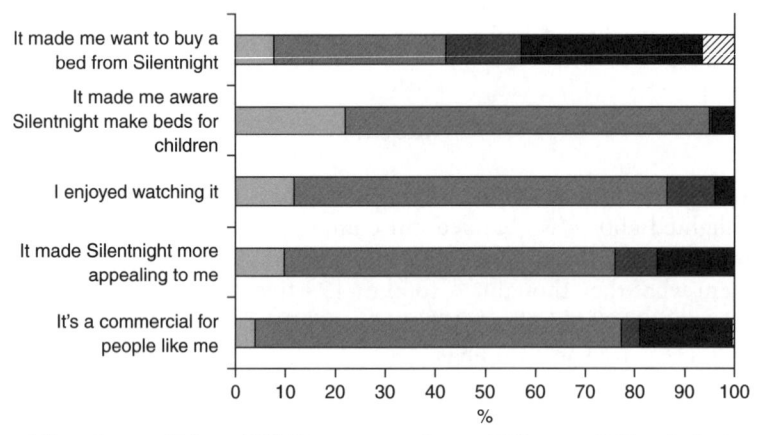

Figure 4: *Attitudes to cinema advertising*
Source: Dipsticks Research, September 2003

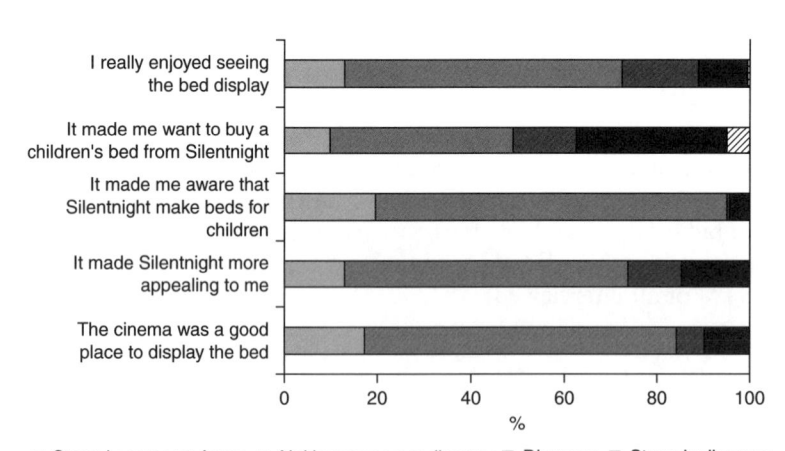

Figure 5: *Attitudes to bed display*
Source: Dipsticks Research, September 2003

- the foyer stunt did the job very well and evoked *trust* – over 50% agreed that it made them want to buy a children's bed from Silentnight (see Figure 5)
- 75% felt more favourably towards the brand after seeing the display
- 78% said that, if they were going to purchase a children's bed, they would be likely to choose Silentnight (see Figure 6).

MY FIRST BED

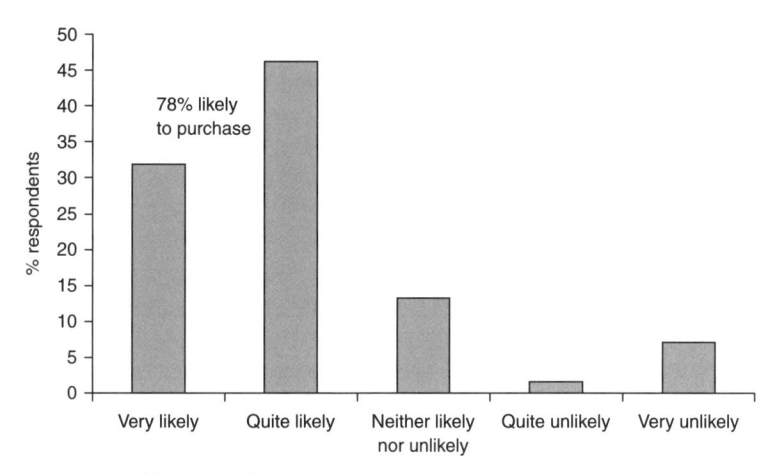

Figure 6: *How likely to purchase*
Source: Dipsticks Research, September 2003

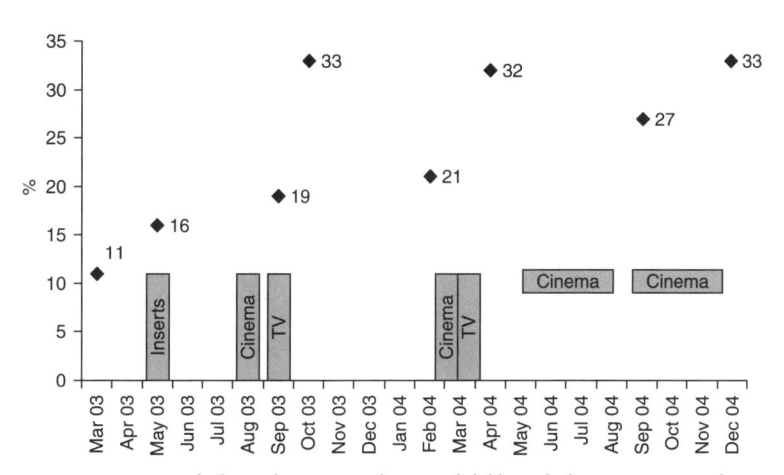

Figure 7: *Awareness of Silentnight as a manufacturer of children's beds (spontaneous and prompted)*
Base: 1000 women
Source: BMRB Access

In addition to this research, a BMRB access study has been used from launch to the present day. Figure 7 clearly shows the effect of advertising – with an uplift of 22 percentage points.

Did we achieve our second objective: to maintain awareness of the main Silentnight brand, even though budget was shifted to the My First Bed product? Yes. Overall brand recall is higher now than it was in January 2003 (see Figure 8).

WHAT ABOUT SALES?

Aim

To achieve 25% market share of single beds bought at the £300 to £400 price point.

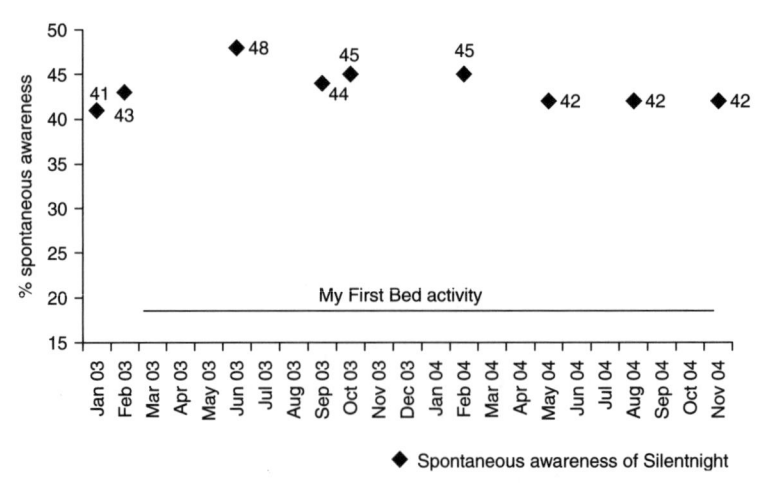

Figure 8: *Spontaneous recall for Silentnight*
Source: BMRB Access

Result

Over 14,500 My First Beds sold to date – 50% market share (source: Silentnight).

SUMMARY

We successfully launched My First Bed as a unique product into a traditional marketing environment and far exceeded the objectives that we had set out to achieve.

Our media was far from traditional:

- we used cinema when no other bed manufacturer was using it
- we put beds in cinema foyers for the first time ever and let kids *play* with them
- we timed the campaign carefully, so that each medium had a specific role to play in a specific order
- we established a future for the branded kids' bed market
- the media we chose engaged our audience in such a way that we managed to develop a relationship that provoked pester power, initiated intrigue and was, crucially, founded on trust.

BRONZE

13

Nambarrie

Going from strength to strength

Principal author: Julie Amers, The Leith Agency
Media agency: Universal McCann

EDITOR'S SUMMARY

A strong case study from The Leigh Agency, with good use of research and consumer insight to create new energy for Nambarrie in a declining, competitive market, made more challenging by the need to address the brand's customers in two very different regions. The judges felt that a more rigorous analysis of ROI was needed to make this paper complete, but liked the commitment to a focused positioning based on strength of flavour to give Nambarrie its competitive rationale.

INTRODUCTION

This paper will show how, by taking a calculated risk and focusing sharply on a single-minded but potentially polarising product benefit, Nambarrie's advertising achieved a step-change in the brand's fortunes. Not only that, but it managed to do this in two very distinct markets: a mature home market and also in Scotland where the brand was less well established.

BACKGROUND

Nambarrie tea is one of the most popular and well-known brands in Northern Ireland. Based in Belfast, Nambarrie has been blending mainstream teas for over 140 years. However, it faces tough competition both from Tetley and from local competitors such as Punjana and Lyons. The market is highly competitive, with much emphasis placed upon fierce price-fighting promotional activity (offers such as 50% and even 100% extra free are not uncommon).

In 1989 Nambarrie tea was introduced in Scotland. The Scottish tea market is also very competitive, with two brands dominating the sector: Tetley and Brooke Bond's Scottish Blend. In the face of these massive competitors, Nambarrie has struggled to make sufficient inroads. Again price promotions are common, with the two leading brands regularly undercutting each other's prices in a battle for market dominance.

A DIFFICULT SECTOR TO CHANGE

For the vast majority of consumers, mainstream teabags are a commodity and a habitual purchase. Perceived brand differences are negligible. With consumer choice largely dictated by family tradition and habit, it's very difficult to get consumers to switch brands without aggressive promotions. The assurance of taste and the perceived quality afforded by brands appears to be paramount.

'As far as buying standard tea is concerned, some 89% of housewives questioned claimed to always buy their favourite brand of tea. 59% look for a well-known brand name. For 62% taste is the most important factor in choice of brand'.

Shopper Insight Research, SPA Scotland, July 2004

The mainstream tea market is also fairly static. The biggest change has been the increase in the popularity of speciality teas, and herb, fruit and green teas, fuelled by consumer health interest. By comparison there has been very little innovation in the mainstream tea bag sector since the launch of pyramid bags by Brooke Bond in 1996.

NAMBARRIE

ONE BRAND: TWO DISTINCT MARKETS

In Northern Ireland

In Northern Ireland, Nambarrie is a fabric brand, part of everyday life, with a rich heritage behind it. Despite this enviable brand status the market was becoming increasingly price competitive. Aggressive price promotions by powerful competing tea brands continually challenged Nambarrie's position.

Nambarrie had few choices – sit tight and hope that the big brands would bring their prices back in line, cut its own price or take some alternative action. New product developments were not a viable option. To engage in dramatic counter-price cutting was not the best route if Nambarrie was to retain its brand equity in the long term. The only feasible way for the brand to engender loyalty was to somehow strengthen consumers' emotional closeness to the brand.

In Scotland

Tracking research revealed that Nambarrie's previous advertising activity raised levels of brand and advertising awareness. Spontaneous brand awareness had more than doubled between 1996 and 2002. Advertising awareness had also risen dramatically over the same period.

However this was not reflected in significant improvements in market share, as indicated in Figure 1.

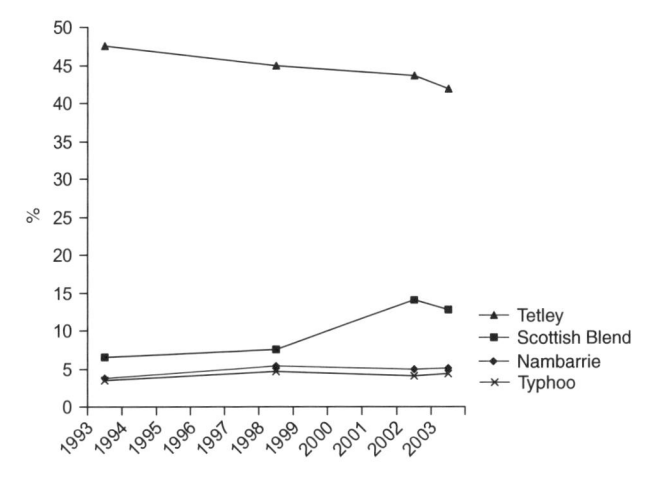

Figure 1: *Scottish standard tea bag market shares, 1993–2003*
Source: ACNielsen Scantrack

We needed to understand why awareness-building advertising was not having a significant positive impact on sales. One critical factor was that brand penetration and trial remained low (see Figure 2).

Qualitative research also highlighted that, in the absence of product trial, consumers in Scotland did not have a clear view of what Nambarrie would taste like.

SCOTTISH ADVERTISING WORKS 4

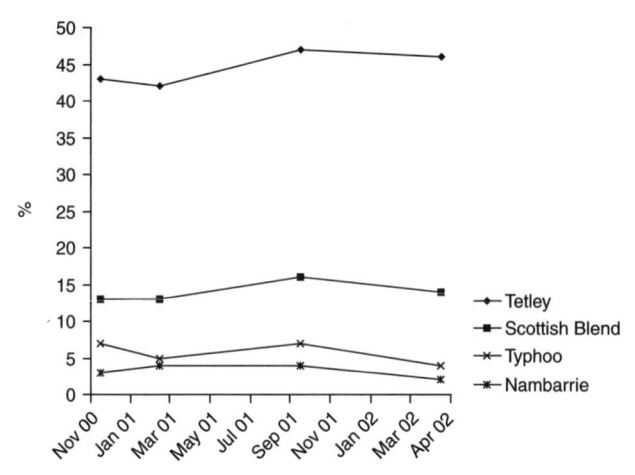

Figure 2: *Brand of tea purchased most frequently*
Base: all respondents, 1016
Source: Millward Brown Ulster Scotland Omnibus

'I've heard of it, but I've never tried it and I couldn't tell you what it was like.'

Creative development research, November 2002

At a basic level, consumers did not have a clear idea of what the brand stood for. It was just another tea brand in a busy marketplace. The most recent qualitative research put the brand's position bluntly:

'The problem for Nambarrie in Scotland is simply lack of a clear positioning:
- literally non-descript for potential users
- no brand personality
- nor any sense of heritage or provenance.'

The Research Practice, May 2003

MARKETING OBJECTIVES

The marketing objectives for the brand were different in each region:

- to substantially grow market share in Scotland
- to maintain the brand's pre-eminence in Northern Ireland.

The Leith Agency was tasked with developing a single advertising campaign that would meet the marketing objectives for Scotland and Northern Ireland.

TOUGH ADVERTISING COMPETITORS

Over the years, the tea sector has produced some of advertising's best-known and well-loved campaigns. Traditionally, tea advertising has been generic, focusing on 'tea moments' and the relaxing, reviving, pick-me-up emotional effects delivered by a nice cup of tea.

NAMBARRIE

The most memorable campaigns have embodied these generic messages using engaging characters – the Tetley Tea Folk, the PG Tips Chimps, the Scottish Blend Café Owner – to bring tea moments to life in a warm, lighthearted fashion. In fact, these campaigns have dramatised the most natural and potent advertising area for tea.

Nambarrie's task – to establish a distinctive and motivating campaign in this advertising sector, and have one approach that also worked across two distinct markets – was going to be a massive challenge.

THE ADVERTISING CHALLENGE

In Scotland we had to raise awareness of Nambarrie in a way that would also make the brand stand for something. Moreover, we needed to give people a motivating reason to change their habitual buying behaviour.

In Northern Ireland the situation was equally tough, although different. Under pressure from powerful competition, we needed to reinforce the loyalty of our existing users.

STRATEGY

The strategy was all about back to basics. The generic, tea moment high ground was already effectively 'owned' by leading competitors supported by famous, long-term campaigns. We needed to find a genuine point of difference that both distinguished Nambarrie from its competitors and was relevant to both market situations.

Our first task was to assess the activity of our core competitors in each region and to look for gaps in communication. In Scotland the key competitors were Tetley and Scottish Blend. Tetley had recently dispensed with its Tea Folk and had used a couple of new creative routes: one based on 'we love our tea' and a more recent one positioning tea as a reviver in difficult situations. Typically both approaches were relatively generic. Scottish Blend, by contrast, focused on the brand being 'specially blended for the softer waters of Scotland'.

One strategic area unoccupied by any of our competitors was strength of flavour. This presented us with a great opportunity for Nambarrie. Over the course of many years of research in Northern Ireland, strength of flavour had consistently been mentioned as a brand virtue. Recent qualitative research evidence supported the idea that Nambarrie made a stronger cup of tea that was ideally suited to the Northern Irish palate.

> 'Nambarrie is associated with strength – a local brand, created to satisfy local tastes for stronger tea ... only differentiating versus Tetley and Typhoo – "English", weak tea.'
>
> *The Research Practice, May 2003*

When Scottish consumers tasted Nambarrie for the first time, strength of flavour was also frequently the main attribute that was mentioned spontaneously.

> 'A wee bit strong, but not that tarry taste or bitter.'
>
> *Older Nambarrie users, Glasgow*
> *The Research Practice, May 2003*

Strength of flavour was an exciting area for advertising as no other tea advertiser occupied this territory in either Scotland or Northern Ireland. However, we were also concerned that it could be potentially off-putting for consumers.

To determine the appeal of a strength of flavour positioning we conducted quantitative research among Scottish consumers. A significant minority of Scots consumers (33%) considered themselves to be drinkers of strong tea. Furthermore 16% claimed to find the concept of a strong tea 'very appealing', with a further 25% finding this idea 'quite appealing'. Most encouraging of all, 8% claimed that they would 'definitely buy' a strong tea, with a further 20% claiming that they would 'probably buy' a strong tea. Those consumers who were most positive about the concept were also the heaviest tea drinkers and represented the segment that accounts for 10% of all consumption.

So although most people didn't like the idea of a strong cup of tea, those who did were heavy tea drinkers and exceeded the current market share of the brand. We therefore had a significant and valuable group of potential converts to go for among Scottish tea drinkers.

From this research we concluded that there was potential to position Nambarrie as a strong tea brand in Scotland. And our research in Northern Ireland confirmed that drinkers there liked the idea of a strong cup of tea.

MANAGING THE COMMUNICATION OF STRENGTH

A tea strategy centred on strength of flavour was new and different, but it was always going to be difficult to execute successfully. For many (even those who prefer strong tea) the idea of a 'strong cup of tea' conjures up a dark-brown brew that is stewed and bitter. Certainly it is not everybody's idea of a good cuppa. So the task we set ourselves was to communicate a point of difference in a way that won over strong tea lovers without putting everyone else off.

In order to identify how we should be communicating the idea of a strong tea, we undertook further qualitative research.

This research confirmed that while strength of flavour was indeed a credible route for Scottish consumers, extreme care needed to be taken in the communication of this benefit. Strength was deemed to be a double-edged sword – it was not always necessarily a good thing, as for some the notion of a 'strong' cup of tea was off-putting.

'Flavoursome or full flavour is better, as strong could mean stewed.'

Younger Nambarrie users, Edinburgh
The Research Practice, May 2003

'I like a strong cup of tea, nice and hot – it's very refreshing if you've got a real thirst.'

'A good, strong cup of tea ... Tea that you really enjoy is more comforting.'

Younger Nambarrie users, Belfast
The Research Practice, May 2003

From this research we determined that the strategic positioning for Nambarrie was 'balanced strength'. By this we mean Nambarrie is strong in a smooth, full-flavoured sense, but not so strong as to be deemed stewed or bitter-tasting. We also determined that the execution of the advertising must not undermine the brand's quality credentials or give the impression of excessive product strength. The strength had to be in the overall brand character.

Qualitative research in Northern Ireland also confirmed that strength of flavour was indeed recognised as a brand truth and that, as long as it was treated in the suggested 'balanced' fashion, there was no danger of this alienating current Nambarrie users.

THE CAMPAIGN IDEA

We decided that the best way to articulate Nambarrie's new strength positioning was to say that it was 'strong, but also nice'. This became our advertising proposition. This led to a creative idea where Nambarrie produces strong but nice behaviour in people who drink it.

The television commercial featured a lady, coming home laden with shopping bags, who rushes to get the phone, only to find out that it is a cold-caller from 'Creativity Kitchens'. She then nonchalantly puts the caller on hold, leaving him to listen to the music from a discarded child's toy, while she makes herself a nice cup of Nambarrie tea. When she is ready she comes back to the phone to thank the caller 'for holding' before she finishes her cup of tea. The end frame shows a mug with muscular arms and uses the strap-line 'Nambarrie. Nice and strong'.

Figure 3: *TV campaign end frame*

As the commercial needed to work in both Scotland and Northern Ireland, qualitative research was conducted in both areas. This revealed that in Northern Ireland, where the brand was already known to deliver a strong-tasting tea, the end frame gave the impression that there had possibly been a change to its blend to make it even stronger, potentially too strong. To avoid any suggestion that the product was too strong, this final frame was removed from the commercial for use in Northern Ireland.

In Scotland, where consumers had fewer preconceptions about the brand, research showed that the commercial successfully communicated our point of difference and conveyed a motivating reason to purchase Nambarrie. The muscular end frame was therefore ideal for Scotland.

'I never knew Nambarrie was strong; at least I know something about it now. I like strong tea so I might try it if I see it on the shelf.'

Out of the Box Research, August 2003

MEDIA SELECTION

TV was the lead medium in both Scotland and Northern Ireland. In Scotland only, this was supported by a six-sheet poster campaign, featuring the 'Muscle Mug'. A total of 369 poster sites were used in the central belt of Scotland in one burst of activity during January 2004.

The TV advertising ran in both areas in a series of four-week bursts covering the period 5 January to 19 December 2004. There were a total of 1850 TVRs in Scotland and 2150 TVRs in Northern Ireland.

TEST MARKET EVALUATION

Prior to the national launch, a store test evaluation was conducted in the Grampian TV region. The purpose of this was to establish whether the commercial would have the required short-term impact on sales of Nambarrie.

Comparative tests conducted by ACNielsen indicate that in more than half of all cases, TV campaigns show no short-term uplift in product sales. In our test there was an average uplift of 7.5% in sales over a four-week period in which the advertising was on air. Even more impressive was that the 80-pack format (the most popular size) had an uplift of 19% in the final week of advertising and an average uplift of 11.9%. ACNielsen regarded this result as being 'exceptional' given the brand's status in Scotland and the market conditions. Following these encouraging results we were in a position to launch the campaign nationally with confidence.

SALES EFFECTS

Following the national launch of the campaign the results have been impressive, with Nambarrie's share of the Scottish mainstream tea bag market growing by some 14.5%. The improvement in Nambarrie's MAT value shares between 2003 and 2004 is shown in Figure 4.

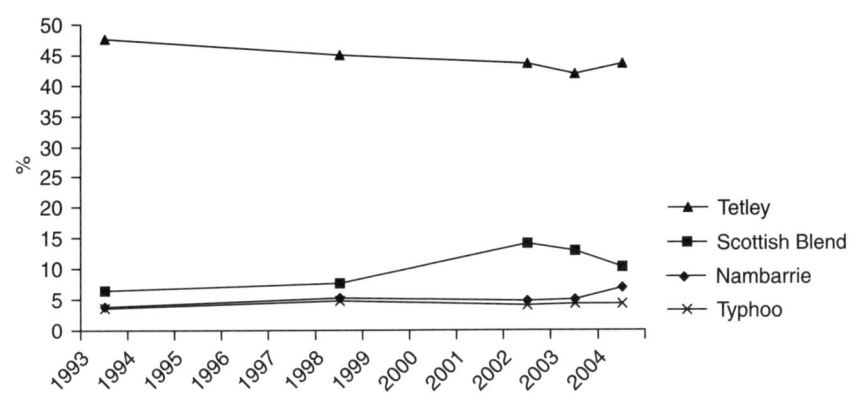

Figure 4: *Scottish Standard Tea Bag Market Shares, 1993–2004*
Source: ACNielsen Scantrack

The total market in Scotland has declined over the same period. The market value (£s) growth was –3.6% between September 2003 and 2004.

In Northern Ireland Nambarrie has maintained its market share, despite powerful and aggressive competition. In fact, sales grew by 2.2% between December 2003 and December 2004, as indicated in Figure 5. The total market in Northern Ireland declined over the same period. The market value (£s) growth was –7.6% between September 2003 and 2004.

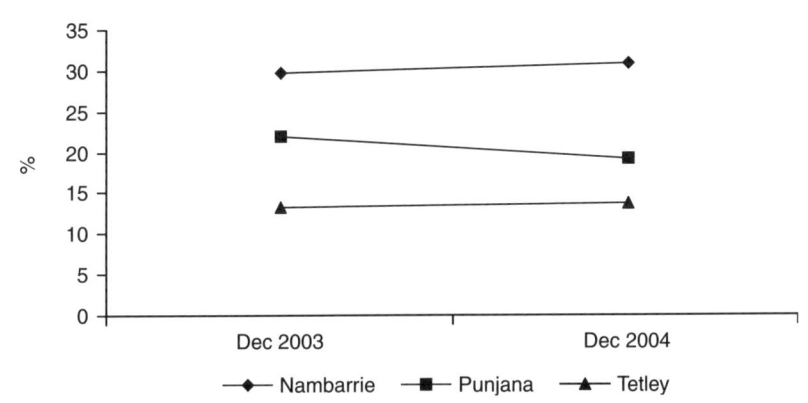

Figure 5: *Northern Ireland standard tea bag market shares, 1989–2004*
Source: ACNielsen Scantrack

THE WIDER MARKET CONTEXT

Nambarrie's performance is all the more impressive given the wider market context.

Although the National Food Survey still shows tea as the most popular beverage in 2000 (latest full-year data available), consumption has fallen since 1990 (see Table 1).

TABLE 1: CONSUMPTION OF HOT BEVERAGES PER PERSON PER WEEK, 1990–2000

	1990 grams	1995 grams	2000 grams	% change 1990–2000	% change 1995–2000
Tea	43	39	34	–20.9	–12.8
Coffee	18	16	15	–16.7	–6.3
Cocoa and drinking chocolate	5	2	4	–20.0	+100.0
Branded food drinks	4	5	5	+25.0	
Total	70	62	58	–17.1	–6.5

Source: NFS, National Statistics/Mintel

There is increasing competition and new product development in the hot beverage sector – for example, from herbal, green, fruit, speciality, organic, fair trade and Ayurvedic teas. It is the fruit, herb and speciality teas that are driving sales in the sector (see Table 2).

TABLE 2: UK RETAIL SALES OF TEA AND HERBAL TEA, BY TYPE AND VOLUME*, 2000 AND 2002

	2000 000 tonnes	%	2002 (est.) 000 tonnes	%	% change 2000–02
Standard tea bags**	113.9	87.0	109.5	86.2	–3.9
Specialty	3.2	2.4	4.7	3.7	+46.9
Decaffeinated	1.7	1.3	1.9	1.5	+11.8
One cup	2.4	1.8	2.2	1.7	–8.3
Loose tea	6.6	5.0	5.8	4.6	–12.1
Instant	2.1	1.6	1.6	1.3	–23.8
Herbal/fruit	1.0	0.8	1.3	1.0	+30.0
Total	130.9	100.0	127.1	100.0	–2.9

* Excludes sales through health food shops, garage forecourts and CTNs
** Excludes speciality, decaffeinated and one cup
Data may not equal totals due to rounding
Source: Mintel

'This whole area is one in which consumers are bombarded with new products, meaning that tea is no longer the automatic hot drink of choice.'

Mintel, Market Intelligence, February 2003

When we look at the hot drinks market in Scotland, it is in line with the national trends, and it is clear that although tea is still dominant, it is increasingly losing volume share to sales of coffee (see Figure 6).

This overall picture does not represent an easy backdrop to a campaign aiming to grow market share of Nambarrie in Scotland.

WHAT ELSE HAPPENED AS A RESULT OF THE CAMPAIGN?

In Scotland

Indications from ACNielsen Scantrack were that Nambarrie was gaining share from all three of its main competitors in Scotland (Tetley, Scottish Blend and

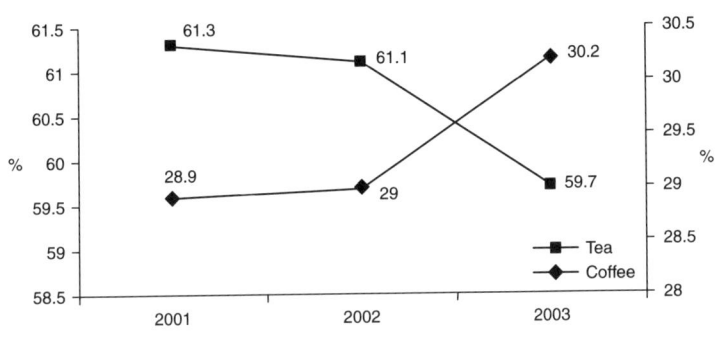

Figure 6: *Volume share of hot drinks market in Scotland*
Source: ACNielsen Scantrack, w/e 27 December 2003

Typhoo). The implication of this was that the strength proposition was appealing to consumers regardless of brand choice.

Tracking research in Scotland revealed that Nambarrie's unprompted brand awareness doubled over the course of the activity. Post-advertising levels of spontaneous awareness were at the same level as Tetley, Scottish Blend and Typhoo.

Brand awareness was also significantly higher among those who found the idea of a strong tea appealing (see Table 3).

TABLE 3: BRAND AWARENESS

	December 2003 pre (1000) %	February 2004 post (1000) %	Post among those finding the proposition appealing (222) %
Nambarrie (first mentions)	3	6	14
Nambarrie (total mentions)	14	16	40

Source: Scottish Opinion, December 2003 and February 2004

The strength message came through clearly in the advertising. There was a 60% increase in the percentage of consumers associating the brand with strength following the advertising.

There was also an uplift in advertising awareness for Nambarrie. This grew from 17% pre-advertising to 22% post-advertising – a significant achievement in such a tough advertising sector.

The majority of respondents who had seen the commercial agreed that it communicated a strength message (see Table 4).

TABLE 4: HOW STRONGLY DID THE COMMERCIAL COMMUNICATE THAT NAMBARRIE IS A STRONG CUP OF TEA?

	Those claiming to have seen (224) %
Very strongly	21
Quite strongly	29
Not very strongly	19
Not at all strongly	9
Don't know	22

Source: Scottish Opinion, February 2004

In Northern Ireland

We wanted to maintain the brand's status and salience. In terms of brand awareness, this was already high to begin with in Nambarrie's home market. Levels of brand awareness remained stable post-advertising. However, in terms of brand saliency (first brand mentioned) it was pleasing to see that, following the campaign, Nambarrie was on a par with Tetley (at 32%) on this important measure.

Most encouragingly, emotional closeness to the Nambarrie brand showed no signs of declining. To measure this we asked consumers to score Nambarrie on a 10-point scale to indicate whether or not it was 'a brand for people like me', where 10 represented the highest level of agreement with the statement and 1 the lowest. This score remained stable across this period with a mean score of 6.05, 35% endorsing the top three scores (8, 9 or 10 out of 10).

There was also significant uplift in advertising awareness for Nambarrie. This built significantly from 26% pre-advertising to 35% post-advertising.

Reassuringly, the strength message did not entirely dominate the quality/taste reassurance messages and certainly did not undermine previous quality perceptions. In fact, it added another dimension to the brand's communication (see Table 5).

TABLE 5: BRAND DIMENSIONS

	Spontaneous communication
A good-quality tea/tastes good	16
A good, strong cup of tea	14
There is always time for a cup of tea	10
Makes you relaxed/good pick-you-up	7
To sell tea	6
Enjoy your tea and make the sales person wait	4

Source: Millward Brown Ulster, February 2004

DISCOUNTING FACTORS OTHER THAN ADVERTISING

Distribution

There was no change in the distribution of Nambarrie in either Scotland or Northern Ireland over the period of advertising activity.

Price

The retail shelf price remained unchanged in both Scotland and Northern Ireland over the period of advertising activity.

Product quality

There was no change in the product specification or quality of Nambarrie in Scotland or Northern Ireland over the period of advertising activity.

NAMBARRIE

Other factors

Nambarrie was the fastest and only growing mainstream tea brand in Great Britain (source: MAT, August 2004, value sales).

SUMMARY

In a habitual market with stiff competition, Nambarrie took a chance and ran a campaign with a distinctive, but potentially polarising 'strong tea' message. This campaign has demonstrably contributed to maintaining the brand's dominance in Northern Ireland. At the same time, it has helped make it the fastest-growing tea brand in Scotland.

BRONZE

14

Overgate
The drive of your life

Principal author: Helen Crosthwaite, family
Media agency: Trident Media

EDITOR'S SUMMARY

A very neat case, with an intelligently applied small budget generating an immediate (short-term) response in increased mall traffic. By making a real event out of a promotion, family's advertising brought new shoppers to the location with an apparently sparkling ROI. An example of excellence in promotional execution delivering the goods.

INTRODUCTION

In a fiercely competitive retail environment, achieving standout is an increasingly difficult task. Overgate was suffering at the hands of a loyal audience of window shoppers who were happy to visit the Centre, but were less happy to actually spend when they got there. We were tasked to turn this situation around and convert this audience from window shoppers to big spenders.

By examining market trends and identifying key learnings from research undertaken about existing visitors to the Centre, we were able to construct a promotion that appealed to the Centre's core audience enough to get the tills ringing. At the same time, it created a talking-point that served to support the brand and its core values as well as garnering some impressive local and trade press coverage.

This paper demonstrates how a tactical promotion for Overgate achieved a 13% increase in sales, a 16.5% increase in footfall, a 42% increase in spend per head and successful penetration of high-value secondary and tertiary customers. The campaign broke the norms of a normal promotion, creating word of mouth and an external talking-point, which was born from an intuitive understanding of the customer.

It thereby both met and exceeded the objectives that were set out by the client. Not a bad result for a giant carrier bag, albeit a carrier bag that turned into a contender for the *Guinness Book of World Records*!

BACKGROUND

Overgate, Dundee, was launched in March 2000 as Tayside's premiere shopping destination, with a vision to deliver an unexpected and positive experience to its guests on every visit. With an abundance of competition on the high street and the increasing development of out-of-town retail parks in Dundee, Overgate has always understood that shopping is much more than the products you buy – it's an emotional experience, not just a rational one.

THE RETAIL ENVIRONMENT

The UK retail market is widely recognised as one of the most sophisticated in Europe. Total shopping centre floorspace stands at almost 13 million square metres, more than any other country in Europe, with an extra 370,000 square metres of floorspace added in 2001 alone.

After the initial panic that the high street would perish at the hands of the out-of-town retail park, the last decade has seen a revival of its fortunes. But rather than an 'either/or' decision, shoppers are now faced with a plethora of retail choices, with hypermarkets, discount retailers, warehouse clubs, factory outlet centres and the retailer's worst nightmare: e-tail.

OVERGATE

FIERCE COMPETITION

Despite the competition, UK shoppers are still displaying significant loyalty to their shopping centres. Cushman & Wakefield Healey & Baker's 2002 study, 'Where People Shop', discovered that UK customers visit shopping centres on average 21 times a year, the equivalent of one trip every two or three weeks. This is significantly more than the survey average, which covered the whole of Europe, and reflects the established nature of the shopping centre market in the UK.

Unsurprisingly, the major reason for last visiting a shopping centre was to buy something (as cited by 41% of UK respondents). However, the growing trend for shopping centres to become destinations for spending recreational or leisure time is reflected by the 19% of British respondents who cited 'window shopping' as the main reason for visiting. And therein lies our problem.

UNDERSTANDING OUR EXISTING AUDIENCE

Based on guest exit research conducted by an independent research company, Croft Marketing, on behalf of Overgate in October 2002, it was established that 81% of customers who visit Overgate are from the core catchment area of Dundee, with 12% from the secondary and 6% from the tertiary areas, and 1% from 'pull-in' customers – in other words, those who are visiting Dundee in some other capacity and visit the shopping centre (see Table 1 and Figure 1).

TABLE 1: INCREASING SECONDARY, TERTIARY AND 'PULL-IN' CATCHMENTS AFTER THE PROMOTIONAL ACTIVITY

Catchment	2002 figures	2003 target	Actual achieved (promotion)
Core	81%	75%	69%
Actual footfall	559,596	559,596	555,461
Secondary	12%	14%	13%
Actual footfall	84,903	96,720	104,652
Tertiary	6%	8%	7%
Actual footfall	41,452	55,269	56,351
Pull-in	1%	3%	11%
Actual footfall	6,909	20,727	88,552
Total footfall	690,859	732,312	805,016

Note: this assumes that the target core catchment footfall remains equal; a targeted 6% increase in footfall from catchment areas outside the core.

The average spend of those who visited from the core catchment area was less than £25. In line with wider market trends, this same research established that 31% of customers visiting the Centre did not make any purchases while there.

Thus, as 81% of customers originated within 26 minutes' drive-time, it was clearly evident that the Overgate customer profile was the core catchment area, who were high-frequency visitors with low or no spend occurring while they were in the Centre.

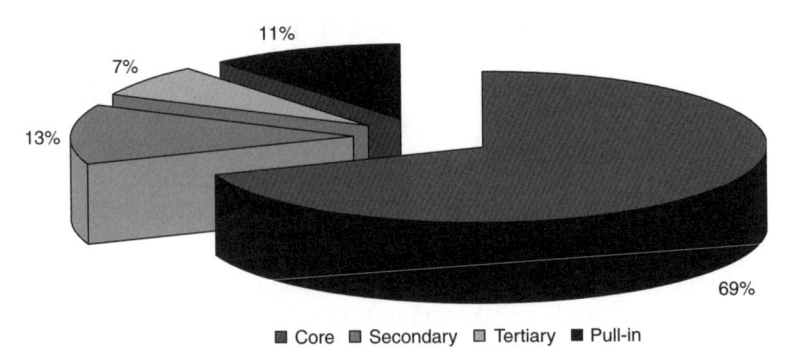

Figure 1: *Increased secondary, tertiary and 'pull-in' catchments achieved after the promotional activity*

OUR CHALLENGE

This represented a great deal of untapped potential. We were reaching footfall capacity for the Centre of 12.3 million guests but individual customer spend levels were falling far short of Overgate's targets. In short, sales were stagnating, with many visitors not spending at all. To address this, we set the following business objectives:

- increase spend per head within the existing core catchment customer base by 20%, from £25 to £30
- increase the frequency of secondary and tertiary catchment visitors; as higher-value shoppers than the core catchment, this group represented a huge revenue opportunity; we set annual targets for 2003 to increase secondary customers by 2%, tertiary customers by 2% and 'pull-in' customers by 2%
- increase overall sales of the total retail offering by 10%, during and as a result of any promotional activity.

Clearly we needed some kind of promotion to kick-start this activity, but it had to sit comfortably alongside the existing brand campaign for Overgate, which we had evolved at the Centre's launch.

'YOU'LL FIND A REASON'

The brand positioning for Overgate was evolved from an understanding of its core audience – broadly speaking, women.

Perhaps the most significant trend affecting our marketplace at the time was the increasing number of working women. More working women, with flexible working hours, means more women with money to spend on themselves, their families and homes. Such shopping tends to be a leisurely experience: they browse. With our variable climate, the shopping centre is an ideal location.

Having established this, our brand proposition was born from a core human truth: women love to shop. Thus we evolved our campaign strap-line: 'You'll find a reason'. The brand campaign was formed from a series of statements giving ever more ridiculous reasons why our audience needed to go to Overgate. A visual of a pair of red stiletto-heeled shoes sat alongside the headline 'Now I can change light bulbs', and so forth.

The campaign was flexible enough to work at both a brand and a tactical level. And initial research suggested that our audience loved it.[1] The female audience were able to laugh at themselves and the male audience felt as if they were in on the joke. We had to be sure that our promotion would not sit out of kilter with this positioning.

OUR MARKETING OBJECTIVES

Any promotional activity that we undertook had to excite the target audience, generate a desire to visit and ultimately encourage them to spend more than they had originally anticipated. We also set out to create sufficient 'word of mouth' to make Overgate the most talked-about shopping destination in the local area. We would thereby continue to build the Overgate brand.

Overgate allocated £40,000 of its marketing budget to support the initiative during the spring 2003 period and this had to include any prize elements. This represented 10% of the overall annual marketing budget.

'JUST ANOTHER CAR'

Many tactical promotions are overused and can be seen to devalue a brand, erode margins and diminish brand loyalty. So it was important that our offering was perceived as high value in order to maintain the brand's premium image.

What could entice the secondary and tertiary visitors to Overgate more regularly? And could the same tool be used to encourage loyal core catchment visitors to spend more?

Through a considered process of options, the winning answer came in the form of a three-week tactical competition. To appeal to our mainly female audience, Overgate gave customers the opportunity to win a stylish Hyundai Coupé, one of the UK's most aspirational and chic female sports car models at that time (see Figure 2).

To meet our business targets, a £30 or more spend per head was specified as the entry requirement for the prize draw. Customers were entitled to enter the draw as often as they liked, to encourage repeat visits. We hoped that this would ultimately lead to Overgate becoming a 'habitual' choice over the longer term.

Giving away a car in a prize draw is arguably nothing innovative or unique, so our challenge was to present the promotion in a differentiating way that would make Overgate stand out from its competitors.

CREATING A TALKING-POINT

Returning to our core human truth – that women love shopping – we decided to create a visual reminder of this. So we built a giant carrier bag in the heart of the

---

1. Source: GSR October 2002, Croft Marketing.

Figure 2: *A competition to win a stylish Hyundai was part of the Overgate promotional campaign*

shopping centre, in which the car was displayed. At 22 feet high and 16 feet wide, this oversized bag was designed to create a focal point within the mall and a 'talked-about' event externally. It did both. In bagfuls.

This focal point was further supported by an above-the-line creative campaign. As promotions are all too often deemed to devalue a brand in the retail sector it was important that the tone of all communications surrounding the promotion was consistent with both the premium values of the core Overgate brand and the advertising proposition of 'You'll find a reason'.

THE MEDIA STRATEGY

At the heart of the media strategy was a requirement for the advertising message to be intrusive and to reach the outlying catchment areas. We abandoned the traditional retail advertising medium of local press and chose high-impact vehicles to grab attention and maximise response. Outdoor advertising in the form of four-sheet posters and 'special build' advans were supported by a tactical radio campaign. A targeted door-to-door leaflet campaign took the consistent message into people's homes.

The competition ran for a three-week period from 24 May to 15 June 2003.

THE RESULTS

- Average spend per head increased by 42% over the three-week promotional period, from £25 to £35.53. This represents an increase of 22% over and above the original target of 20%, which was set by achievements in similar previous campaigns.
- Overall Centre sales during the period were £5.4 million, giving a 13% increase in additional sales against the same period during 2002 (£4.8 million). This represents a 3% increase beyond the original target of 10%.

- Footfall increased by 16.5% over the promotional period, based on comparable footfall of 690,859 visitors in 2002 and 805,016 visitors during the same period in 2003. Although an increase in footfall was not identified as a key objective at the outset of the promotion, the marked increase in visits was accompanied by an increase in spend per head so contributed to the overall targets.
- Previous tactical promotions linked to spend had attracted, on average, 1200 entries over a three-week period. To make a meaningful contribution to overall Centre sales and profitability the activity had to achieve in excess of this number. A total of 5498 entries were received to win the car – an increase of 458%.
- Catchment area visits increased from 12% to 13% in secondary and from 6% to 7% in tertiary areas. Pull-in visitors increased from 1% to 13% during the period of activity. Although this represented a 1% increase in secondary and tertiary areas, it achieved 50% of our annual target in just three weeks.
- Sales generated as a direct result of the promotion were £168,770 (from entry receipts), with £50,099 of additional sales revenue generated over the £25 average spend per head. The total investment in this campaign was £40,000, including all media, production, promotional staff and prizes.

WERE THESE RESULTS ALL DOWN TO OUR PROMOTION?

Other factors that may have influenced the market have been investigated and eliminated. No new retailer opened in Overgate during the promotion that could have attracted new or lapsed visitors. There were no price promotions or seasonal discounts on offer from individual retailers. No additional brand activity was running and there were no key events taking place in Dundee to attract customers that might not normally visit the area. Competitor advertising and promotional activity was maintained at a normal frequency throughout the period. Attributing the above results to our promotion therefore seems like a fairly safe bet.

'A RUN-OF-THE-MILL PROMOTION'

'A run-of-the-mill promotion, yet executed fabulously, the big carrier bag was a major talking point that caused great excitement in the Centre. We noticed an increase in visitors coming from surrounding areas, including Perth, St Andrews and Aberdeen.'

Store Manager, Debenhams (Anchor Tenant)

A total of 5498 people found a reason to enter our promotion for Overgate – the highest number of entries to a promotion Overgate had ever experienced. The promotion struck a chord with our target audience – a clear demonstration of its effect on the uplift in footfall, sales and spend, and confirmation that customer insight can lift an ordinary sales promotion out of the ordinary and into one of excellence.

BRONZE

15

s1jobs.com
Leading from the front

Principal authors: Mark Reid, The Union, and Ewan Colville, s1.com
Collaborating author: Beverley Hart, The Union
Media agency: MediaCom

EDITOR'S SUMMARY

This clear and well-written story of sustained momentum continues the s1jobs.com case from 2002. Leadership status is a powerful competitive advantage for an online recruitment site, but keeping a brand leader ahead of the pack still requires constant fresh thinking and The Union's smart through-the-line work in this case maintained s1jobs.com's dominance. A stronger demonstration of cause and effect between the advertising activity and the brand's strong growth, accounting for other variables, would have made the paper even stronger.

THE CHALLENGE

At the start of 2004, s1jobs.com occupied the enviable position of Scotland's number-one recruitment site. However, it also recognised that, over the next 12 months, it would face unprecedented competition from global, local and niche job boards – all upping their game and with the objective of knocking s1jobs.com off its pedestal.

The continued growth of online recruitment through 2003–04 was as much a problem as an opportunity. An abundance of new and relatively poorly informed customers represented a 'land grab' opportunity for all those purporting expertise in online recruitment. Misinformation was rife.

The massing of diverse customer groups created clearly segmented channels – dictating the need for better-targeted communications. Furthermore, s1jobs.com was tasked with the challenging target of delivering 25% growth on 2003 revenues.

The specific marketing challenges were as follows.

- Maintain first-choice status among Scotland's job-seekers through memorable brand advertising and by communicating meaningful product benefits.
- 'Checkmate' misinformation with incontestable proof of s1jobs.com's number-one status.
- Segment customer channels across the full spectrum of employers and develop channel marketing strategies to support and augment the sales resource.
- Extend the brand proposition into key niche sectors.

S1JOBS.COM: A BRIEF HISTORY

s1jobs.com is published by s1now, the Scottish internet division of Newsquest (Herald & Times) Ltd. Launched in January 2001, s1jobs.com quickly overtook then market leader monster.co.uk as Scotland's most heavily trafficked job site, and over the following two years not only strengthened its number-one position but also helped grow the online recruitment sector in Scotland. In 2003 the sector in Scotland was estimated to be worth £5 million.[1]

By October 2003, s1jobs.com was attracting 137,000 unique users every month, publishing double the number of Scottish jobs than any other media source and had been named Best Regional Job Site in the 2003 National Online Recruitment Awards.[2]

S1JOBS.COM: THE POWER OF THE BRAND

Much of the initial success of s1jobs.com was down to an incredibly powerful launch advertising campaign. However, sustaining a constantly strong branded presence is critical to success in the online recruitment sector. The dynamics of the

---

1. Source: Advertising Association Survey, April 2004, estimating UK-wide online recruitment ad revenue in 2003 at £51.39 million.
2. Source: ABC Electronic Audit.

sector encourage promiscuous consumer behaviour. Access to job boards is free and, with the click of a mouse, job-seekers can switch sites. It's that easy.

Without brand saliency, job-seekers use search engines for information – and the vagaries of searching can be unpredictable. With individuals in job-seeking mode for only a short period, the audience effectively churns every six months. Furthermore, job-seekers are confronted with an overwhelming range of vacancy information sources: press, radio, outdoor and even television advertising.

In this environment it is the battle for share of mind that dictates who is most successful in the online jobs market.

IT'S A WAR ZONE OUT THERE

The challenge of winning this battle for share of mind was complicated by the fact that there was an increasing amount of competitor activity, as outlined in the lists below.

Direct job boards

- Trinity Mirror launched scotcareers.co.uk in early January 2004, supported by a large media spend.
- Local rival scottishjobs.com committed to a £1 million investment in marketing.
- Global job board monster.com was preparing a fresh assault on Scotland, with a new sales team plus brand advertising.
- Scotsman Publications was relaunching its online recruitment offering.
- Specialist job boards were trying to dominate their niche sectors, and competed directly with generalist job sites like s1jobs.com.

Traditional media

- Newspaper brands aggressively defended their substantial share of recruitment advertising spend.
- Local radio was promoting recruitment advertising packages.

Middlemen

- Recruitment 'middlemen' with a vested interest in press advertising – namely commission – actively discouraged their clients (HR professionals) from spending online where rates were much cheaper.

Other factors that complicated the challenge for advertising in 2004 were as follows.

- The requirement to refresh s1jobs.com's 'In The Wrong Job' TV campaign. While hugely successful in launching the brand, the executions were three years old and at risk of wearing out.
- The appearance of new, heavy-spending online job sites meant that s1jobs.com's share of voice was declining.

- As market leader, s1jobs.com had sustained and justified a premium rate card. But while s1jobs.com ushered in 2004 with a rate card hike, its competitors were blitzing the market with free advertising trials and discounted rates.
- As the online recruitment market matured, the strategic role of advertising needed to evolve to reflect some of the new dynamics at play in the market.

MAKING THE MOST OF ADVERTISING

Retaining and strengthening its number-one market position was, and remains, s1jobs.com's primary business focus. To achieve this, and to counter the wide array of threats, the following advertising strategies and tactics were deployed.

Consumer advertising

TV
Television remains a key medium for s1jobs.com. Brand prominence, as highlighted before, is crucial to online recruitment brands. Television remains the best medium at generating awareness, but the challenge for the advertising had also moved on.

The previous brand claim, 'Scotland's no. 1 recruitment site', was underpinned with a more rational and meaningful consumer benefit: 'More Scottish jobs than anywhere else'. That s1jobs.com had more Scottish jobs than anywhere else was incontestable and to job-seekers the message was clear: if you're looking for a job in Scotland, look no further than s1jobs.com.

This strategic shift also had the advantage of communicating a very potent message to the other key audience for s1jobs.com: employers seeking employees. The communication of 'more jobs' very much gave them permission to use s1jobs.com in so far as it positioned s1jobs.com as the best way to attract the greatest number of relevant eyeballs.

Two new 30-second TV treatments were developed – 'Wrestling' and 'Nursery' – as a continuation of the 'In The Wrong Job' campaign. Memorable and engaging, they most certainly were ('Nursery' was voted 'Best TV Commercial over 30 seconds' at the 2004 Scottish Advertising Awards), and as a call to action they showed instant results.

Press
While television remained the primary driver of awareness, press could be used to further establish real reasons to believe that s1jobs.com had 'More Scottish jobs than anywhere else'.

To this end a new style of testimonial-driven advertising was introduced: 'Real People: Real Jobs'. These executions featured real people who had found their new position through s1jobs.com alongside the HR manager who recruited them via s1jobs.com. The ads could therefore reflect an employee or employer perspective.

A range of 'Real People' treatments targeted the consumer and business pages of national dailies (see Figures 1 and 2). These ads reflected a more serious side to s1jobs.com and provided believable and rational reasons to use the site; complementing the brand recall created by the 'In The Wrong Job' TV campaign.

Found the right job?

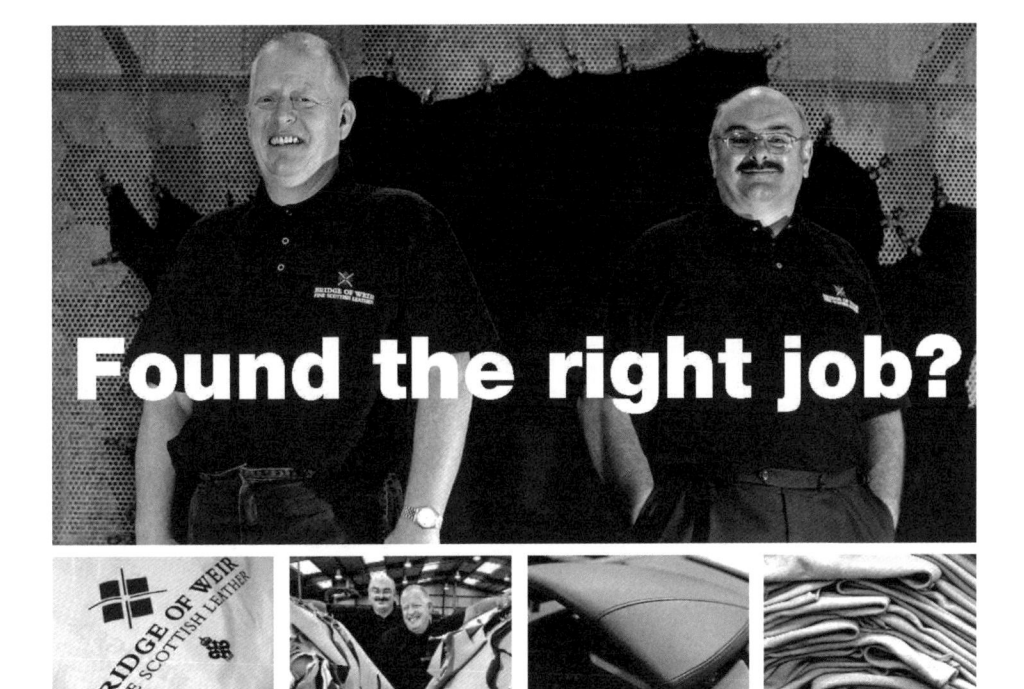

Ian Reid (that's him on the left) did.

Thanks to s1jobs.com, he's now a Mechanical Fitter with Bridge of Weir Leather, one of Europe's leading leather specialists. Considering he was looking for a specialised job in his local area, that's quite a result.

s1jobs found Ian an opportunity he wasn't expecting.
"I've worked in the local area most of my life and with the general decline of engineering I thought that picking up another job was going to be a real uphill struggle."

"But, a quick search on s1jobs showed me what was available locally. Then I applied straight from the site, secured an interview and was lucky enough to be offered the position. I'm totally chuffed," said Ian, pictured above with Bridge of Weir Leather HR Manager Peter Mackay.

But it wasn't just the job that Ian found perfect. "Now, with work just a few miles from home, I get a few minutes extra shut-eye every morning."

s1jobs got me the perfect job in the right location - could anyone ask for more than that?"

s1jobs.com
Scotland's no.1 recruitment site

Figure 1: *'Real Jobs' – press ad and mailer*

Online
The campaign very naturally extended into online media with a number of viral emails helping to keep the profile of s1jobs.com high in an extremely relevant environment (see Figure 3). By definition, those people willing to use online recruitment sites are most susceptible to online marketing.

Outdoor
A contra-deal with ScotRail enabled s1jobs.com to target the New Year back-to-work occasion – when individuals are more highly disposed to messages about changing jobs. Commuters on the Glasgow/Edinburgh shuttle found s1jobs.com

Figure 2: 'Real Jobs' – press ad and mailer

flyers in their 'seat reserved' slots. Again this was felt to be a very suitable environment to communicate the benefits of s1jobs.com.

Trade activity

Clearly, attracting prospective employees is a hugely important part of the advertising challenge for s1jobs.com. Of increasing importance, however, is to ensure that those employers looking for employees regard s1jobs.com as the online recruitment website they have to use (see Figures 4–8).

s1jobs.com

Figure 3: *'Berti' tactical viral*

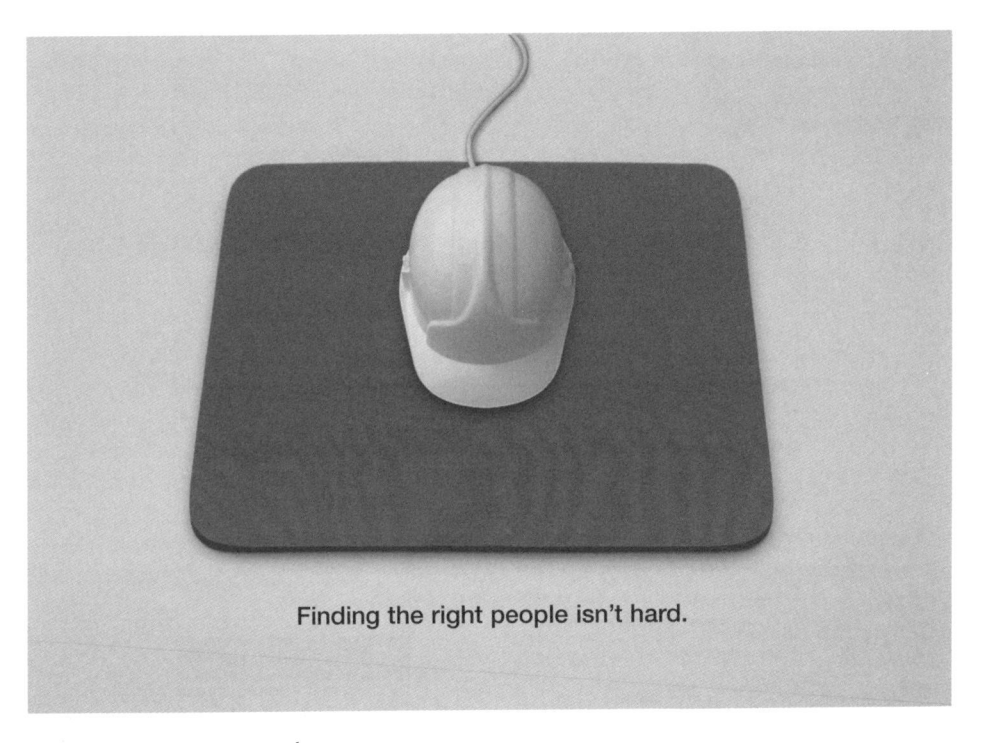

Finding the right people isn't hard.

Figure 4: *Construction sector mailer*

BLOODY NORAS!

NORAS Winter 2004 confirmed that s1jobs reaches 106% more job seekers in Scotland than any other job site.

Contact frank.skivington@s1now.com or call 0141 302 7507.

s1jobs.com
Scotland's no.1 recruitment site

Figure 5: *Trade ad targeting HR decision makers*

s1jobs.com reaches 10 times more Scottish job seekers than Monster.

How can we be so sure? Because our traffic claims are independently audited and verified by ABCe. Monster's Scottish traffic figure is around one tenth the size of ours, even though it's audited by, well, Monster. s1jobs is in fact the 9th biggest recruitment site in the UK (yet it only operates in Scotland). What's more, we offer unrivalled value for money. Unlimited listings for a full year on s1jobs (that's 365 days) costs less than the price of a single mono page recruitment ad in The Scotsman (that's 1 day).

So if you want to reach more job seekers in Scotland, reach for the phone.
Call Frank Skivington on 0141 302 7507. Or email frank.skivington@s1now.com

s1jobs.com
Scotland's no.1 recruitment site

Figure 6: *Direct mail targeting all s1jobs.com customers, prospects and canvassed Monster advertisers*

Figure 7: *Trade ad targeting marketing sector employers*

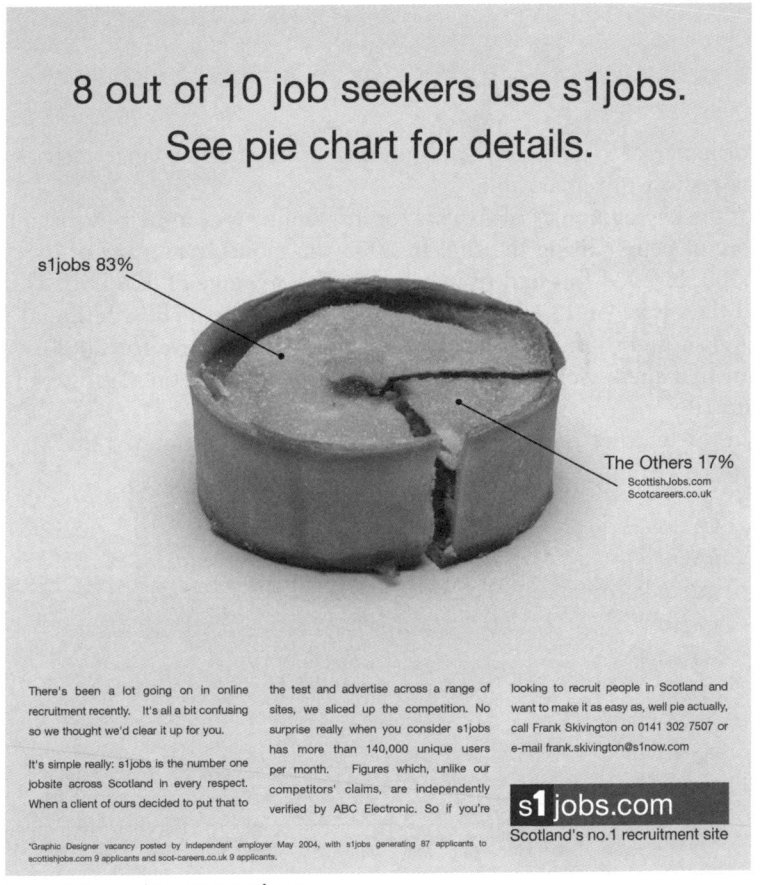

Figure 8: *Press ad targeting employers*

Hence a multimedia campaign targeting employers with messages regarding the scale of s1jobs.com was developed. Much of this activity was undertaken to emphasise the credentials of s1jobs.com. It is the only Scottish-based job board to allow itself to be audited so thoroughly and this strand of activity legitimised s1jobs.com's position as Scotland's number one.

This in turn helps create the virtuous circle that allows online recruitment operations to thrive (see Figure 9).

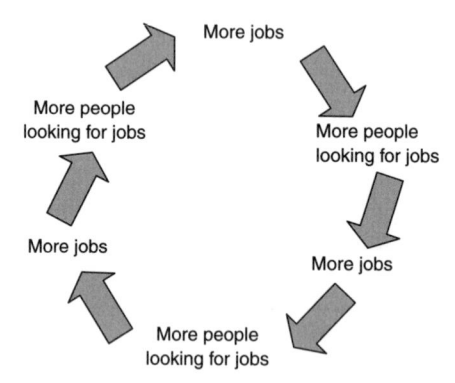

Figure 9: *Online recruitment sector virtuous circle*

RESULTS

The performance of s1jobs.com on a number of key performance metrics in 2004 was nothing short of remarkable.

One of the key dynamics of success for any online recruitment website is simply the number of people using the site. In 2003 the monthly average of user sessions was 218,000. In 2004 this had risen to a monthly average of 336,000. This greatly surpassed the target of 230,000 that s1jobs.com had set. The additional 118,000 user sessions a month on average represents a 54% increase for 2004 over 2003, and meant that there were over four million user sessions on s1jobs.com in 2004 (see Figure 10).

Growth of internet users over the period had been estimated at 7% – clearly s1jobs.com had dramatically outperformed the sector.

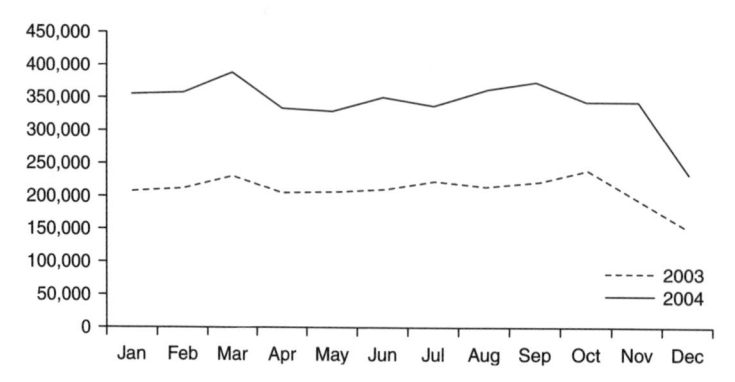

Figure 10: *s1jobs.com user sessions 2003 vs 2004*

s1jobs.com

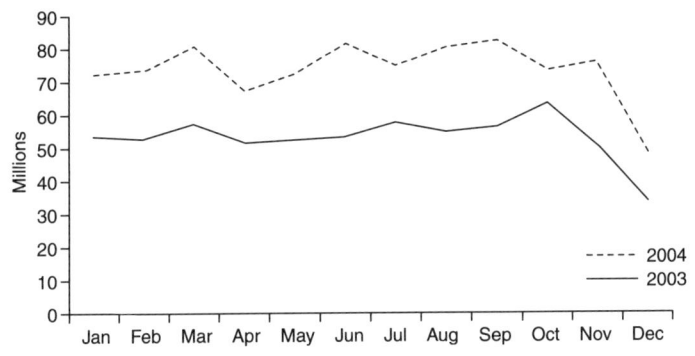

Figure 11: *s1jobs.com page impressions 2003 vs 2004*

All this meant that there were around 88 million pages viewed on the s1jobs.com site in 2004. This was compared to 63 million in 2003 (see Figure 11).

Over the course of 2004, s1jobs.com attracted an average of 186,223 unique users each month. This is at least double that of the two main competitors (Scotcareers and Scottish jobs) combined (see Figure 12). The number of unique users increased by 36% from 2003.[3]

On average, on each day of 2004 there were 10,000 unique users who visited the s1jobs.com site. With greater traffic to the site it is logical to see an increase in applications from those people visiting s1jobs.com. And this is indeed the case, with the site generating over 850,000 applications to vacancies advertising on s1jobs.com. This equates to 2500 applications from those visiting the site every day (see Figure 13). Again, these figures were both well ahead of 2003 (45%) and much better than s1jobs.com's own targets.

As highlighted elsewhere in this paper, momentum is crucial to the success of any online recruitment website. A crucial part of creating momentum is to attract more employers with jobs available to use the site.

In 2003 the number of clients using s1jobs.com to market their vacancies was 171. In 2004 this figure had grown to 259. This represents an increase of 51% in the number of employers using the site (see Figure 14).

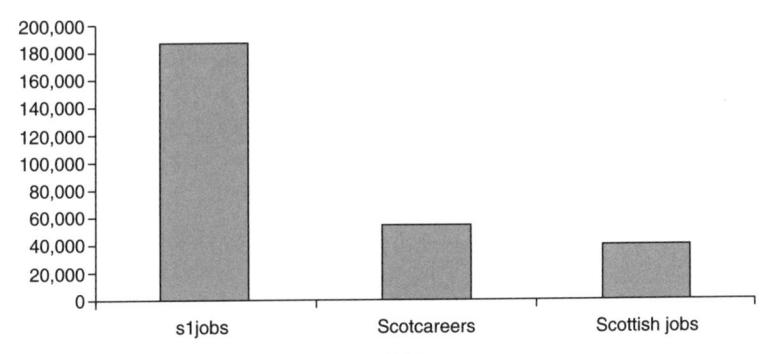

Figure 12: *s1jobs.com Unique Users 2003 vs 2004*

---

3. Source: NORAS/competitor data.

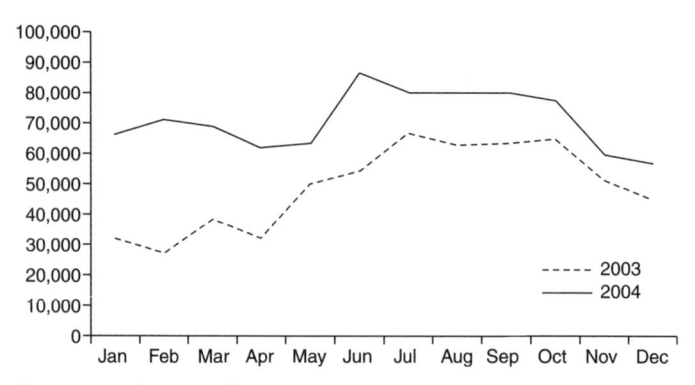

Figure 13: *s1jobs.com applications to recruiters 2003 vs 2004*

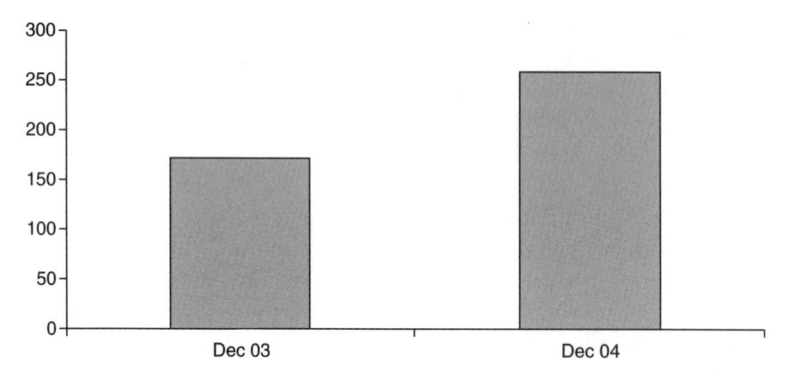

Figure 14: *s1jobs.com recruiters on site 2003 vs 2004*

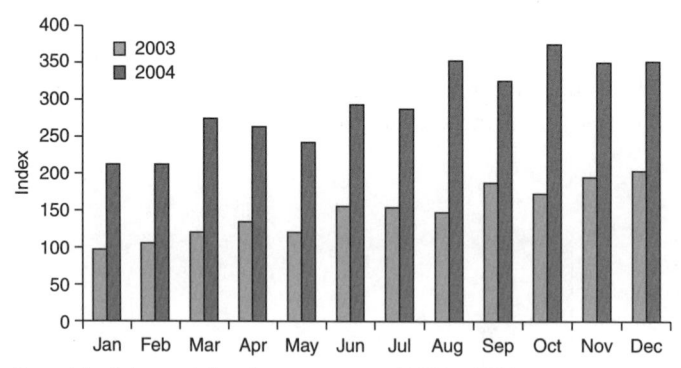

Figure 15: *s1jobs.com index of revenue generated 2003 vs 2004*

The upshot of this was that the revenue generated by s1jobs.com grew by an impressive 97%. This widely surpassed the projected 15% growth in revenues. Revenue in December 2004 was 3.5 times greater than it had been in January 2003 (see Figure 15).

s1jobs.com

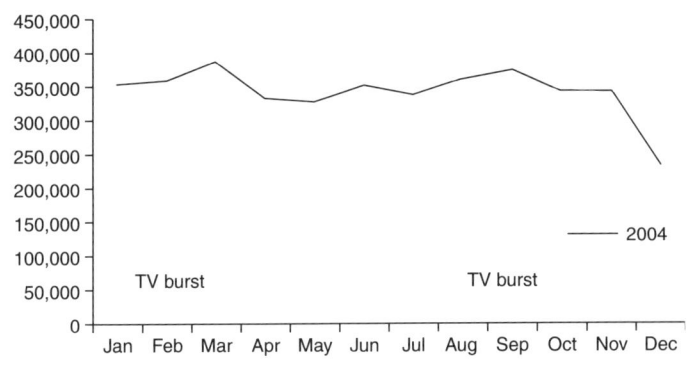

Figure 16: *s1jobs.com responsiveness to advertising*

THANKS TO THE ADVERTISING

Levels of traffic to s1jobs.com are remarkably responsive to advertising activity. The graph in Figure 16 shows how traffic peaks on the site coincide with television advertising bursts.

This again demonstrates the powerful contribution advertising has made in helping to make s1jobs.com a success.

In addition to this, data from the National Online Recruitment Audience Survey (NORAS) emphasises the potency of s1jobs.com's advertising. NORAS is the biggest independent survey of online job-seekers: it surveys 18,000 respondents. This survey highlighted the strength of s1jobs.com's brand and marketing.

According to NORAS, s1jobs.com has:

- 141% more Scottish job-seekers than any other website
- 74% of users from ABC1 social class
- 50% who are degree educated
- 20% who say they were first attracted to s1jobs.com as a result of advertising.

CONCLUSION

The online world is littered with dotcoms whose demise has been hastened by some less than effective advertising.

Since its launch, s1jobs.com has come to depend on powerful, persuasive advertising to help establish itself as the most successful recruitment website in Scotland.

Through innovative evolution of the advertising strategy and use of media, s1jobs.com cemented its position as Scotland's number one recruitment site throughout 2004. This was despite a competitive environment that was becoming increasingly brutal.

All the key metrics influencing the business improved as s1jobs.com evolved its advertising strategy to reflect the changing dynamics of the market.

Despite increased competition in 2004, s1jobs.com in 2004 attracted more job-seekers to the site more often. So it's no surprise that s1jobs.com generated almost twice as much revenue in 2004 as it did in 2003.

BRONZE
BEST NEW AUTHOR

16

Scotch Beef
Raised the way you want it

Principal author: Giles Moffatt, The Union
Collaborating authors: Andrew Ovens and Suzie Carlaw, Quality Meat Scotland
Media agency: MediaCom

EDITOR'S SUMMARY

A credible and straightforward story of effective planning and creative development, with the 'Glen' character on TV and in-store contributing a solid set of results for Scotch Beef. The judges' view was that some more detailed analysis of advertising's specific contribution to the recovery in Scotch Beef sales and of ROI was needed for this paper to receive a higher award but, in Glen, The Union undoubtedly created a popular spokesman for the brand, who worked effectively through the line.

SCOTTISH ADVERTISING WORKS 4

INTRODUCTION

Quality Meat Scotland (QMS) is responsible for marketing the Scottish red meat industry on behalf of farmers and producers.

It is impossible to overestimate the importance of the Scotch Beef industry, not just to Scottish farmers and the economy, but also to perceptions of Scotland as a high-quality environment producing high-quality exports.

In the past, advertising for Scotch Beef has been sporadic, with no consistent long-term strategy. The Union's remit was to devise and develop a brand advertising solution that would deliver immediate results, but also offer a long-term vehicle for promoting Scotch Beef in any chosen medium.

In 2001, the foot-and-mouth disease crisis loomed large over the beef industry. The media was rife with images of burning pyres and despairing farmers. The epidemic reached the north of England, but thankfully did not make it into Scotland. All the same, the crisis followed a number of years of bad press for red meat, and other meat types had become increasingly popular. BSE had been extremely destructive – who can forget the sight of empty Angus Steakhouses all over London in the mid-1990s?

Perversely, if handled correctly, the crisis provided an opportunity for, in particular, Scotch Beef – the product is high quality, can be rigorously traced and is produced under stringent quality controls. Foot-and-mouth had also been kept at bay.

With this in mind, QMS appointed The Union, with a brief to create a big idea that would deliver:

- a marked increase in awareness of the Scotch Beef brand
- a famous and durable advertising property
- rapid increases in all key brand health measures as measured by Millward Brown, designed to counter any lack of confidence about beef in general, and position Scotch Beef as the best available
- work later, in key markets such as the south-east of England.

The campaign ran across 2002, 2003 and 2004. This paper aims to demonstrate how the advertising that resulted not only exceeded all expectations, but gave QMS one of the most recognised and popular brand icons in Scotland of recent times.

This paper also aims to demonstrate the benefits of applying 'big agency processes' and proper advertising development tools, even when dealing with a tactical issue, a limited budget and a small-scale client organisation. Since 2001, QMS has introduced strict qualitative and quantitative planning and measurement tools. We believe that this professional approach made the advertising development possible. In the face of foot-and-mouth, it would have been easy to panic. Instead, the response was strategic, measured and highly successful.

BACKGROUND TO THE CHALLENGE

Scotch Beef is one of the iconic products of our country. It has a worldwide reputation for quality and taste. In recent years, fierce competition between retailers has become the prevailing dynamic, and with it there has been an influx of cheaper foreign imports from countries like Ireland and Argentina.

SCOTCH BEEF

The foot-and-mouth crisis of 2001 sparked the realisation that there was an immediate need to create a powerful consumer campaign designed to underpin the brand's quality credentials. The fallout from the crisis effectively created a hiatus, or breathing space, and we took the opportunity to investigate the best way to get beef back on the agenda.

In Scotland, the key marketing challenge for Scotch Beef is to retain its market position by giving consumers a reason to believe it is the finest beef available. The price point for Scotch Beef is higher than the competition, and a key role for communication is to justify this premium by reinforcing quality cues.

The marketing challenge is not exclusively a consumer one either. There is an ongoing task to keep the retailers on side and add value within their channel. There is also a need to excite the producers in the industry, as it is they who are effectively funding the activity.

This paper will demonstrate how we created a compelling consumer campaign that placed Scotch Beef back at the top of people's shopping lists. It will also demonstrate how the advertising idea was adapted to provide an extremely powerful sales promotion tool for the retailers involved. Finally, it's worth pointing out that the advertising is the longest-running campaign QMS has ever done. This means the farmers (who fund it) are, more than ever, behind it.

THE BUSINESS STRATEGY

QMS is a public-sector organisation. It receives funding from the Scottish Executive and the EU, and levies raised from subscribing farms. In return for the levies, the farming community gets accreditation and quality assurance certification. More significantly, it gets a centralised marketing resource whose mission is to promote Scotch Beef-branded beef throughout the UK and beyond.

The QMS mission is to 'work with the Scottish red meat industry to improve its efficiency and profitability, and to maximise its contribution to Scotland's economy'.

The business objectives for Scotch Beef are to:

- maximise profitability for the industry
- maximise the value of the Scotch Beef brand
- promote the Scotch Beef brand to consumers
- sustain a price premium for the brand through marketing activity.

The role for advertising covers the last two points.

THE STRATEGIC SOLUTION

QMS commissioned insight groups (qualitative) early in 2001. This study was designed to probe attitudes towards Scotch Beef, and identify any potential threats and opportunities. It aimed also to understand the effects of the foot-and-mouth crisis on the nation's state of mind. The one key objective of the research was to try to establish exactly what it was about Scotch Beef that would position it in the consumer's mind as a high-quality product worth paying a premium for. The aim was to get beef back on the map and to make sure Scotch Beef was at the top of the list.

Research very quickly identified that:

- although confidence in beef per se was at an all-time low, it was recognised that Scotch Beef had strong quality associations
- the Scottish provenance of the brand was a key strength as Scotland as a country is one of space, ruggedness, greenery and health.

Though clearly aware of the foot-and-mouth situation, consumers did not want to see it overtly referenced in any kind of brand activity. They actually took a sense of pride in the product, as they do with other national products like whisky and salmon (how things can change ...). The name of the game was to sing the brand's praises in the advertising – to reinforce positive perceptions and rally consumer confidence. A decision was made to deal with the foot-and-mouth issue separately with public relations activity and straight-talking information-only press.

The insight for the brand campaign we arrived at was effectively as follows:

'Scotch Beef is so good because it takes on all the qualities of the land in which it is raised. Scotland is the UK's biggest area of natural beauty with wide, unpolluted open space. In other words, the phrase "you are what you eat" also applies to the livestock. Its natural diet and open, fresh living conditions all contribute to better-quality meat and a better-quality taste. The implication being that meat from Scottish-reared animals is better than meat from other animals.'

The proposition the agency therefore worked to was: *raised the way you want it*.

A number of advertising ideas were tested in further qualitative research, and one clear winner emerged.

THE COMMUNICATION ACTIVITY

Most people in Scotland will be familiar with the advertising that resulted. In fact, the 'Glen' character (see Figure 1) is now one of the most recognised icons in Scottish advertising. On a number of occasions, tracking even demonstrated that the brand's awareness is as high as that of brands like Tennent's Lager and McDonald's.

The agency developed the Glen character as shorthand for Scotch Beef. We knew that consumers don't like associating the food on their plate with a beast in a field, and we needed a visual metaphor for Scottish cattle.

Attractive, sturdy, strong and silent, Glen embodies all the attributes of Scottish-reared livestock. On top of this we emphasised the quality of his environment and diet to reinforce his natural, healthy provenance.

The results of the next round of qualitative research were phenomenal. On a rational level, Glen symbolised all that is good about Scotch Beef. On an emotional level, his good looks and masculine appeal endeared him hugely to Scottish housewives. It became clear very quickly that here was an advertising property that would deliver against the key

Figure 1: 'Glen'

brand health measures – and capture the housewife's imagination. Subsequent quantitative and qualitative research would reveal massive levels of awareness (from only 1800 TVRs across two years) as well as huge levels of involvement with the main character. These points are elaborated upon later.

TV was chosen as the main medium, given that the job was to build trust and stature rapidly. The beauty of the Glen idea, however, was that it offered great scope for field marketing and sales promotion. Branded 'Glens' were sent into supermarkets, railway stations and shopping centres, to take the message into the retail environment in an imaginative and eye-catching way. You will see that the results of this tactical activity were almost as impressive as the advertising performance itself, with huge uplifts seen in-store.

Figure 2: Branded 'Glens' took the message into the retail environment

THE RESULTS

The primary objective was to increase sales of Scotch Beef following a fallow period when consumption was declining and the foot-and-mouth crisis presented a very real threat. The secondary objective was to rebuild and reinforce affinity for the brand.

With the launch of the new advertising going into 2002, you can see from the TNS sales data that there was the beginning of a recovery (see Figure 3).

The activity was up-weighted across 2003 and 2004, and the following main effects were seen.

- Total awareness of the Scotch Beef brand was catapulted from a long-term base of 16%, to 60% in the space of two-and-a-half years.
- Declining year-on-year volumes and value were overturned.
- Despite the increasing popularity of white meats following the foot-and-mouth crisis, Scotch Beef sales began to rise again in 2003 and 2004.

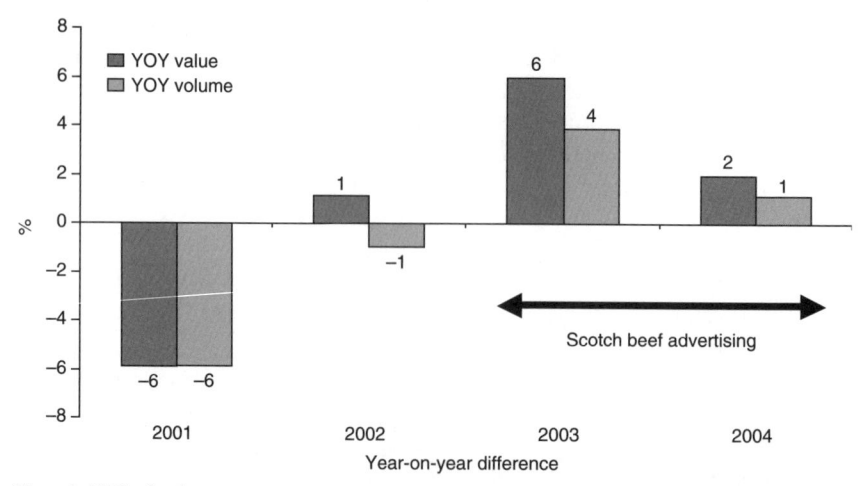

Figure 3: *TNS sales data*

Millward Brown tracking: total brand awareness

The base level awareness rose from 16 to over 60 (see Figure 4).

Consumer confidence in Scotch Beef also rallied, with the brand's key health measures scoring all-time highs as a result of the advertising:

- 'Worth paying more for' – 69% of consumers agreed (up by 7 percentage points)
- 'The best available' – 77% of consumers agreed (up by 7 points)
- 'Produced to the highest standard' – 79% of consumers agreed (up by 6 points).

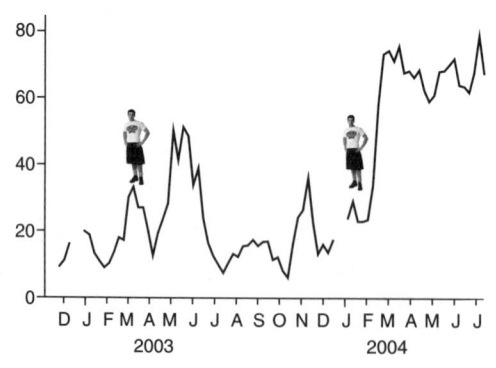

Figure 4: *Millward Brown tracking – total brand awareness*

QUANTITATIVE BRAND HEALTH MEASURES

We set up a tracking study at the outset. The Millward Brown data show a massive increase in the importance of Scottish provenance – now the main driver of brand choice. Similarly, the brand's key health measures are also at an all-time high (see Figure 5).

SCOTCH BEEF

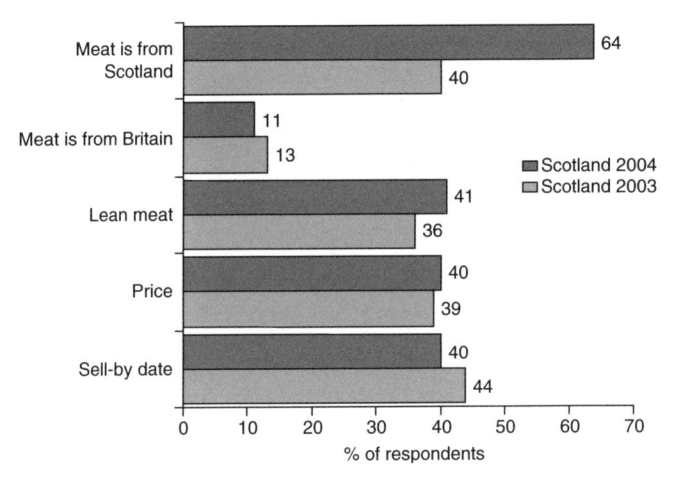

Figure 5: *Key health measures*
Source: IGD, June 2004

Bar chart showing % of respondents for Scotland 2004 vs Scotland 2003:
- Meat is from Scotland: 64 / 40
- Meat is from Britain: 11 / 13
- Lean meat: 41 / 36
- Price: 40 / 39
- Sell-by date: 40 / 44

PROMOTIONAL ACTIVITY

The strength of Glen as a brand character and promotional device was exploited below the line. There was a rolling programme of 'Glens' conducting in-store leafleting and bringing theatre to the shopping aisles. The results in stores showed some huge uplifts in sales versus test stores (see Figure 6).

Scotch Beef sales increased by 10%. Not only that, but there was a significant halo effect on other 'Scotch'-branded products.

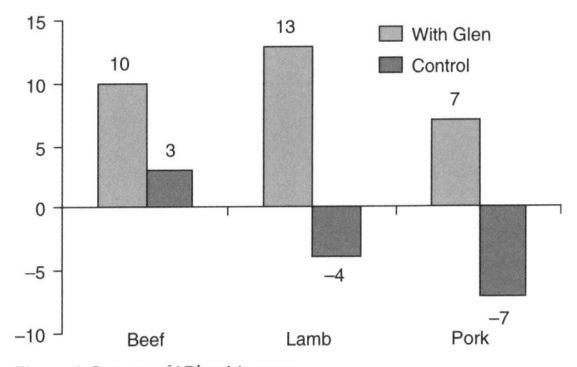

Figure 6: *Impact of 'Glens' in-store*
Source: Tesco, 2004

Bar chart (With Glen vs Control):
- Beef: 10 / 3
- Lamb: 13 / -4
- Pork: 7 / -7

PAYBACK/RETURN ON INVESTMENT

Before foot-and-mouth, the market was worth £158 million in annual sales of beef in Scotland (see Figure 7). In 2001 that plummeted to £149 million. When the campaign began in 2002, the market started to recover. In 2003, there was a leap to £160 million, followed by £164 million in 2004. With an annual spend of circa £800,000 over three years, the market saw an increase in value of £15 million.

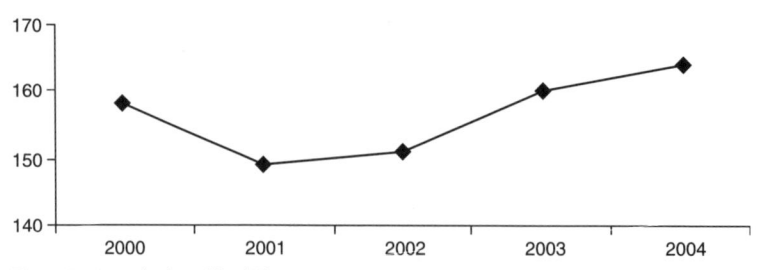

Figure 7: *Annual sales of beef (£m)*
Source: TNS

All this despite the fact that Scotch Beef's share of voice was *nothing* compared to the hundreds of millions in TV adspend from food brands that Scots were exposed to. Similarly, the increases occurred in an environment where conditions favoured other types of food. Chicken was (and still is) being given away for practically nothing in major retailers like Asda.

It's worth mentioning the 'Atkins' word at this point. It would be easy to imagine from all the hype in the media and the USA that the 'low-carb' fad in some way contributed to the recovery in consumption of red meat. This most definitely wasn't the case. A recent DEFRA[1] UK study reports only a minute increase in all meat consumption between 2000 and 2003 (less than 0.03 of a per cent). The phenomenon simply isn't mainstream. In stark contrast, overall volume sales of beef in Scotland rose by a net 7% across the same period.

CONCLUSIONS

Glen wasn't just an idea that housewives found sexy. He has become an emblem for Scotch Beef with far greater power than that. Millward Brown reported only recently that the advertising achieved an AI score of 17. Only Budweiser's 'Whassup?!' campaign to our knowledge has scored better (24).

Beef seemed to be in terminal decline before the foot-and-mouth crisis came along. It's good to see it back on the menu again.

---

1. Office of National Statistics, 2003 report on family expenditure.

BRONZE

17

ScottishPower
Energising The Energy People

Principal authors: Alan Clarke and Brian Crook, The Bridge
Media agency: Feather Brooksbank

EDITOR'S SUMMARY

ScottishPower's continuing battle with Scottish/British Gas made for another good paper from The Bridge. With an all-staff commitment to 'do more for you' and by exploiting a price advantage to the full, ScottishPower was able to re-engage with its customers to reduce churn. The reported ROI impressed the judges, although 'lifetime values' are never guaranteed unless loyalty can be assured, so the key to success will be if ScottishPower keeps its customers and delivers the promised returns.

INTRODUCTION

In 2003 The Bridge and ScottishPower entered an IPA Advertising Effectiveness paper identifying that, to ensure the future prosperity of the latter's UK customer supply business, two challenges had to be addressed:

1. losses among existing customers needed to be stopped quickly (success in this was detailed in the 2003 paper)
2. there was a need to establish a clear positioning for ScottishPower that would provide a platform on which it could build the business.

This year's paper addresses the second challenge and demonstrates how advertising played a crucial role in helping ScottishPower become one of the UK's leading energy supply companies. It played an internal role in helping align ScottishPower's various departments. And it played an external role in re-establishing ScottishPower as the key player (in its homeland) and helping ScottishPower 'own' the critical territory of value for money.

The result was that losses fell, acquisitions improved and overall customer numbers in Scotland grew by 11%, a return on the advertising investment of 1600%.

On a UK-wide basis customers have increased from four million to five million and, critically, the UK customer supply business has begun to offer the plc the kind of critical mass that it enjoys in other aspects of its portfolio.

THE CHALLENGE

The challenge ScottishPower faced in its customer supply and service business was both internal and external.

The internal challenge stemmed from the legacy of the various strategies that the company had followed over the previous five years. Brand extensions into and subsequent exits from areas such as telecoms and financial services had left a lack of internal focus. There was also a lack of certainty as to what the business stood for and where it was headed. This is particularly dangerous in a business where customer service and customer interaction is a fundamental part of the offering. The management knew that it was critical that this was addressed.

The external challenge had some similarities. Customers were unclear as to what ScottishPower's offering was. This was exacerbated by some of the market's basic characteristics. Energy supply is about as low-interest, low-involvement a sector as one can find. The basic product is fundamentally undifferentiated (it doesn't matter who supplies your gas and electricity, the same 'product' comes out of the pipe and through the wire). Research consistently reported that, provided they felt they were getting a good deal on price and continuity of supply, consumers were happy. This inertia was only overcome when someone literally knocked on consumers' doors offering them a 'cheaper' deal. In the chaotic market that had followed deregulation, acquisition success across the industry was driven by the promise of a substantially better price and the convenience of signing up on the spot, with around three-quarters of all 'switches' made face to face. Advertising (and branding for that matter) played little role.

ScottishPower had to re-engage with its audiences. Internal and external.

SCOTTISHPOWER

BECOMING 'THE ENERGY PEOPLE'

ScottishPower established a multi-departmental working party for Project Nirvana – a project that would define both the positioning of the company and the executional manifestation of that positioning. The Bridge was appointed to help facilitate the project and to execute the creative work – advertising and design.

In 2001 ScottishPower enjoyed brand values similar to the other energy suppliers who had retained their pre-deregulation brands – trust, heritage, size and respect – but the company was also considered to be cold and faceless.

Desk research provided an understanding of the essential role competitive prices and continuity of supply played. It also provided an insight into how an energy company could differentiate by delivering a more proactive, customer-focused approach.

Following a stage of exploratory field research, a range of broad positioning areas was identified. Each was investigated to see how it stacked up against ScottishPower's values and a range of customer touchpoints (see Figures 1 and 2).

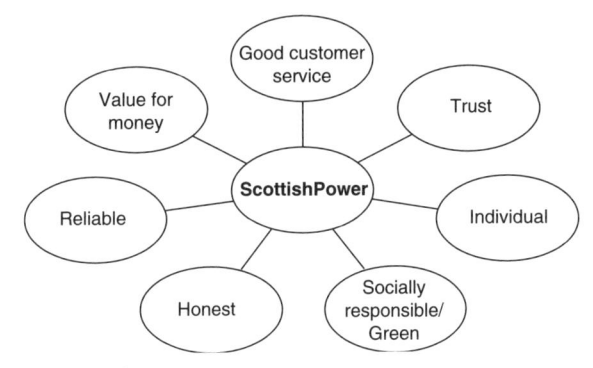

Figure 1: *Values*

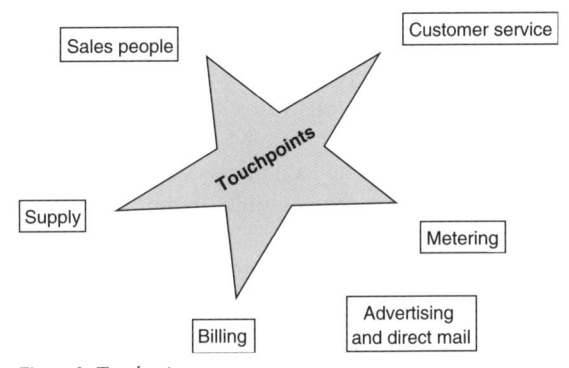

Figure 2: *Touchpoints*

A series of internal workshops was followed by more consumer and B2B research, exploring different positioning statements and what they meant in practice for how the business delivered its products and service. Further research validated a refined positioning and sanity checked it against both consumer and business customers. From that came the finalised positioning statement:

'We specialise in gas and electricity so we can do more for you and your environment.'

What was critical was the recognition that this would come to life only from the bottom up – through the different touchpoints. It had to be brought to life via demonstrating the 'more for you' in each of the touchpoint areas. And a critical one in the medium term was the area of price. Consumers needed reassurance about ScottishPower's price competitiveness. (Effectively 'doing more for you on price' could be being competitive versus the 'gold standard' in the market at the time – British Gas – or it could be in new and more imaginative payment methods, e.g. 'capped' or 'online'.) Beyond that we would eventually extend into other manifestations of 'doing more for you' that customers valued (e.g. Green products or more accurate, more user-friendly bills). A whole internal multi-departmental project looking at the implications of 'doing more for you' was implemented.

DEVELOPING THE CREATIVE

Executing a fully integrated campaign required a communications idea that could work across all communication channels, so it had to be much more than just an advertising idea – it had to be flexible enough to work across all the touchpoint areas of price, product and service. It had to be an idea where different specific propositions could still be held together with strong branding running throughout the commercial (even more important than usual in this low-interest market).

Four routes were developed and researched with consumers and business audiences. The Energy People route emerged as the strongest.

BRINGING THE CAMPAIGN TO LIFE

The communications idea uses simple, distinctive animation and illustration with a light, refreshing tone of voice to demonstrate the benefit of being a ScottishPower customer. The simplicity of the style is meant to help underline the simplicity and focus of ScottishPower's offering. The executions acknowledge that the consumer may find the whole subject dull but they emphasise that, among that dullness, there is important information (see Figure 3).

Learnings from the losses reduction campaign meant the roles for advertising, direct marketing and direct selling were well understood.

The advertising was tasked with the context-setting role of bringing the new positioning to life, building brand awareness and improving brand perceptions. It would also play an important role internally by communicating the business's new confidence and step-change in approach in the most public of environments.

Direct marketing would continue its role in delivering tightly targeted messages that sold higher-value, 'stickier' products to existing customers either through a direct response or in conjunction with direct selling.

Direct selling would continue to be the key channel for actually signing up new customers.

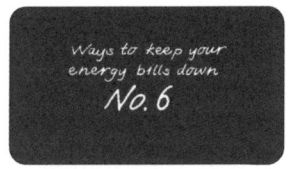

SCOTTISHPOWER

BRONZE

VO: Ways to keep your energy bills down, number 6

SFX: Parade noises growing louder

VO: Now please pay attention, because some people still seem to be missing the point

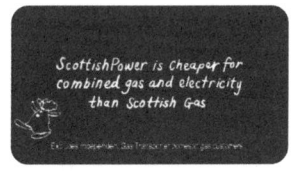

VO: For the average customer ScottishPower is cheaper for combined gas and electricity than Scottish Gas

VO: So to save money switch to us

ScottishPower
gas and electricity
0800 027 9018

The energy people

VO: Another great way to keep your energy bills down from the energy people. ScottishPower

Figure 3: *Examples of the creative work*

MEDIA

The media strategy was also driven by the learnings from the losses reduction campaign, which had validated TV's awareness-building and attitude-changing strengths in such a low-interest, low-involvement market. It also validated the strategy of making sure that whenever the advertising ran it did so at a sufficiently heavy weight. The rule of thumb established was that the effective weight for this type of message in this type of market was as high as 8 OTS.

Posters were used to up-weight certain messages locally. The media lay-down in Scotland during 2003 and 2004 involved a total spend of £1.6 million.

The advertising that ran

Consumer research during the development of The Energy People positioning reinforced the critical role competitive price (not necessarily cheapest) played in acquiring and retaining customers. Consequently, the communications plan was developed to lead with advertising demonstrating that ScottishPower offered customers a range of ways to keep their energy bills down and a core price proposition that ScottishPower was cheaper than British Gas, the biggest player in the market (and the company that was taking 75% of ScottishPower's customer losses).

WHAT HAPPENED?

Internal success

The internal success of the campaign can be observed in the revised structures within the business; in the project teams that were developed to address the different touchpoints; in the number of new (focused) products that were developed and launched; and in the business's growing confidence in the role for advertising and subsequent increase in investment. The internal success can also be witnessed in the atmosphere within customer supply and service.

External success

To be deemed a success the advertising would need to achieve the following:

- show that it was cutting through in a low-interest market
- demonstrate that it was changing perceptions – and, critically, winning the battle with British Gas
- show that it was establishing ScottishPower as a value-for-money supplier
- show that it was establishing ScottishPower as a preferred supplier.

Evidence comes from three main sources:

1. advertising tracking in the Scottish TV region
2. 'voice of the Customer', ScottishPower's principal barometer of customer satisfaction
3. internal customer numbers and lifetime value data.

SCOTTISHPOWER

The advertising successfully cut through in a low-interest, low-involvement market

Although low when compared to some fmcg brands, it is ScottishPower's relative position that matters. It has risen from 12% to 22% and ScottishPower's spontaneous advertising awareness is consistently the highest in the sector, higher than Powergen and dramatically overtaking British Gas despite British Gas having higher TV and total media spends (see Figure 4).

Prompted advertising awareness has more than doubled from 18% to 41% (see Figure 5).

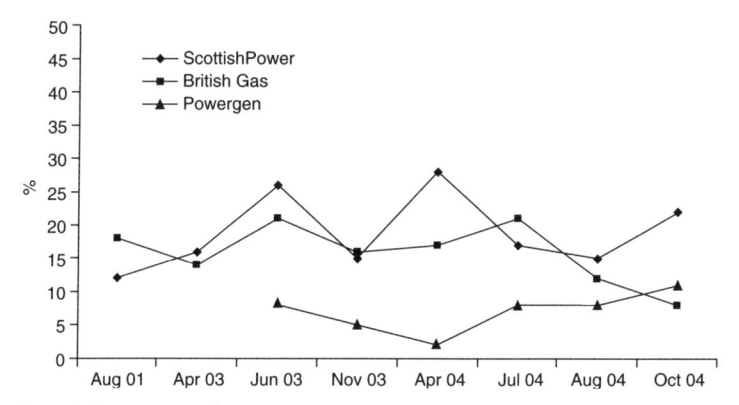

Figure 4: *Spontaneous advertising awareness*
Source: advertising tracking

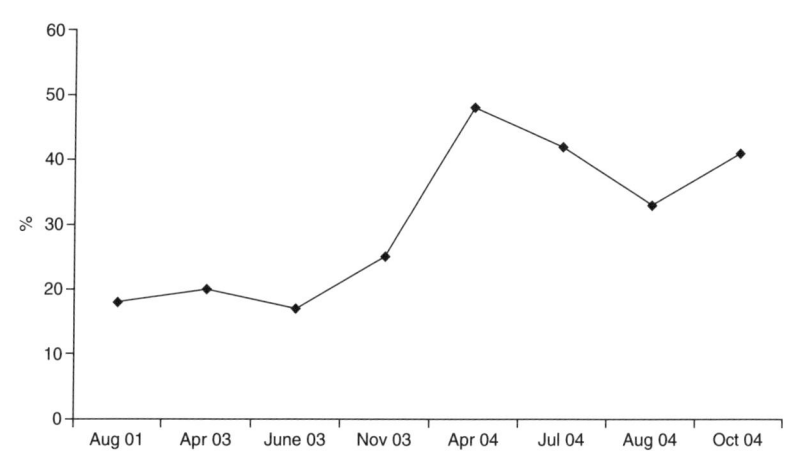

Figure 5: *ScottishPower prompted advertising awareness*
Source: advertising tracking

Not only did it cut through, it communicated the desired 'competitive prices' message ...

'Attributable recall' grew during the campaign, reaching 83%. 'Attributable recall' records very specific ad message codes such as 'ScottishPower is cheaper for gas and

215

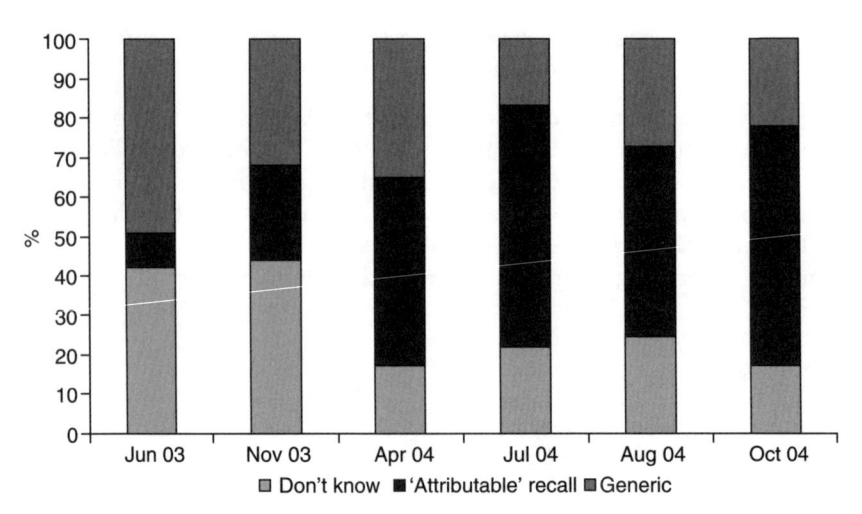

Figure 6: *Attributable recall*
Base: respondents who recalled ScottishPower advertising
Source: advertising tracking

electricity', 'cheaper than British Gas', 'keeping bills down'. Generic recall records codes such as 'cheaper' and 'switch to ScottishPower' (see Figure 6).

... which has driven forward price perceptions

'Voice of the Customer' reports ratings on five out of seven value-for-money measures improved among those aware of the advertising. All seven fell among those not aware of the advertising.

This positive movement is supported by the advertising tracking, which reports that the period of heaviest advertising coincided with peak agreement that 'ScottishPower is cheaper than British Gas for ...

- both gas and electricity'
- gas only'
- electricity only'.

Similar findings were reported for 'Offers competitive prices', 'Reassures you on competitiveness' and 'Willing to help reduce bill'.

The advertising also had a positive impact on brand perceptions ...

While brand measures on 'Voice of the Customer' go up and down over time (reflecting the broader profile of the company in the media) the difference in ratings between those aware of the advertising and those not aware of the advertising has widened on the key measures 'ScottishPower is the best supplier of gas and electricity' and 'Overall, how satisfied are you with ScottishPower?'

The advertising tracking reports every brand attitude statement improving, with peak levels again coinciding with the period of heaviest advertising.

SCOTTISHPOWER

... with The Energy People positioning becoming increasingly established among those aware of the advertising (see Figure 7)

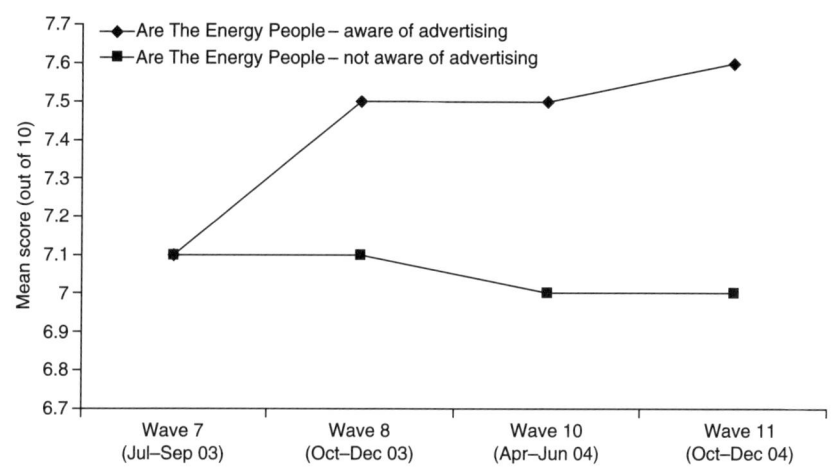

Figure 7: *'ScottishPower are The Energy People'*
Source: Voice of the Customer

The outcome was that ScottishPower has become established as the consumer's front-of-mind supplier ...

First-mention brand awareness of ScottishPower has risen from 20% to 69%, while British Gas has fallen from 53% to 26% (see Figure 8).

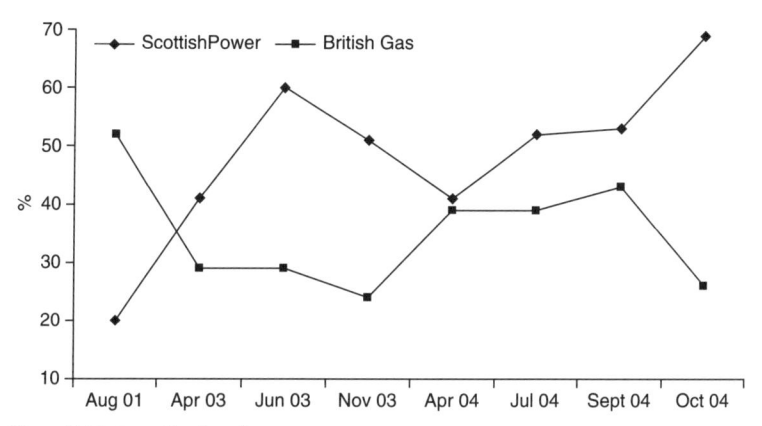

Figure 8: *First-mention brand awareness*
Source: advertising tracking

Spontaneous brand awareness has reached almost saturation point and leads British Gas (see Figure 9).

The brand is almost as high profile among non-customers (i.e. those ScottishPower could hope to recruit), spontaneous brand awareness having grown by half to reach 90% (see Figure 10).

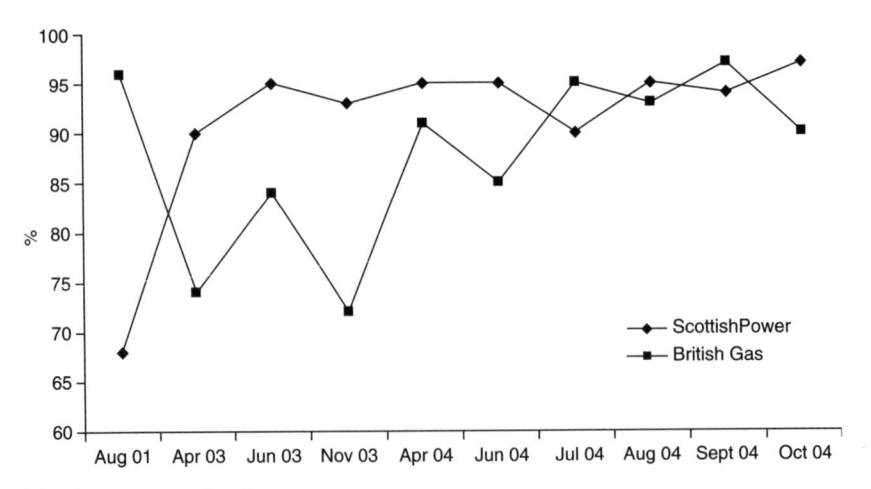

Figure 9: *Spontaneous brand awareness*
Source: advertising tracking

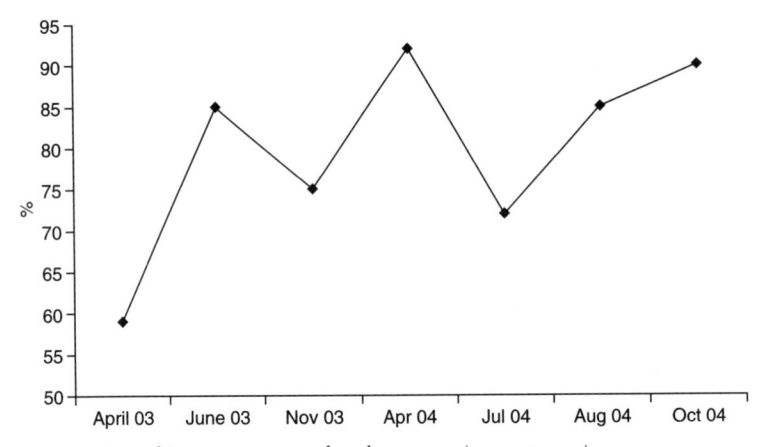

Figure 10: *ScottishPower spontaneous brand awareness (non-customers)*
Source: advertising tracking

... and as the market's preferred supplier

When asked who they would choose if they could choose only one company to supply all their energy needs, twice as many consumers picked ScottishPower than picked British Gas (see Table 1).

TABLE 1: FAVOURED ENERGY SUPPLIER, NOVEMBER 2004

	November 2004
ScottishPower	51%
British Gas	26%

Source: advertising tracking

SCOTTISHPOWER

This has resulted in a reduction in customer losses and growth in the total customer base

ScottishPower's customer number data report that the customer base has grown every month since the advertising launched to sit at an all-time high. Churn (ScottishPower's measurement of customer turnover) among core customers has fallen during the campaign.

DISCOUNTING OTHER FACTORS

It wasn't because ScottishPower's relative price position changed

ScottishPower's core products maintained their position as competitive on price but not cheapest on the market.

It wasn't because we had the advertising market to ourselves

British Gas outspent ScottishPower each year (see Figure 11).

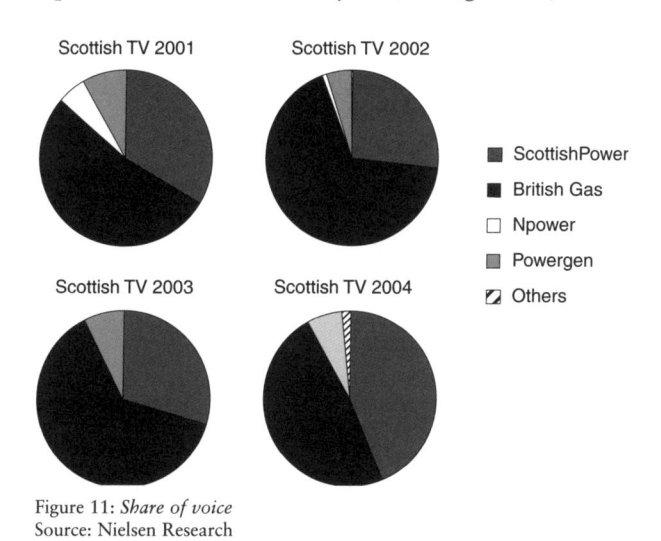

Figure 11: *Share of voice*
Source: Nielsen Research

It wasn't because of additional investment in other communications activity

ScottishPower didn't significantly increase spend in other communications channels.

MANIFOLD EFFECTS

ScottishPower is the only big winner in the customer numbers game

In a nil sum game, ScottishPower is the only major player to have significantly increased its net customer base over the last two years. British Gas has been a major net loser; all the others have held pretty steady.

The impact in Manweb

While this paper focuses on the impact in the Scottish market, the advertising also ran on Granada TV to support the ScottishPower Manweb region (ScottishPower bought the local electricity company Manweb shortly after deregulation and has taken on the role of 'legacy' supplier). The marketing environment means the advertising worked differently and it would need another paper to describe it; however, the bottom-line result has seen ScottishPower grow its customer base by more than 20,000 during the last two years, which generated an additional £5 million in lifetime value, a 223% return on the media investment.

The impact nationally

The scale considered necessary by the industry to compete effectively is five million customer accounts. When this activity was conceived, ScottishPower had just 3.5 million. The Energy People positioning strategy has driven all ScottishPower's marketing activity over the last two years, during which time it has become the UK's fastest-growing energy company, with more than one million new customers in the last 12 months. In January 2005 ScottishPower broke through the five million customer barrier.

Marketing communications resource

Recognising the success of the campaign and the important role it now has in the success of its business, the resource allocated to marketing communications within the marketing team at ScottishPower has grown from two to a team of five, headed by the newly created position of Head of Campaigns.

PAYBACK

Between May 2003 and November 2004 ScottishPower's customer base in central Scotland grew by 146,563, an increase of 11.1%. The cost of advertising (including all TV production) was £2.3 million. Customer lifetime value varies and is confidential; however, we can say that it typically averages in the mid-£hundreds. Even based on an average lifetime value of £250 (which would be at the bottom end of the spectrum), that would equate to a return on the advertising investment of nearly £16 for every £1 spent. And while we accept that advertising can't claim to have been directly responsible for every acquisition made or retention saved, there is no doubt that the new brand positioning and advertising have been fundamental to the success of ScottishPower.

BRONZE
BEST INSIGHT AND INNOVATION

18

Standard Life
It's not easy to be liked

Principal author: David Amers, The Leith Agency
Collaborating author: Gillian Cairney, Feather Brooksbank
Media agency: Feather Brooksbank

EDITOR'S SUMMARY

Low-involvement processing has generated a lot of comment and here was a campaign shown by The Leith Agency overtly based on its principles, that moved the brand on from its well-known 'Baby James' advertising with 'quiet confidence'. The insight and innovation impressed the judges, as did the evidence of attitudinal improvement for a brand under pressure in a stressed and negatively viewed market. Again, better evidence of ROI would have boosted this paper's scores, to clarify the value of what was a defensive campaign to protect the Standard Life brand and minimise policy surrenders.

INTRODUCTION

It's not easy to be liked, especially when you're a large, financial company responsible for over five million customers' finances in very uncertain and unfavourable economic times.

This paper shows how, by embracing a new model of advertising, The Leith Agency created a campaign that has made consumers feel better about Standard Life despite an unprecedented onslaught of negative press. In doing so, it maintained the brand's value and made a downturn in the company's fortunes far less damaging than it would have been without successful advertising.

THE IMPORTANCE OF A BRAND CAMPAIGN

In 2002, Standard Life (an Edinburgh-based financial company) and The Leith Agency agreed that there was a need for a new corporate brand campaign.

Brand-building advertising was essential to Standard Life for a variety of reasons:

- the brand lacks high-street presence and regular customer contact. Advertising is the best means of shaping what the brand stands for;
- consumers want the reassurance of strong financial brands when choosing something as important as a pension or an investment product.

'You're more liable to take out a policy with someone who has a good reputation.'

25–35-year-old, London, Aspect Research

- Research[1] shows that being a well-known brand is important to independent financial advisers (IFAs) when recommending a provider.

'Brands are becoming more important regardless of whether the purchase is mediated by an adviser. Advisers find it easier to sell brands to consumers.'

Prospektus: Planning for the Future of Financial Services

A TROUBLED ECONOMIC CLIMATE

Brand-building advertising was made even more important by the uncertain and unfavourable economic climate of the time. As the MORI survey depicted in Figure 1 shows, economic uncertainty was reducing consumer confidence.

Consumer confidence in financial companies had started to plummet, caused by daily references to falling returns on investments, pensions and endowments.

Negative media coverage, like that shown in Figure 2, made the task of brand-building advertising extremely difficult. Research shows that consumers' impressions of brands and companies are far more influenced by editorial coverage than they are by advertising. Unless the advertising was powerful enough to make people feel genuinely more favourable towards the brand, it was likely to be

---

1. Source: ORC study among IFAs, 2004.

STANDARD LIFE

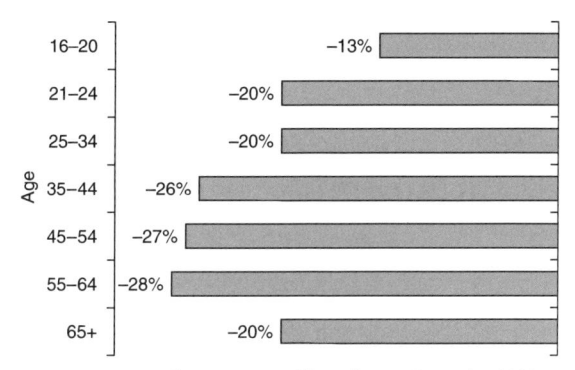

Figure 1: *Net general economic confidence by age, December 2003*
Base: all
Source: MORI Financial Services, December 2003

Figure 2: *Example of negative media coverage,* Daily Mail, *July 2002*

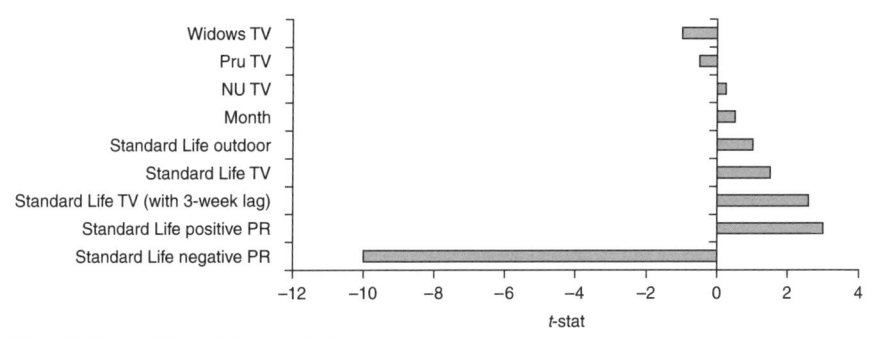

Figure 3: *Favourability – influencing factors*
Source: Nunwood tracking/AIM

overwhelmed and countered by negative press coverage (as the modelling shown in Figure 3, undertaken at the planning stage, shows).

Modelling highlighted that negative PR was, by far, the biggest influence on brand favourability. Given the increasing climate of negative press coverage, this made the challenge for advertising even tougher.

'In 2002 there were 11,809 negative press mentions on financial products (all companies).'

Press Watch

THE ADVERTISING OBJECTIVES

These focused on strengthening the brand by increasing:

- *saliency* – keeping the brand at the forefront of consumers' minds
- *predisposition* – making people feel favourable towards the brand by building positive associations.

Research shows that there is a strong causal link between saliency and consumer predisposition: brands at the forefront of people's minds tend to be those thought of most favourably.

A DEMANDING REQUIREMENT

It is easy to underestimate how difficult it is to establish a truly successful brand-building advertising campaign, especially in the largely uninteresting world of long-term finances.

In order not to fall foul of the usual brand advertising pitfalls, we set ourselves a rigorous and demanding strategic and creative checklist. We wanted nothing less than a big advertising property that would be:

- well branded (not easy with a name like Standard Life and products like pensions and life assurance)
- engaging, even at low levels
- able to run and run
- flexible, suited to all media channels.

THE STRATEGY

We wanted a campaign that would make customers and non-customers feel more favourable towards Standard Life and make staff feel proud.

To determine our advertising proposition, research was conducted with both consumers and Standard Life staff. Research showed that consumers were daunted by financial decision-making and wanted, above all, to feel confident that they have made the right financial choice (see Figure 4).

Internal research with staff confirmed that, given the company's stature and history, consumers could have confidence in Standard Life.

Our research led to a campaign proposition of:

'Confidence that your financial future is in good hands.'

Attitudes to financial services	Desired feelings
• Hard to make decisions you can feel confident about • Hard to know who to trust • Daunted by choice • Loss of sense of control over future	• Confidence • Trust • Security

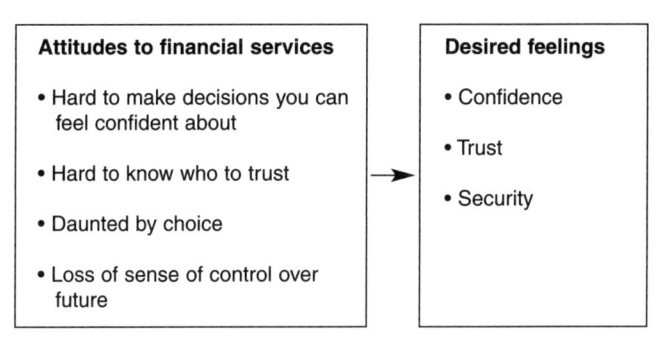

Figure 4: *Financial services – attitudes and desired feelings*
Source: Scott Porter Development Research, July 2002

A NEW APPROACH WAS REQUIRED

Two fundamental problems meant that we had to explore new ways of approaching our brand-building advertising.

1. First, we wanted to communicate a message about confidence in a way that made people feel favourable. But this ran counter to the financial market conditions and the frequent negative press coverage at the time. Consumer confidence was waning. Consumers were not inclined to feel favourable.
2. Second, financial advertising is notoriously low interest (not least because the audience is rarely in the mood to purchase when the advertising reaches them).

We therefore needed a model of advertising that would overcome these key barriers.

We realised we couldn't have advertising that asked consumers to have confidence (the advertising equivalent of someone saying to you 'Trust me'). We also knew that the brand messages available to us could easily be deflected in the current climate. What we needed was an advertising approach that would somehow make people feel confident towards the brand and that would sneak messages under the viewer's radar.

We concluded that our advertising had to work at a low level of consciousness.

LOW-INVOLVEMENT PROCESSING

We were aware of a new (at that time) advertising model developed by Robert Heath and introduced in his article 'The hidden power of advertising'. Essentially, this highlighted the link between the emotional nature of decision-making and the latest understanding of how information is processed and stored by the brain. Specifically, it shows how advertising can work powerfully both at low levels of consciousness and at a visceral level. It argues that the success of a campaign should be measured primarily by the impact it has upon the viewer's awareness of, and predisposition towards, the brand rather than their recall of the ads themselves.

Given our need to get under consumers' radar and make them feel favourable towards the brand, this model seemed ideally suited to our task.

We invited Robert to come into the agency and to brief the creative department on low-involvement processing and how it would apply to our brief. There's no doubt this innovative briefing process helped liberate our creatives from the usual constraints of a financial service brief.

THE CAMPAIGN IDEA

The creative breakthrough was also influenced by the depth interviews we conducted with key stakeholders within Standard Life. There was remarkable consistency in how they described the way they wanted Standard Life's culture to be reflected.

> 'We're not an arrogant company. We're quietly confident.'
>
> 'I'd like the fact that we're confident but quietly so to come across ... not brash.'
>
> *Stakeholders, Leith Qualitative, 2002*

The notion of 'quiet confidence' was extremely important to staff and they wanted this reflected in the advertising. In fact, 'quiet confidence' became the seed of the campaign idea itself.

Think of a quietly confident person. The person who comes to mind is someone who knows what he/she likes. It was a short walk from here to the idea of liking Standard Life.

'I like Standard Life' seemed like our big brand property. It had the emotional power we wanted. (A measure of its power is simple: say to someone you know, 'I like you'. The impact of these few words becomes obvious.)

In order to generate feelings of confidence, we wanted the advertising to make people feel warm and positive. The tone we established was evocative and empathetic.

> 'The campaign has the potential to have a strong impact ... and at a positive emotional level. The tone is entirely appropriate for the Standard Life brand at this point in time.'
>
> *Scott Porter Development Research, March 2003*

Research helped us overcome a dilemma: how to convey dry financial messages in TV advertising without undermining the appealing tone. We decided to move the viewer from empathetic 'I likes ...', through symbolic financial references, to an explicit Standard Life message. This approach we called 'the financial funnel' (see Figure 5).

This simple discipline enabled us to communicate a positive financial message without it eroding the warm feel of the TV advertising.

> 'All of these make you feel good.'
>
> 'It's satisfying because it relates to me.'
>
> *Respondents, Scott Porter Development Research, March 2003*

STANDARD LIFE

THE FUNNEL EFFECT

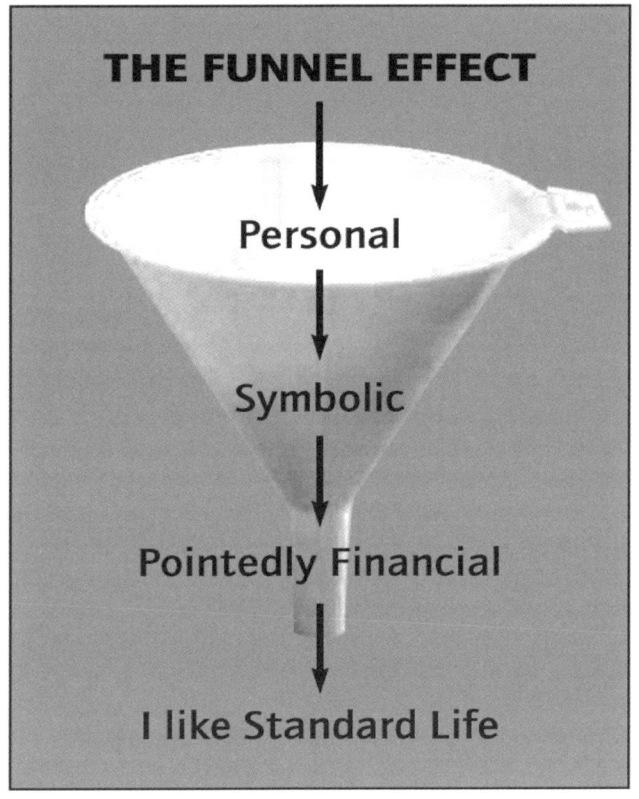

↓ Personal
↓ Symbolic
↓ Pointedly Financial
↓ I like Standard Life

Figure 5: *The funnel effect*

CAMPAIGN AND MEDIA ACTIVITY

We wanted staff to feel positive towards the campaign so it kicked off with a big internal launch. By the time the campaign was launched to the public, there wasn't a member of Standard Life who wasn't fully aware of, and behind, the new campaign.

The consumer campaign, aimed at a broad, all-adults audience (25–55 ABC1C2) comprised four key elements: posters, 40- and 20-second TV executions, tactical Christmas TV, and broadcast sponsorship. Feather Brooksbank's media strategy reflected the two key advertising objectives: increase both brand saliency and predisposition.

Creating saliency or awareness was the priority for the launch phase of the campaign because we wanted to establish our new campaign property quickly.

The campaign launched on 29 September with unbranded posters (see Figure 6). Executions such as, 'I like waking up and realising it's Saturday', created intrigue – so much so that the posters were actually discussed on the Terry Wogan breakfast show on BBC Radio 2. This activity ensured that the television advertising, which featured some of the lines from the unbranded posters, was launched with maximum impact.

I like knowing my dependants can depend on me.

I like Standard Life.

STANDARD LIFE

I like my hard earned money to work hard for me.

I like Standard Life.

STANDARD LIFE

I like waking up and realising it's Saturday.

Figure 6: *The poster campaign – examples*

Media overview	2003				2004											
	Sep	Oct	Nov	Dec	Jan	Feb	Mar	Apr	May	Jun	Jul	Aug	Sep	Oct	Nov	Dec
LAUNCH																
48/96 sheets																
Bus supersides																
Television																
Ambient media		←——— Including baggage reclaim, Taxi tip-ups, Ticket barriers														
2004																
							'Cherry-picking' programming									
Television																
Television sponsorship					←———→ Life begins, William and Mary, Fat friends											
49/96 sheets																
Ambient media		Including baggage reclaim, Petrol nozzles														

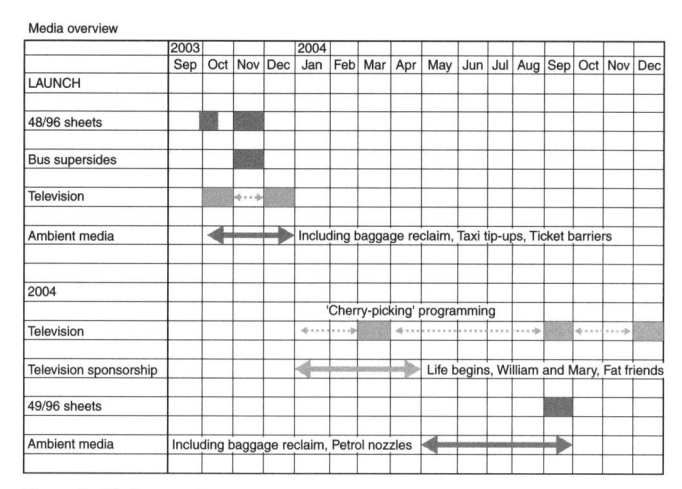

Figure 7: *Media overview*

Once the launch phase was complete the media strategy was then shifted towards the second advertising objective: building brand favourability (see Figure 7).

As discussed, the TV creative work looked to build warm and positive feelings towards Standard Life. We believed that exposure to these messages in media environments that consumers felt positive and favourable towards would enhance campaign effectiveness. We therefore began to identify 'I like' media moments.

We looked at television first. We moved from the initial burst TV strategy to cherry-picking TV programming that our audience had real affinity to, programmes they really looked forward to watching. We were able to do this using quality rating points (QRPs), a means of identifying 'must watch' programmes and the level of quality of viewing.

Standard Life also sponsored three high-profile ITV dramas our audience had real affinity to (*Fat Friends*, *William and Mary* and *Life Begins*). A series of 'I like …' idents broadened our audience's exposure to the campaign idea in a highly cost-effective fashion.

To reinforce the three 40-second TV commercials that ran throughout the year, 10- and 20-second tactical Christmas TV ads were also aired. Family viewing over the holiday period provided perfect 'I like' media moments. Moreover, Christmas provided us with the opportunity to introduce talked-about subject matter (one ad featured a turkey, with the strapline – 'I like vegetarians'). It also gave us real standout because none of our competitors advertised at that time.

Finally, ambient media featuring executions such as, 'I like it when my bag comes first' on baggage reclaim carousels, and 'I like stopping it on zeros' on petrol pump nozzles, really helped build the 'I like Standard Life' property.

HOW THE ADVERTISING WORKED

The advertising worked even better than planned.

We wanted to increase the brand's saliency knowing that this had a positive impact on favourability. The advertising pushed the brand to the consumer's front

SCOTTISH ADVERTISING WORKS 4

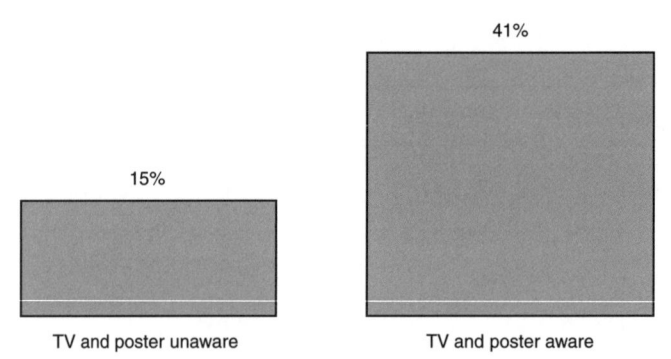

Figure 8: *The stark contrast between those who were aware of the TV and poster ads and those who were not*

of mind. Prior to the campaign launch, overall spontaneous awareness was 16% (fourth position among key competitors). Only four weeks after the 2003 launch, spontaneous brand awareness jumped to 30%.

This dramatic increase made Standard Life *the* most well-recalled company, a first for the brand. Since launch, awareness levels have remained generally above the 20% level, with uplifts coinciding with TV bursts.

Research shows that front-of-mind brand awareness is much higher among the ad aware (see Figure 8).

Although low-involvement processing values brand measures more highly than advertising recall ones, it is worth noting that advertising awareness and advertising recognition built consistently and in line with advertising bursts (see Figure 9).

The strategic thrust was to increase favourability towards the brand. Enhanced favourability would make it more likely that customers would retain their policies with Standard Life during difficult times and that non-customers would still consider the brand when making financial decisions.

Low-involvement processing determines that there should be a statistically significant difference in brand perceptions between those who have seen the ads

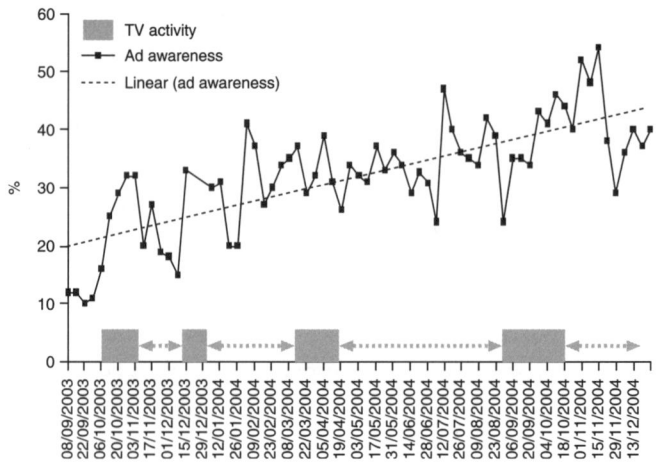

Figure 9: *Standard Life advertising awareness*
Source: Nunwood tracking

STANDARD LIFE

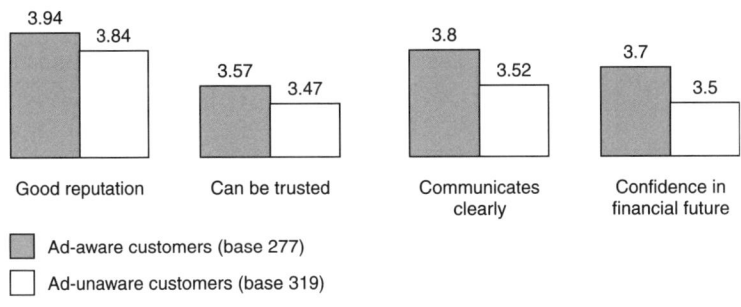

Figure 10: *Standard Life brand statements – customers (cumulative results, October 2003 to January 2005)*

and those who haven't. To put it another way, people who have seen our ads more than once should definitely feel more favourable towards the brand.

This proved to be the case exactly.

Over the campaign period (October 2003 to December 2004) the cumulative favourability shows that ad-aware customers are significantly more favourable towards Standard Life (a mean score of 7.47 versus an ad unaware score of 7.09). Not only that, the ad-aware segment who claim to be 'extremely favourable' is 50% greater than the non-ad-aware segment. These figures tie in with the brand associations conveyed by the advertising. Consistently, the ad-aware customers had more positive associations towards Standard Life than the non-ad aware (see Figure 10). The same goes for personality associations (see Figure 11).

Significantly, for the key dimension of 'likeable', the difference was very marked (ad aware 51% versus ad unaware of 38%).

The low-involvement processing worked as well, if not better, among non-/potential customers.

In terms of favourability, the cumulative score (October 2003 to December 2004) shows that ad-aware non-customers were more favourable (mean score of 5.84 versus 5.52 for the non-ad aware).

Positive associations with the brand were also consistently heightened among the ad-aware non-customers. The scores are even more marked for the personality traits (see Figures 12 and 13).

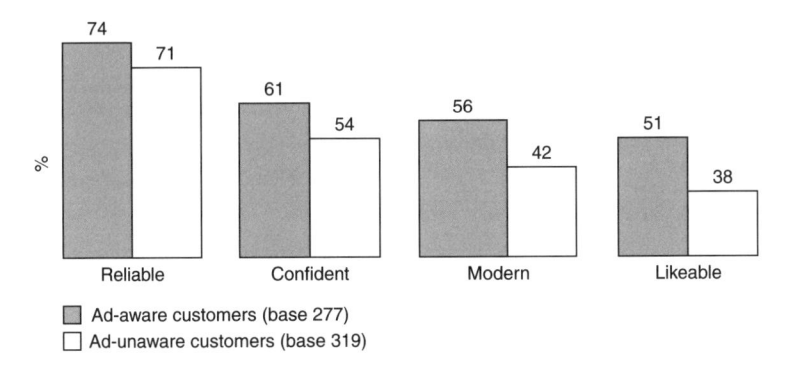

Figure 11: *Standard Life personality traits – customers (cumulative results, October 2003 to January 2005)*

	3.8	3.74	3.44	3.33
	3.67	3.65	3.35	3.26
	Financially strong	Good reputation	Can be trusted	Confidence in financial future

■ Ad-aware non-customers (Base 1403)
□ Ad-unaware customers (Base 2383)

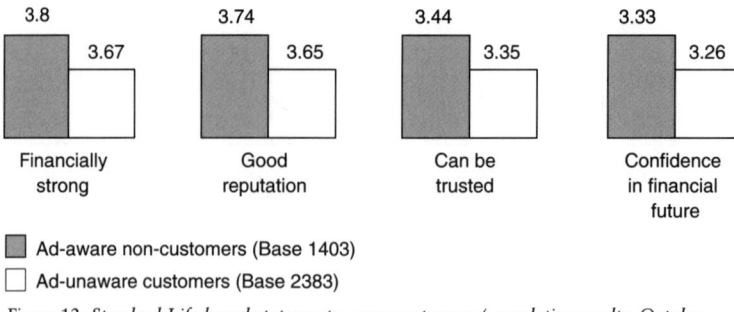

Figure 12: *Standard Life brand statements – non-customers (cumulative results, October 2003 to January 2005)*

	Reliable	Confident	Approachable	Modern	Intelligent	Likeable
Ad-aware	61%	55%	54%	51%	46%	48%
Ad-unaware	49%	44%	43%	39%	34%	35%

■ Ad-aware non-customers (base 1403)
□ Ad-unaware non-customers (base 2383)

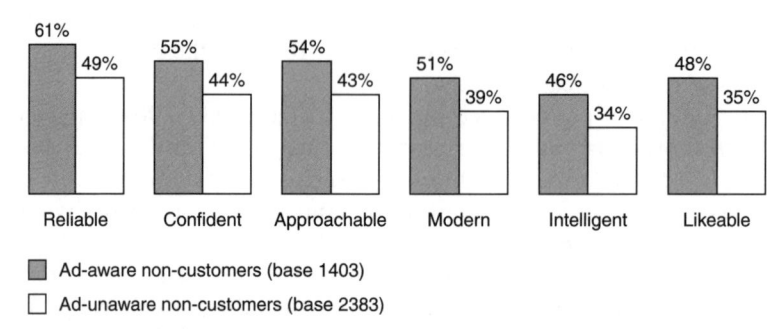

Figure 13: *Standard Life personality traits – non-customers (cumulative results, October 2003 to January 2005)*

Again, for the core communication of 'likeable', the gap was very marked: 48% of ad aware versus 35% of the non-ad aware. Given that the only communication other than advertising that the non-customers will have received is a mass of ongoing negative press coverage, these previously outlined differences in brand associations were both impressive and important.

Qualitative research confirmed that it was the campaign that made Standard Life memorable in a very positive way.

> 'Response to the campaign was very positive ... it drives memorability and a strong emotional response ... The tone generated a warm response and reinforced the brand values ... solid, secure, confident, reliable, caring, empathetic.'
>
> *Scott Porter Evaluation Research, May 2004*
>
> 'Gives you a secure feeling that everything is going to be all right.'
>
> *Female, 41–55, Nunwood Research, November 2004*
>
> 'If you're with Standard Life, everything's going to be fine'
>
> *Customer, Scott Porter Evaluation Research, May 2004*
>
> 'You can rely on us, and not just for today but for the future.'
>
> 'Standard Life make you feel comfortable and secure.'
>
> *Non-customers, Scott Porter Evaluation Research, May 2004*

We wanted the advertising to reflect Standard Life's 'quietly confident' culture and make staff feel proud. Research shows that this was successfully achieved.

'The campaign conveys a confidence of tone without seeming bullish.'

Scott Porter Research, March 2003

We would not have been successful had we fallen foul of the massive pitfall in financial advertising: misattribution. Attribution scores for the previous 'Talking Baby' TV advertising peaked at 33%.

The latest (January 2005) figures show an all-time attribution high for Standard Life of 51%. Just over one year into a new campaign and one in two people link 'I like ...' with Standard Life – a huge achievement.

In summary, we sought a campaign with a big, sustainable property, flexible enough to work across all media, high on branding and capable of making viewers feel more favourable towards the brand. As all the research shows, the 'I like ...' campaign achieved this.

THE CAMPAIGN ACHIEVED ITS OBJECTIVES

Because the campaign ran through an extremely difficult business period for Standard Life, accurately gauging return on investment (without recourse to elaborate econometrics) is beyond this paper's scope.

However, we clearly achieved our main priority: creating a brand-building advertising campaign powerful enough to support Standard Life for years to come. Indeed, 18 months after launch, 'I like ...' has proven to be efficient advertising property of huge value.

Media coverage shapes financial brand perceptions more than advertising. In the last two years, Standard Life has suffered an unprecedented level of sustained negative press coverage, overwhelming any positive PR communicated by the company.

'In 2002 Standard Life had 135 negative press mentions, in 2003 they had 344 and in 2004 they had 521.'

Press Watch

Without a powerful campaign such as 'I like ...' keeping the brand at the forefront of people's minds in a positive way, negative PR would have seriously damaged their perceptions of the brand. In doing so, it would have made the task of retaining customers and acquiring new ones extremely difficult.

It has been proven that advertising-aware customers and non-customers are markedly more favourable towards the brand and have a more positive set of associations.

Independent tracking by Nunwood examined brand favourability among those who had seen the ads but not the negative press coverage and concluded, 'awareness of the advertising drives brand favourability' (see Figure 14).

Figure 15 shows the gulf between those who were ad aware and those who were press aware. It demonstrates how much consumer favourability would have been damaged without having emotionally powerful advertising to counteract it.

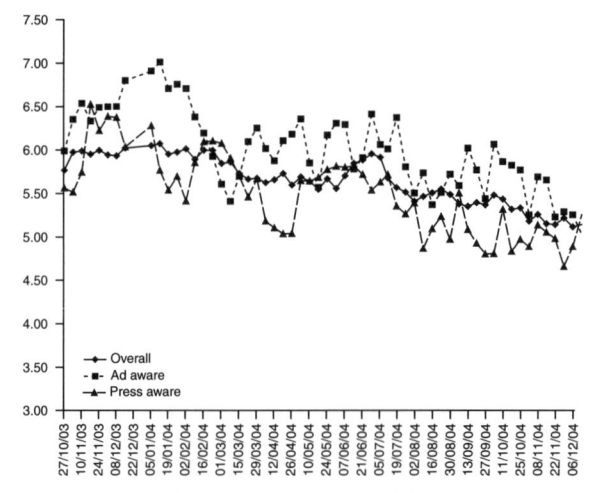

Figure 14: *Favourability means scores are much higher among the ad aware vs the press aware*

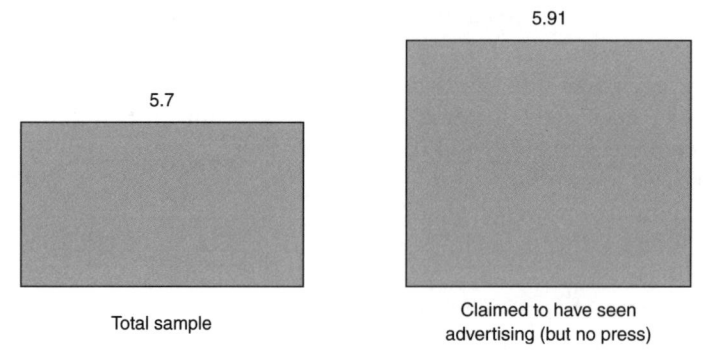

Figure 15: *Impact on favourability (cumulative results, CATI tracker October 2003–October 2004)*
Source: Nunwood

As a result, the campaign has kept the brand on the purchasing consideration repertoire for non-customers. It has allowed the all-important recommendations of IFAs to retain their value.

Crucially, by making customers more favourable the campaign helped increase customer retention. In the campaign launch period (1 October 2003 to 30 September 2004) there was a 20% fall in customer life policy surrenders compared to the same time period in the previous year. In addition, 2003–04 saw the worst of the media coverage directed at Standard Life. Normally, such coverage would have increased surrenders. The fact that customers' favourability was increased by the campaign helps account for this anomaly.

All in all, a difficult period for Standard Life would have been made far worse without the campaign.

How to Access the IPA dataBANK

The IPA Effectiveness dataBANK represents the most rigorous and comprehensive examination of marketing communications working in the marketplace, in the world. Over the 25 years of the IPA Effectiveness Awards competition, the IPA has collected over 1000 examples of best practice in advertising development and results across a wide spectrum of marketing sectors and expenditures. Case histories from the National, AREA and Scottish Awards are included, and papers from the Scottish Effectiveness Awards (1991–2005 only) are listed on page 237.

ACCESS

The dataBANK is held in the IPA Information Centre for access by IPA members only. Simply contact the Centre by emailing *info@ipa.co.uk*. Simple or more sophisticated searches can be run, free of charge, by qualified, professional knowledge executives across a range of parameters including brand, advertiser, agency, target market (by age, sex, class, and so on), medium and length of activity, which can be specified by the user and the results supplied by email or other means as required.

PURCHASING IPA CASE STUDIES

Member agencies will be allowed a maximum number of 25 case studies for download in any given calendar year, after which they will be charged at £17 each. Alternatively, members can sign up to WARC (see overleaf) at a beneficial IPA rate and can download case studies as part of that subscription.

FURTHER INFORMATION

For further information, please contact the Information Centre at the IPA, 44 Belgrave Square, London SW1X 8QS.
Telephone: +44 (0)20 7235 7020
Fax: 020 7245 9904
Website: *www.ipa.co.uk*
Email: *info@ipa.co.uk*.

www.WARC.com

The IPA cases can also be accessed through the World Advertising Research Center (WARC). Reached by logging on to *www.warc.com*, the world's most comprehensive advertising database enables readers to search all the IPA cases, over 2000 case histories from similar award schemes around the world, including the Advertising Federation of Australia and the Institute of Communications and Advertising in Canada, plus thousands of 'how to' articles on all areas of communication activity. Sources include the *Journal of Advertising Research*, Canadian Congress of Advertising, *Admap*, and the American Association of Advertising Agencies, as well as the IPA.

Scottish Effectiveness Awards Cases in the IPA dataBANK

* Denotes publication in the relevant *Scottish Advertising Works* volume
** Paper on WARC.com is version entered into the national awards

NEW ENTRIES 2005
2005 Adventure Sport
2005 Anderson Strathern Solicitors*
2005 Bank of Scotland (Corporate)
2005 Baxters*
2005 Blood Donation*
2005 Broadband for Scotland*
2005 Broadband Registration Drive*
2005 Business Gateway (Young Person's Start-up Grant)
2005 Caledonian MacBrayne (ferry services)
2005 Carling
2005 Children's Hearings*
2005 Glen's Vodka
2005 Go for it – Accelerating entrepreneurship
2005 Grolsch*
2005 My First Bed (Silentnight)*
2005 Nambarrie*
2005 National Trust for Scotland*
2005 Oral Cancer Campaign*
2005 Overgate*
2005 Reid Kerr Enterprises
2005 s1jobs.com*
2005 Scotch Beef*
2005 Scotch Pork
2005 Scotsman, The
2005 ScottishPower*
2005 See Me (Mental health campaign)
2005 Seriously Strong Cheddar*
2005 Standard Life*
2005 Tea and Coffee World Cup Exhibition
2005 The Big Plus (learndirect Scotland)
2005 University of Dundee*
2005 VELUX Roof Windows

A
2003 Age Concern Scotland*
2001 Ardberg Whisky*
2003 Auto Trader*

B
1999 Bahlsen Biscuits*
2003 Bahlsen

1999 Bank of Scotland (Car Loans) *
1999 Bank of Scotland (Mortgage) *
2001 Baxters of Speyside*
2001 Beat 106*
2001 Big Idea, The*
2001 Bowmore Malt Whisky*
2003 Bowmore Single Malt Whisky*

C
2003 Citylink*

D
2001 Direct Holidays*
1999 Drumond Park*

E
2003 Edinburgh & Lothians Tourist Board

F
2003 Falkirk Wheel, The

G
2003 Gala Casinos
1999 General Accident Direct*
1999 Glenmorangie**
1999 Global Video*
2003 Grolsch*

H
1999 HCI Cosmetic Clinic*
1999 Health Education Board for Scotland (Smokeline)*
1999 Health Education Board for Scotland (Big3)**
1999 Historic Scotland*
2003 Historic Scotland
2001 Honda Motors Europe*

I
2001 ID Recruitment*

L
2001 Ladbroke Casinos*
1999 Lanarkshire Health Board*
2003 Limelite Limescale Remover*

237

2005	Scotch Beef	1999	Stakis Hotels
2005	Scotch Pork*	2001	Standard Life
1999	Scotch Quality Beef and Lamb Association	2005	Standard Life
		2001	Standard Life and Standard Life Bank
1999	Scotland Call Centres	1999	Standard Life Bank
1999	Scotland on Sunday	1999	Strathclyde Police
2001	ScotRail		
2005	Scotsman, The*	**T**	
2001	Scottish Conservative and Unionist Party (s)	2005	Tea and Coffee World Cup Exhibition*
2001	Scottish Executive (Domestic Abuse)	1999	Tennent's Lager
2003	Scottish Leader	2005	The Big Plus (learndirect Scotland)*
2003	Scottish Mutual		
1999	Scottish National Blood Transfusion Service	**U**	
		2001	University of Abertay (s)
1999	Scottish Office (Democratising Scotland)	2001	University of Dundee (s)
		2003	University of Dundee
2003	ScottishPower	2005	University of Dundee
2005	ScottishPower**		
2001	Scottish Provident (s)	**V**	
1999	Scottish Tourist Board	2003	VELUX Roof Windows
2001	Seafish Authority	2005	VELUX Roof Windows*
2003	See Me (Mental health campaign)	2003	VisitScotland
2005	See Me (Mental health campaign)*	2003	Vogue Home Furnishings
2005	Seriously Strong Cheddar		
2001	Simply Organic	**Y**	
2003	Small Business Gateway	2003	Young Scot

Index

advertising attribution, Standard Life 233
advertising awareness
    Baxters 39
    Blood Donation 21
    Broadband for Scotland 54
    Grolsch 149
    Nambarrie 167, 175, 176
    Oral Cancer campaign 73
    ScottishPower 215, 217
    Seriously Strong Cheddar 90–1
advertising effect, Baxters 38–9
advertising effectiveness, evaluation, Broadband for Scotland 52–5
advertising efficiency, Grolsch 146
advertising impact, Seriously Strong Cheddar 90
advertising message, understanding, Oral Cancer campaign 73–4
ambient advertising
    National Trust for Scotland 64, 67
    Standard Life 229
Anchor 83
Anderson Strathern
    awards 117
    beginnings of change 113
    business effect 117–18
    challenge 113–14
    communication effect 116
    creative process 114–15
    internal change 116
    launch and turning-point 116
    market perception 112
    objectives 113
    other possible factors 119
    results 117
    return on investment 118
    shared vision 117
    values 114
attributable recall, ScottishPower 215–16

Bannockburn 63, 64–7
Bass 144
Baxters
    awareness 39
    brand image 40
    brand preference 39–40
    bringing new consumers to brand 37
    creative development process 36
    creative idea 36–7
    creative and media brief 35–6
    harnessing brand equity 34–5
    isolating advertising effect 38–9
    market context 34
    results 37
Berlin, Irving 144
Blood Donation
    background 18
    creative work 20–1
    response data 22–9
        donor attendances and blood collection 25–8
        other factors 28–9
        radio advertising 23–5
        television activity 22–3
    results 21
    return on investment 29
    strategy 19–20
brand awareness
    Baxters 39
    Grolsch 146, 151–2
    Nambarrie 167, 175, 176
    Scotch Beef 204, 205, 206
    ScottishPower 217–18
    Seriously Strong Cheddar 85–6, 90–1
    Silentnight 161, 163
    Standard Life 230
    University of Dundee 104, 106
brand equity, Baxters 34–5
brand favourability, Standard Life 224, 229, 230–1, 233–4
brand health, Scotch Beef 206–7
brand identity, Anderson Strathern 114–16
brand image
    Baxters 40
    Seriously Strong Cheddar 85, 94–5
brand loyalty, Seriously Strong Cheddar 93
brand perceptions, ScottishPower 216
brand preference, Baxters 39–40
brand proposition
    Overgate 182
    s1jobs.com 188
    Seriously Strong Cheddar 88
brand saliency
    Nambarrie 176

s1jobs.com 189
Standard Life 224, 227, 229–30
brand wheel, National Trust for Scotland 60
British Gas 212, 214, 215, 217, 219
broadband
   adoption 51–2, 53
   benefits 45
   coverage 45, 51
   market 46–7
Broadband for Scotland
   advertising effectiveness 52–5
   'Angry Man' idea 48, 49
   background 44–6
   business strategy 46
   communication activity 48–50
   marketing context 46–7
   payback/return on investment 55
   results 51–2, 53–5
   strategic solution 47–8
   website 55
Broadband Registration Drive
   campaign phases 128, 129–31
   collaborative group 123
   communication and reporting system 123–7
   comparison with rest of Scotland and UK 141–2
   focus group findings 128–9
   media thinking 132
   objectives 122–3
   results 135, 139–41
   taking message to people 132–5
Broadband Steering Group 44
Brooke Bond 166
BSE 202
BT 46, 51, 122, 128
Budweiser 208

Campbell's 34, 37, 40
cancers, awareness 74
Carling 145
Castle Fraser 63
Cathedral City 80–1, 83, 85, 88, 93–5
cheddar cheese market 80–1
   segmentation 83–4
Children's Hearings
   background 4
   communication activity 8–13
   idea 8
   marketing objectives 4–5
   payback/return on investment 15
   problem 4
   results 13–15
   strategic solution 5–8
   task 5
churn, ScottishPower 219
cinema advertising
   Broadband Registration Drive 133

My First Bed 159, 160, 161, 162
communication effect, Anderson Strathern 116
communication proposition
   National Trust for Scotland 60, 68
   Standard Life 224
communication strategy
   Anderson Strathern 114
   Seriously Strong Cheddar 86–7
consumer demand, University of Dundee 104–5
consumer predisposition
   Standard Life 224
   see also brand favourability
Coors Brewers 144, 145, 154
   see also Grolsch
Coors Fine Light Beer 145
Cracker Barrel 83
Culzean Castle 63

Dairy Crest 81
direct marketing
   Broadband for Scotland 55
   ScottishPower 212
direct selling, ScottishPower 212
Dundee, University of
   brand development 101–2
   brand strategy 100
   brief 99
   changing creative 102–3
   communications 103–4
   geographical growth 107
   impediments 108
   overview 98
   quality of applications 95, 105–6
   results 104–7
   return on investment 107–8
   scale of challenge 98
   'Serious Fun' proposition 98, 101, 102, 103
   understanding market 99–100

econometric modelling, Baxters 38–9
Einon, Dr Dorothy 159
emotional closeness, Nambarrie 176
energy supply 210

Falkland Palace 63
field marketing
   Broadband for Scotland 54
   Scotch Beef 205
foot-and-mouth disease 202, 203, 204, 205, 207

'Glen' character 204–5, 207, 208
Grolsch
   activity summary 148–9
   advertising effect on brand perceptions 151–2

INDEX

advertising implications 145–7
discounting other factors 154–5
recap of past 144
results 149–51
return on investment 155
sales effects 153–4
'Schtop' campaign 145, 147, 148
targets 144–5
Guinness 147

Heath, Robert 225–6
Heineken 155
Heinz 34, 37
Highlands and Islands Enterprise 122, 123, 142
  see also Broadband Registration Drive
household penetration, Baxters 37

'internet rage' 48
IPA dataBANK 235
ISPs (internet service providers) 47

John Smith's 147

Kiernan, Ford 48, 54
Kronenbourg 1664 145, 153, 154

Lineker, Gary 21
Local Enterprise Companies (LECs) 123
Luddites 44
Lyons 166

Mackies Ice Cream 64
Manweb 220
market positioning, University of Dundee 98, 106
market share
  Baxters 34, 37
  Grolsch 153
  My First Bed 163–4
  Nambarrie 167, 172–3, 174
  University of Dundee 107
McLelland 81
  see also Seriously Strong Cheddar
media selection
  Baxters 36
  Broadband Registration Drive 132–5
  My First Bed 160–1
  Nambarrie 172
monster.co.uk/monster.com 188, 189
My First Bed
  advertising objectives 158
  media strategy 158–61
  results 161–3
  sales 163–4

Nambarrie
  advertising challenge 169

advertising competitors 168–9
background 166
campaign idea 171–2
communication management 170–1
difficult sector to change 166
discounting other factors 176–7
distinct markets 167–8
marketing objectives 168
media selection 172
results 172–3, 174–6
sales effects 172–3
strategy 169–70
test market evaluation 172
wider market context 173–4
National Online Recruitment Audience Survey (NORAS) 199
National Trust for Scotland
  Bannockburn event 63, 64–7
  campaign 61–4
  'For You' proposition 60, 68
  future 68
  insight
    searching for 59–60
    using 60
  'National Invitation' 62, 67
  as organisation with 'issues' 58
  task 58–9
  wider campaign results 67–8
Newsquest (Herald & Times) Ltd 188

online marketing, s1jobs.com 191
online recruitment 188, 196, 197
  see also s1jobs.com
Oral Cancer campaign
  case for 70–1
  developing advertising 71–2
  discounting other factors 76–7
  results 72–6
    campaign awareness 73
    impact on primary and secondary care 75–6
    knowledge and awareness of mouth cancer 74–5
    understanding of message 73–4
  return on investment 77
  risk of running 71
Overgate
  background 180
  brand positioning 182
  challenge 182
  competition 181
  discounting other factors 185
  marketing objectives 183
  media strategy 184
  prize draw promotion 183, 185
  results 184–5
  retail environment 180–1

talking-point creation 183–4
understanding existing audience 181–2

PDAs 135, 137
personal relevance, Blood Donation 19–20
personal touch, Baxters 34, 36
Pilgrims Choice 83, 93, 95
Powergen 215
PR
   Broadband for Scotland 54
   Broadband Registration Drive 135
   Oral Cancer campaign 72
   Scotch Beef 204
   Standard Life 233
press advertising
   Anderson Strathern 115
   Broadband Registration Drive 132, 133
   Children's Hearings 8, 12, 13, 15
   My First Bed 160
   National Trust for Scotland 61–2, 63, 64
   s1jobs.com 190–1, 195
print advertising
   Broadband Registration Drive 133
   Nambarrie 172
   Oral Cancer campaign 72
   Overgate 184
   s1jobs.com 191–2, 194
   ScottishPower 214
   Seriously Strong Cheddar 82
   Standard Life 227
   see also press advertising
promotions
   in-store
      Scotch Beef 205, 207
      Seriously Strong Cheddar 89
   prize draw, Overgate 183, 185
public relations see PR
Punjana 166

Quality Meat Scotland (QMS) 202, 203
   see also Scotch Beef
quality rating points (QRPs) 229

radio advertising
   Baxters 36–7
   Blood Donation 23–4, 25
   Broadband Registration Drive 132, 133
   Children's Hearings 12, 13, 15
   National Trust for Scotland 62, 63, 64
   Oral Cancer campaign 72, 75
   University of Dundee 103
recruitment 188–90
   see also s1jobs.com
Reid, John 18
research
   Anderson Strathern 117–18
   My First Bed 158

Nambarrie 167, 170, 171, 172
National Trust for Scotland 59–60
Oral Cancer campaign 70–1
Overgate 181
Scotch Beef 203, 204–5
ScottishPower 211, 214
Seriously Strong Cheddar 83–4
Standard Life 222, 224, 226, 232
University of Dundee 99–100
return on investment
   Anderson Strathern 118
   Blood Donation 29
   Broadband for Scotland 55
   Children's Hearings 15
   Grolsch 155
   Oral Cancer campaign 77
   Scotch Beef 207–8
   ScottishPower 220
   Seriously Strong Cheddar 95
   University of Dundee 107–8

s1jobs.com
   challenge 188
   competitor activity 189
   consumer advertising 190–2
   contribution of advertising 199
   history 188
   power of brand 188–9
   results 196–9
      clients 197–8
      revenue growth 198
      users 196–7
   trade advertising 192–6
Sainsbury's 38–9
scotcareers.co.uk 189
Scotch Beef
   background to challenge 202–3
   brand health 206–7
   business strategy 203
   communication activity 204–5
   payback/return on investment 207–8
   promotional activity 205, 207
   results 205–6
   strategic solution 203–4
Scotsman Publications 189
Scottish Blend 169, 174, 175
scottishjobs.com 189
ScottishPower
   bringing campaign to life 212–13
   challenge 210
   developing creative 212
   discounting other factors 219
   manifold effects 219–20
   marketing communications 220
   media strategy 214
   payback 220
   positioning statement 211–12

INDEX

as preferred supplier 218
Project Nirvana 211
results 214–19
    external success 214–19
    internal success 214
Seriously Strong Cheddar
    awareness 85–6, 90–1
    brand development 83–4, 87–8
    brand image 85, 94–5
    campaign development 87–8
    campaign idea 88–9
    cheddar cheese market 80–1
    communication strategy 86–7
    place in market 81–3
    problem 84
    results 90–5
    return on investment 95
    strength perceptions 85
share of voice
    s1jobs.com 189
    Scotch Beef 208
    ScottishPower 219
Silentnight 158, 161, 163
    see also My First Bed
Slumberland 161
sponsorship
    National Trust for Scotland 64
    Standard Life 229
staff buy-in
    Anderson Strathern 114, 116, 117–18
    Standard Life 227
Standard Life
    advertising objectives 224
    campaign idea 226–7
    campaign importance 222
    campaign and media activity 227–9
    customer retention 234
    economic climate 222–4
    'financial funnel' 226–7
    low-involvement processing 225–6
    new approach 225
    objectives achieved 233–4
    personality traits 231–2

results 229–33
strategic and creative checklist 224
strategy 224–5
Stella Artois 147, 149, 151–2, 153–4

television advertising
    Blood Donation 22–3, 24, 25, 27
    Broadband Registration Drive 132, 134
    Grolsch 145, 146, 147, 148–50
    My First Bed 160, 161
    Nambarrie 172
    National Trust for Scotland 68
    Oral Cancer campaign 72, 73–4, 75
    s1jobs.com 189, 190, 199
    Scotch Beef 205
    ScottishPower 214, 219, 220
    Seriously Strong Cheddar 88–9, 90
    Standard Life 226, 227, 229
    University of Dundee 101, 102–3
Tesco 155
Tetley 166, 169, 174, 175, 176
Tiscali 53
Trinity Mirror 189
trust
    My First Bed 160–1, 162, 164
    Scotch Beef 205
    Standard Life 225
TV advertising *see* television advertising
Typhoo 175

vCJD 18

Wanadoo 53
websites
    unique users, s1jobs.com 197
    user sessions, s1jobs.com 196
    visits
        Anderson Strathern 117
        Broadband for Scotland 55
West of Scotland Cancer Awareness Project (WoSCAP) 70
www.broadbandforscotland.co.uk 55
www.WARC.com 236